THE WALLFLOWER
YAMATONADESHIKO SHICHIHENGE

19

Tomoko Hayakawa

Translated and adapted by
David Ury

Lettered by
North Market Street Graphics

**KC
KODANSHA
COMICS**

The Wallflower volume 19 is a work of fiction. Names, characters, places, and incidents are the products of the author's imagination or are used fictitiously. Any resemblance to actual events, locales, or persons, living or dead, is entirely coincidental.

A Kodansha Comics Trade Paperback Original.

Published in the United States by Kodansha Comics, an imprint of Kodansha USA Publishing, LLC., New York.

Publication rights for this English edition arranged through Kodansha Ltd., Tokyo.

First published in Japan in 2007 by Kodansha Ltd., Tokyo,
as *Yamatonadeshiko Shichihenge*, volume 19.

ISBN 978-1-61262-331-3

Printed in Canada.

www.kodanshacomics.com

9 8 7 6 5 4 3 2 1

Translator/Adapter—David Ury
Lettering—North Market Street Graphics

Contents

A Note from the Author

♥ I WENT TO THE WRAP PARTY FOR THE WALLFLOWER
ANIME. YOU CAN READ ALL ABOUT IT IN THE "BEHIND THE
SCENES" SECTION. IT WAS REALLY FUN, BUT IT WAS SAD
KNOWING THAT IT WAS ALL OVER. I COULD REALLY TELL
THAT EVERYBODY PUT A LOT OF LOVE INTO THEIR WORK,
AND IT MADE ME SO HAPPY. THANK YOU ALL SO MUCH.
♥ AND THANK YOU FOR YOUR SUPPORT. ♥

—Tomoko Hayakawa

Honorifics Explained

Throughout the Kodansha Comics books, you will find Japanese honorifics left intact in the translations. For those not familiar with how the Japanese use honorifics and, more important, how they differ from American honorifics, we present this brief overview.

Politeness has always been a critical facet of Japanese culture. Ever since the feudal era, when Japan was a highly stratified society, use of honorifics—which can be defined as polite speech that indicates relationship or status—has played an essential role in the Japanese language. When addressing someone in Japanese, an honorific usually takes the form of a suffix attached to one's name (example: "Asuna-san"), is used as a title at the end of one's name, or appears in place of the name itself (example: "Negi-sensei," or simply "Sensei!").

Honorifics can be expressions of respect or endearment. In the context of manga and anime, honorifics give insight into the nature of the relationship between characters. Many English translations leave out these important honorifics and therefore distort the feel of the original Japanese. Because Japanese honorifics contain nuances that English honorifics lack, it is our policy at Kodansha not to translate them. Here, instead, is a guide to some of the honorifics you may encounter in Kodansha Comics.

-san: This is the most common honorific and is equivalent to Mr., Miss, Ms., or Mrs. It is the all-purpose honorific and can be used in any situation where politeness is required.

-sama: This is one level higher than "-san" and is used to confer great respect.

-dono: This comes from the word "tono," which means "lord." It is an even higher level than "-sama" and confers utmost respect.

-kun: This suffix is used at the end of boys' names to express familiarity or endearment. It is also sometimes used by men among friends, or when addressing someone younger or of a lower station.

-chan: This is used to express endearment, mostly toward girls. It is also used for little boys, pets, and even among lovers. It gives a sense of childish cuteness.

Bozu: This is an informal way to refer to a boy, similar to the English terms "kid" and "squirt."

Sempai/
Senpai: This title suggests that the addressee is one's senior in a group or organization. It is most often used in a school setting, where underclassmen refer to their upperclassmen as "sempai." It can also be used in the workplace, such as when a newer employee addresses an employee who has seniority in the company.

Kohai: This is the opposite of "sempai" and is used toward underclassmen in school or newcomers in the workplace. It connotes that the addressee is of a lower station.

Sensei: Literally meaning "one who has come before," this title is used for teachers, doctors, or masters of any profession or art.

-[blank]: This is usually forgotten in these lists, but it is perhaps the most significant difference between Japanese and English. The lack of honorific means that the speaker has permission to address the person in a very intimate way. Usually, only family, spouses, or very close friends have this kind of permission. Known as *yobisute*, it can be gratifying when someone who has earned the intimacy starts to call one by one's name without an honorific. But when that intimacy hasn't been earned, it can be very insulting.

THE wallflower

YAMATONADESHIKO SHICHIHENGE

ヤマトナデシコ七変化♡

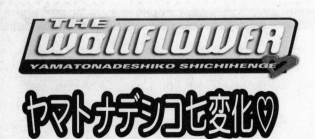

CONTENTS

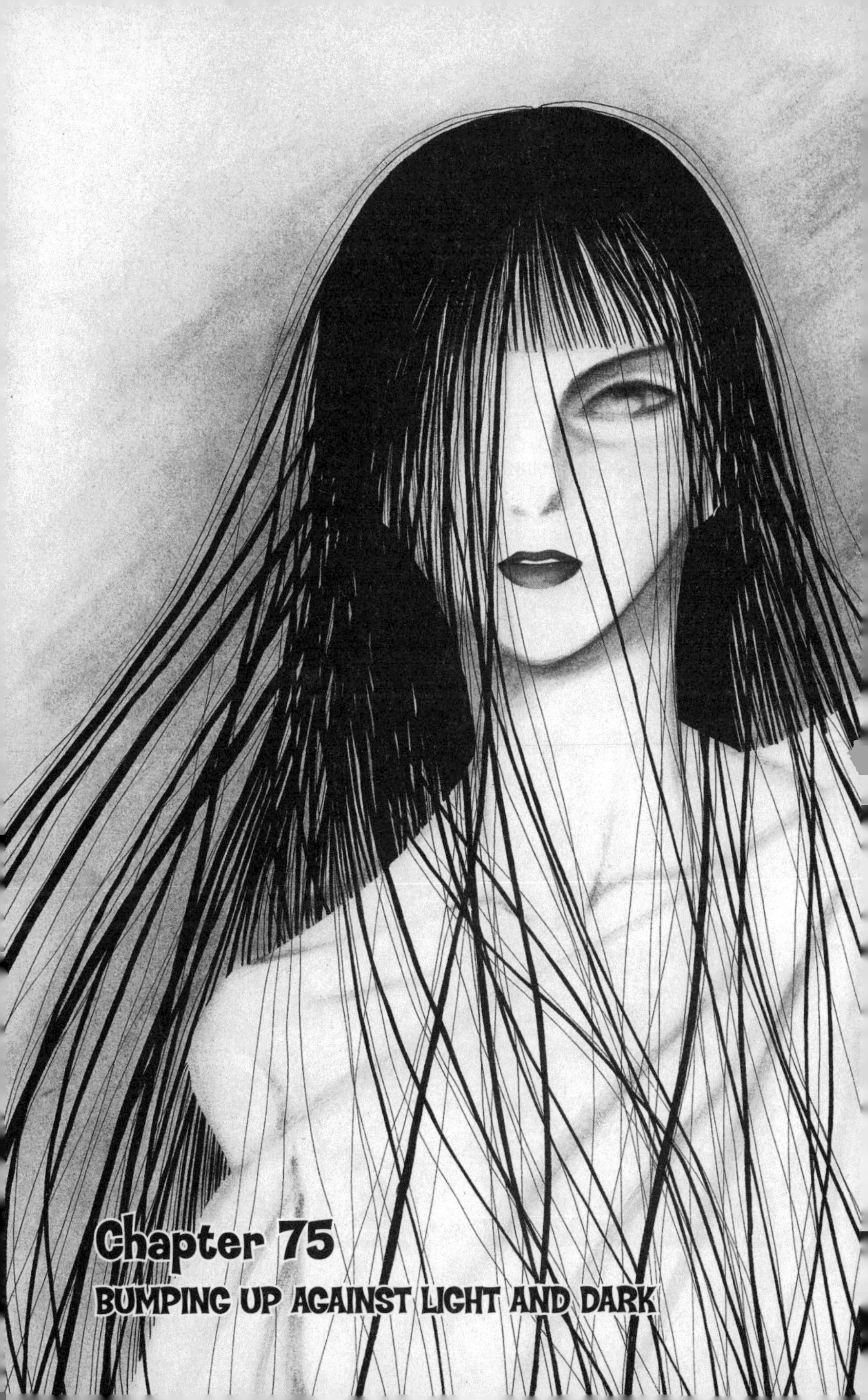
Chapter 75
BUMPING UP AGAINST LIGHT AND DARK

WALLFLOWER'S BEAUTIFUL CAST OF CHARACTERS (?)

SUNAKO IS A DARK LONER WHO LOVES HORROR MOVIES. WHEN HER AUNT, THE LANDLADY OF A BOARDINGHOUSE, LEAVES TOWN WITH HER BOYFRIEND, SUNAKO IS FORCED TO LIVE WITH FOUR HANDSOME GUYS. SUNAKO'S AUNT MAKES A DEAL WITH THE BOYS, WHICH CAUSES NOTHING BUT HEADACHES FOR SUNAKO. "MAKE SUNAKO INTO A LADY, AND YOU CAN LIVE RENT FREE FOR THREE YEARS. TO MAKE MATTERS WORSE, NOI KEEPS TRYING TO SET SUNAKO UP WITH KYOHEI. WHEN KYOHEI SUDDENLY FEELS THE URGE TO KISS HER, SUNAKO IS LEFT LYING IN A POOL OF HER OWN BLOOD.

KYOHEI TAKANO—
A STRONG FIGHTER,
"I'M THE KING"

TAKENAGA ODA—
A CARING FEMINIST

RANMARU MORII—
A TRUE LADY'S MAN

YUKINOJO TOYAMA—
A GENTLE, CHEERFUL, AND VERY EMOTIONAL GUY

SUNAKO NAKAHARA

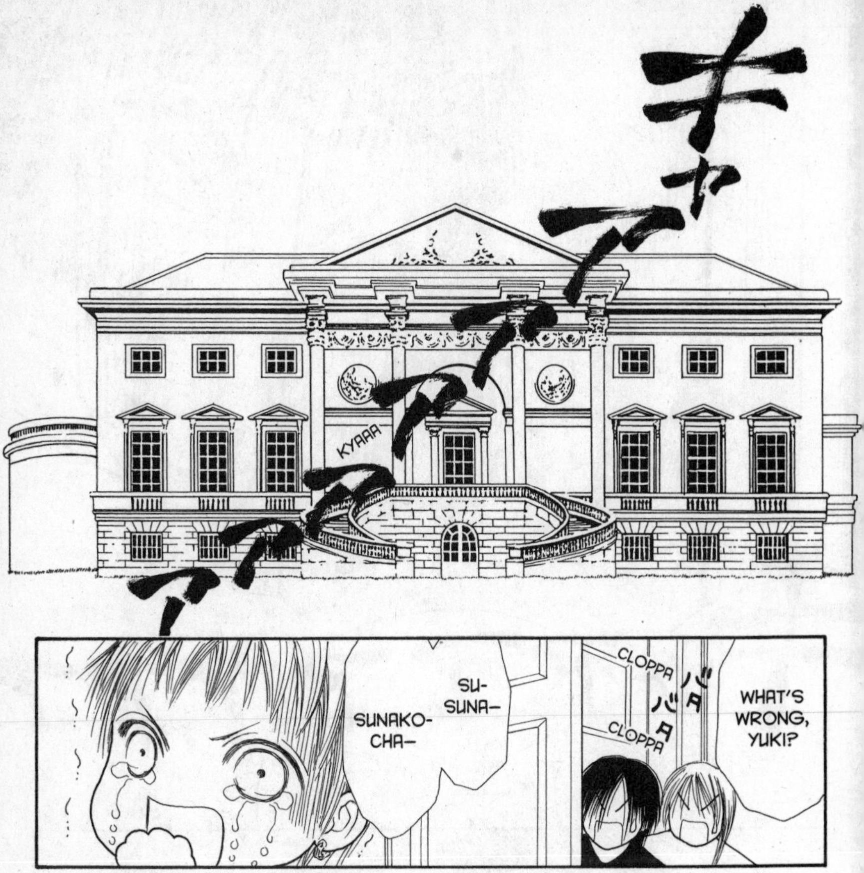
キャアアアア
KYAAA
WHAT'S WRONG, YUKI?
CLOPPA
バタバタ
CLOPPA
SU- SUNA-
SUNAKO-CHA-

BEHIND THE SCENES

THANK YOU FOR BUYING DEL REY MANGA. ♥

BECAUSE OF THE WAY VOLUME 18 ENDED, TONS OF PEOPLE HAVE BEEN ASKING "ARE SUNAKO AND KYOHEI GONNA GET TOGETHER?"

WHAT WILL HAPPEN TO THOSE TWO? I HOPE YOU'LL KEEP READING A LITTLE LONGER SO THAT YOU CAN FIND OUT.

I HAD A HARD TIME WITH MY DEADLINE AGAIN FOR THIS STORY. RIGHT BEFORE MY DEADLINE, I ALWAYS HOPE THAT I'LL BE ABLE TO FINISH WITHOUT CAUSING TOO MUCH TROUBLE... AND THAT I'LL BE ABLE TO GET SOME SLEEP. I HOPE I CAN ACTUALLY ACHIEVE THOSE GOALS SOMEDAY. NO, SCRATCH THAT, I *MUST* ACHIEVE THEM.

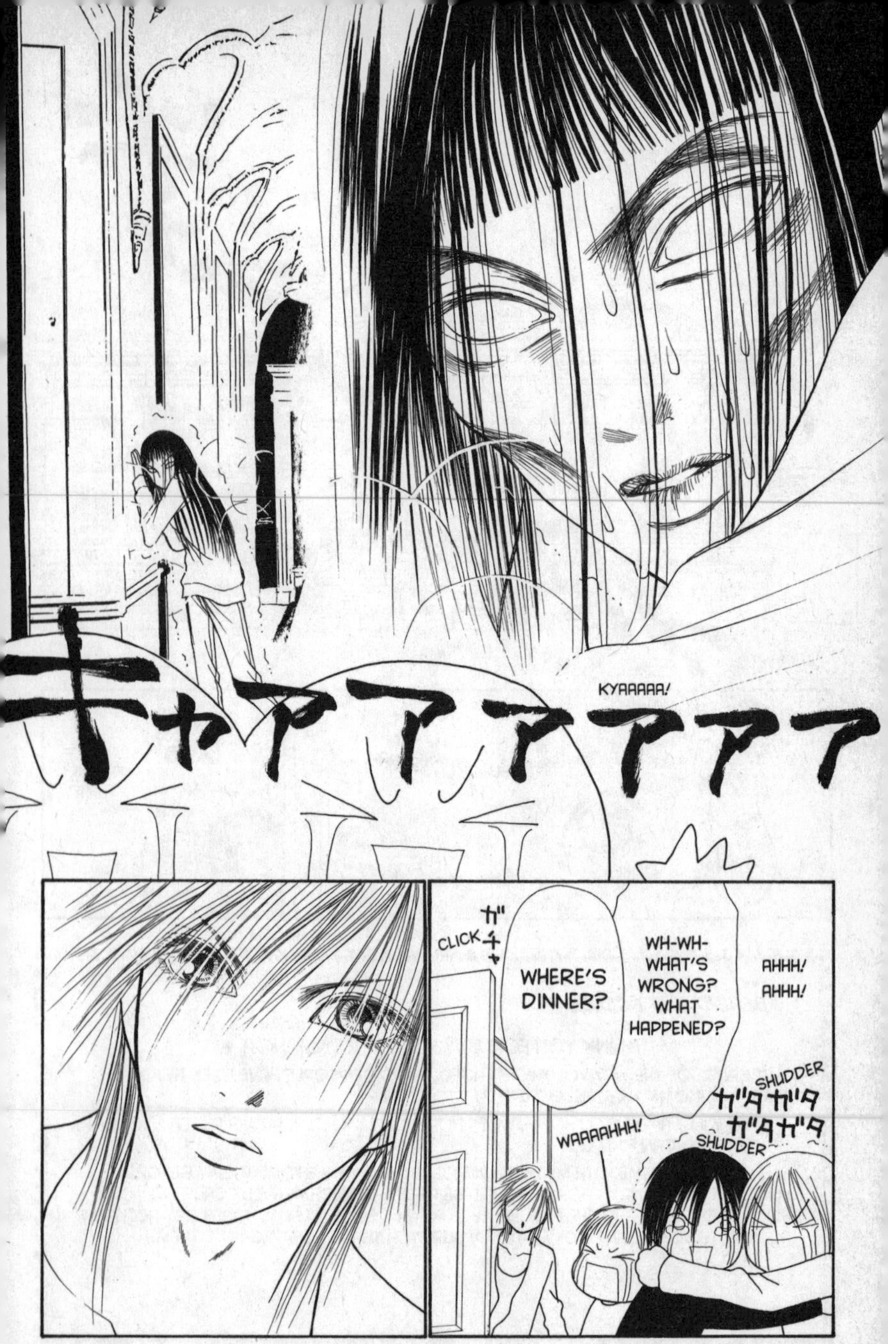
キャアアアアア
KYAAAAA!
AHHH! AHHH!
WH-WH-WHAT'S WRONG? WHAT HAPPENED?
ガチャ
CLICK
WHERE'S DINNER?
ガタガタ
SHUDDER
ガタガタ
SHUDDER
WAAAAHHH!

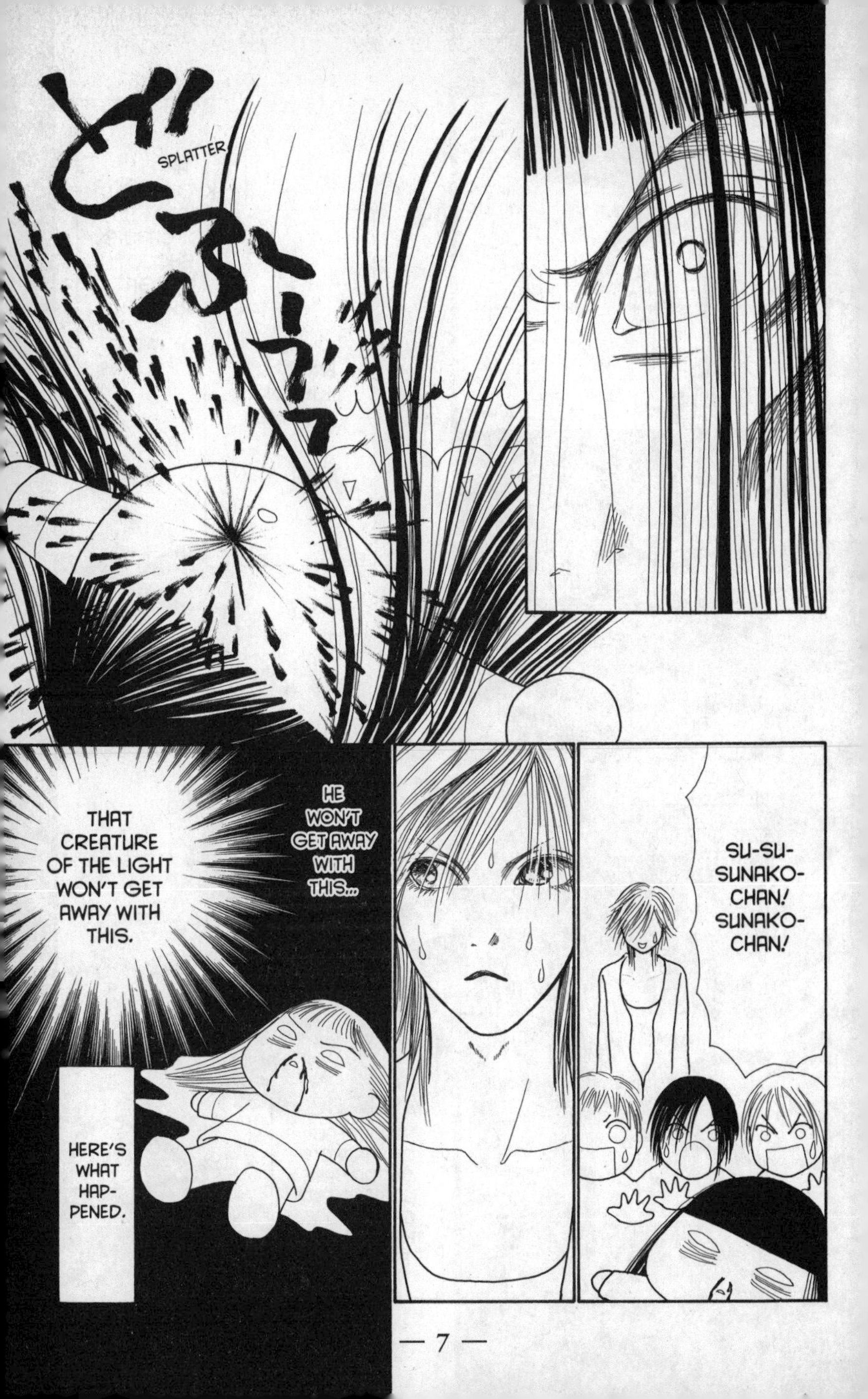
SPLATTER
SU-SU-SUNAKO-CHAN! SUNAKO-CHAN!
HE WON'T GET AWAY WITH THIS...
THAT CREATURE OF THE LIGHT WON'T GET AWAY WITH THIS.
HERE'S WHAT HAPPENED.

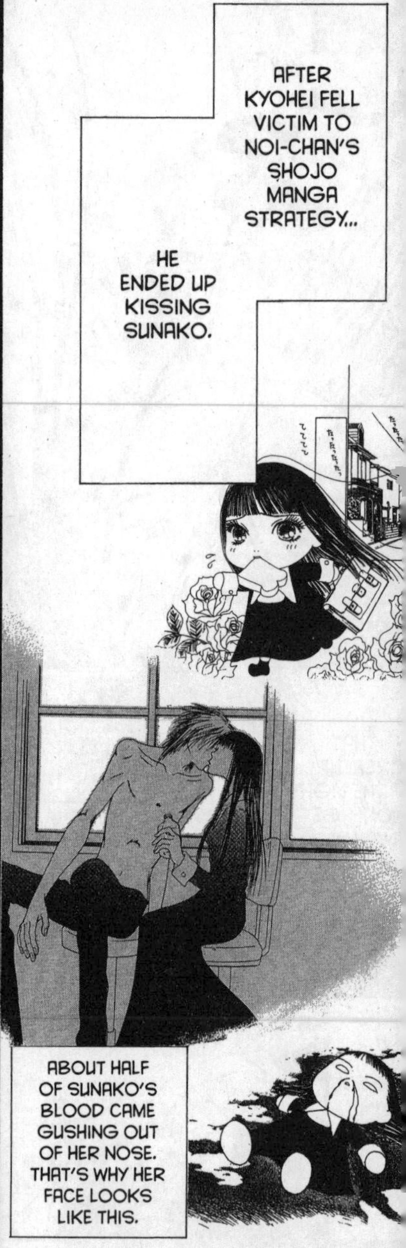
AFTER KYOHEI FELL VICTIM TO NOI-CHAN'S SHOJO MANGA STRATEGY...
HE ENDED UP KISSING SUNAKO.
ABOUT HALF OF SUNAKO'S BLOOD CAME GUSHING OUT OF HER NOSE. THAT'S WHY HER FACE LOOKS LIKE THIS.
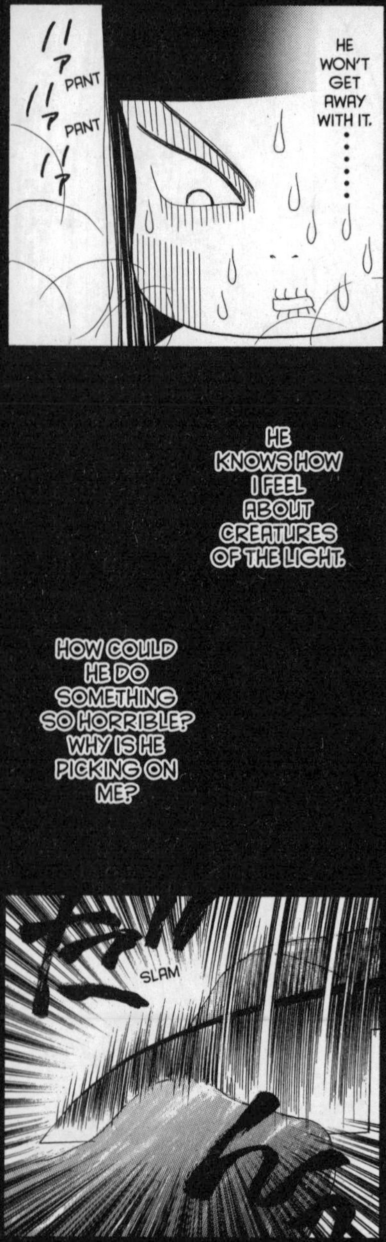
HE WON'T GET AWAY WITH IT......
ハァ PANT
ハァ PANT
ハァ
HE KNOWS HOW I FEEL ABOUT CREATURES OF THE LIGHT.
HOW COULD HE DO SOMETHING SO HORRIBLE? WHY IS HE PICKING ON ME?
SLAM

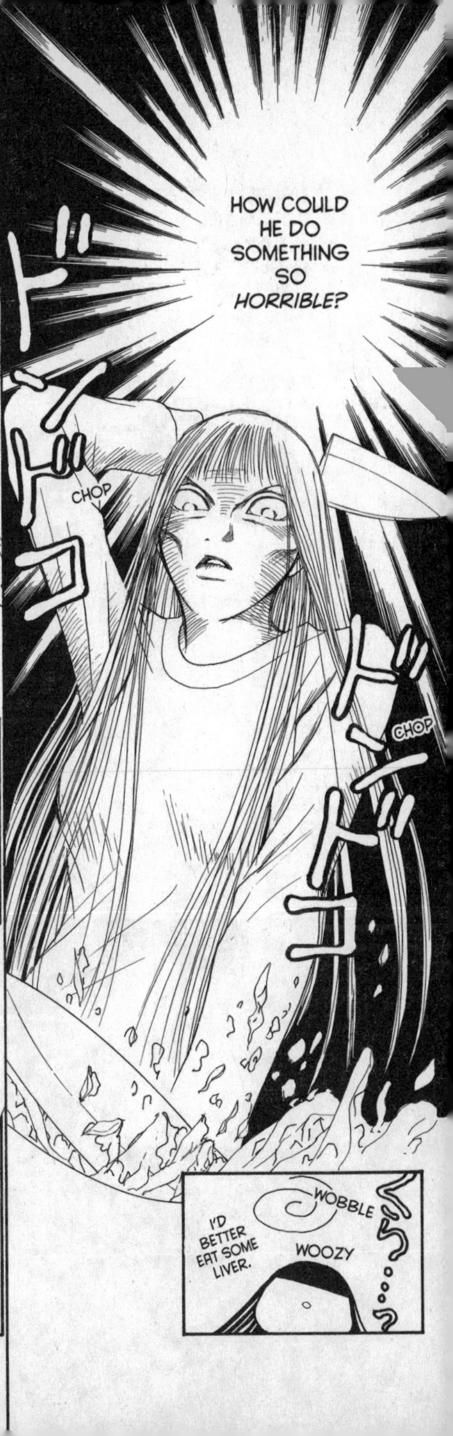
HOW COULD HE DO SOMETHING SO *HORRIBLE?*
CHOP
CHOP
I'D BETTER EAT SOME LIVER.
WOBBLE
WOOZY

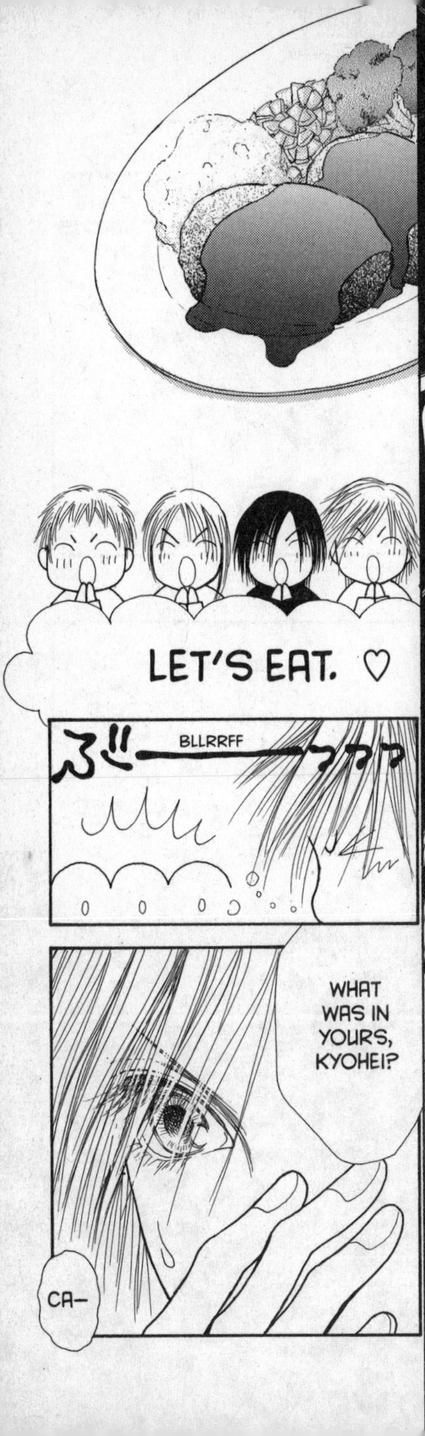
LET'S EAT. ♡
BLLRRFF
WHAT WAS IN YOURS, KYOHEI?
CA—

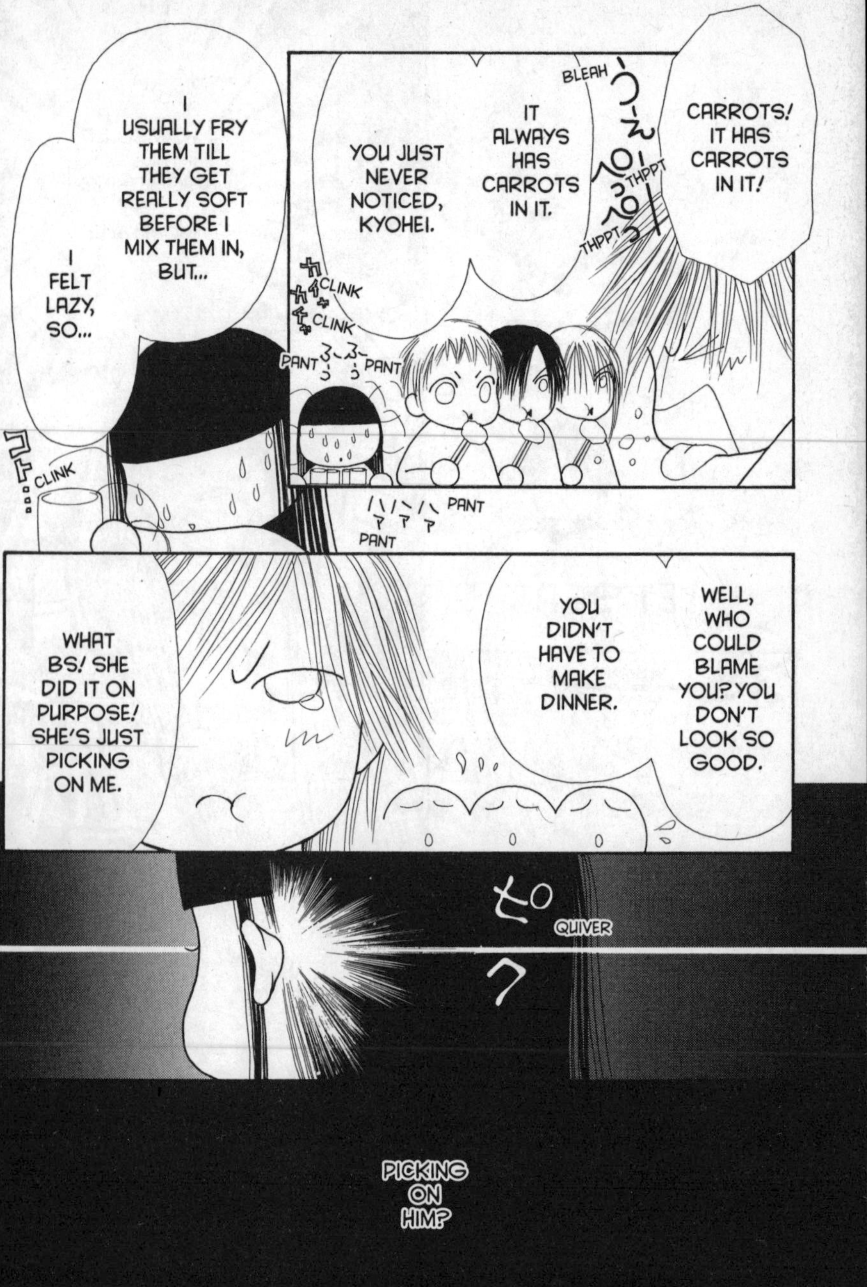
CARROTS! IT HAS CARROTS IN IT!
BLEAH
THPPT
THPPT
IT ALWAYS HAS CARROTS IN IT.
YOU JUST NEVER NOTICED, KYOHEI.
CLINK
CLINK
PANT
PANT
I USUALLY FRY THEM TILL THEY GET REALLY SOFT BEFORE I MIX THEM IN, BUT...
I FELT LAZY, SO...
CLINK
PANT
PANT
WELL, WHO COULD BLAME YOU? YOU DON'T LOOK SO GOOD.
YOU DIDN'T HAVE TO MAKE DINNER.
WHAT BS! SHE DID IT ON PURPOSE! SHE'S JUST PICKING ON ME.
QUIVER
PICKING ON HIM?

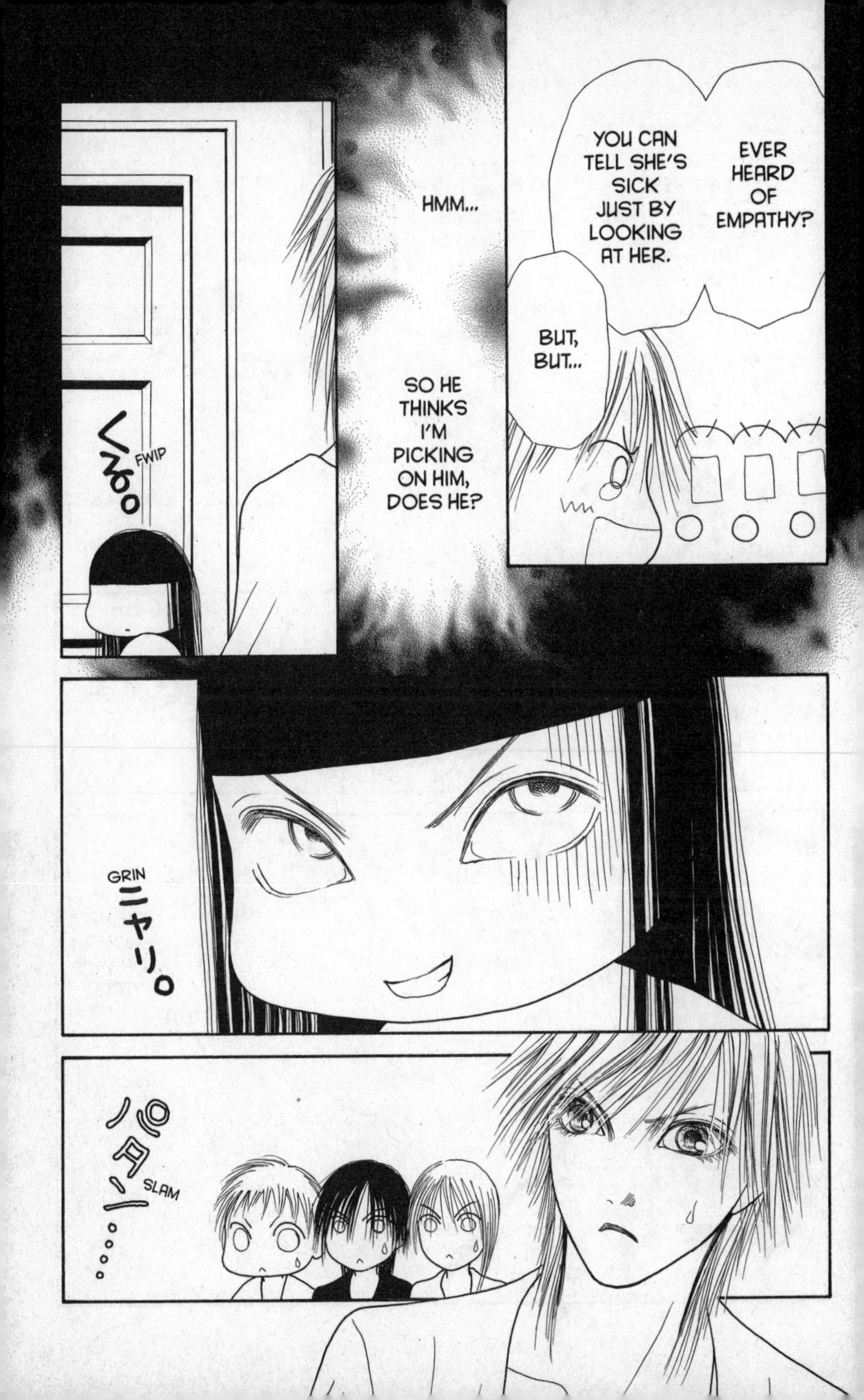
EVER HEARD OF EMPATHY?
YOU CAN TELL SHE'S SICK JUST BY LOOKING AT HER.
BUT, BUT...
HMM...
SO HE THINKS I'M PICKING ON HIM, DOES HE?
くるっ
FWIP
ニヤリ。
GRIN
パタン……
SLAM

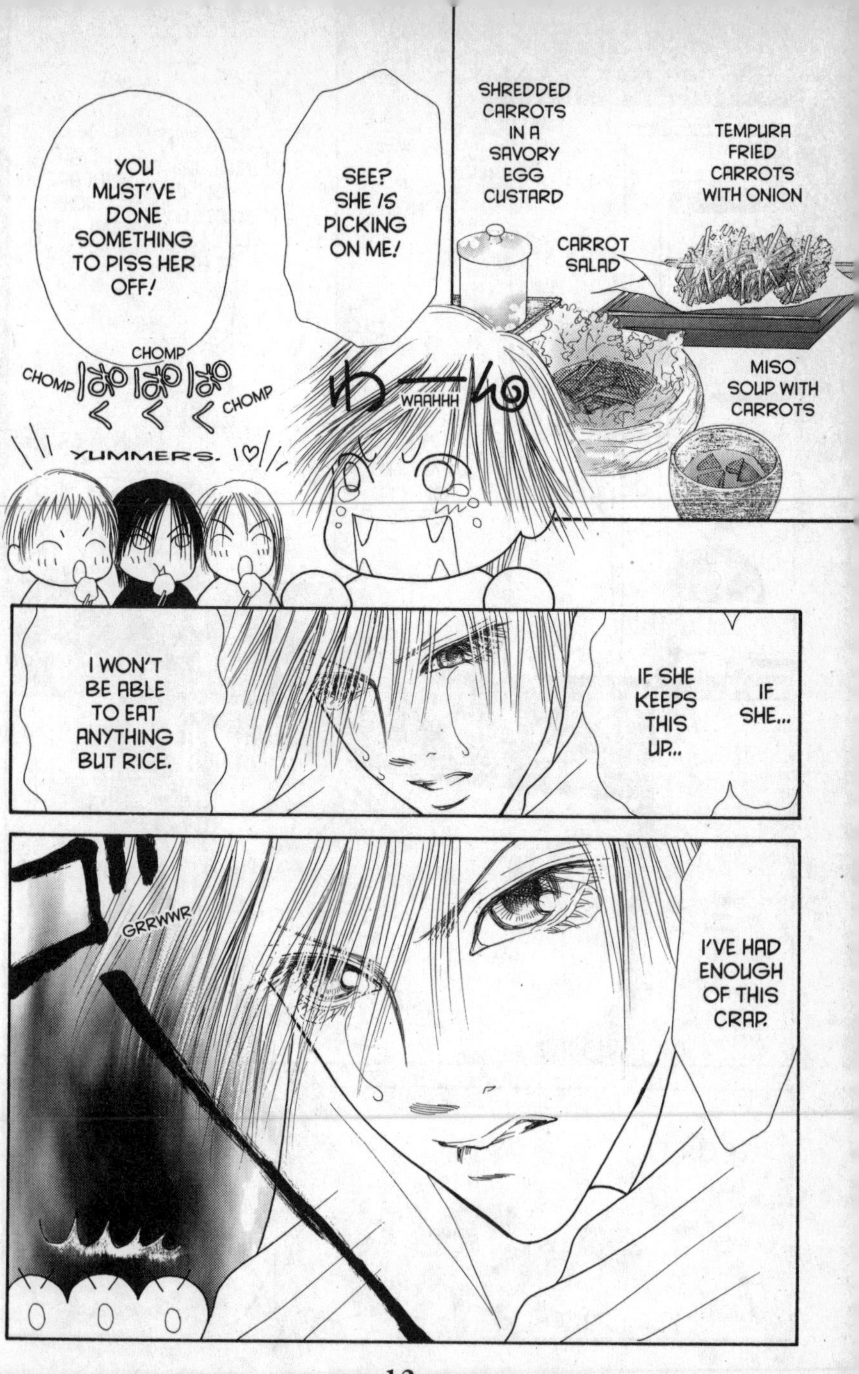
SHREDDED CARROTS IN A SAVORY EGG CUSTARD
TEMPURA FRIED CARROTS WITH ONION
CARROT SALAD
MISO SOUP WITH CARROTS
SEE? SHE IS PICKING ON ME!
わーん
WAAHHH
YOU MUST'VE DONE SOMETHING TO PISS HER OFF!
ぱくぱくぱく
CHOMP CHOMP CHOMP
YUMMERS. ♡
IF SHE...
IF SHE KEEPS THIS UP...
I WON'T BE ABLE TO EAT ANYTHING BUT RICE.
I'VE HAD ENOUGH OF THIS CRAP.
GRRWWR

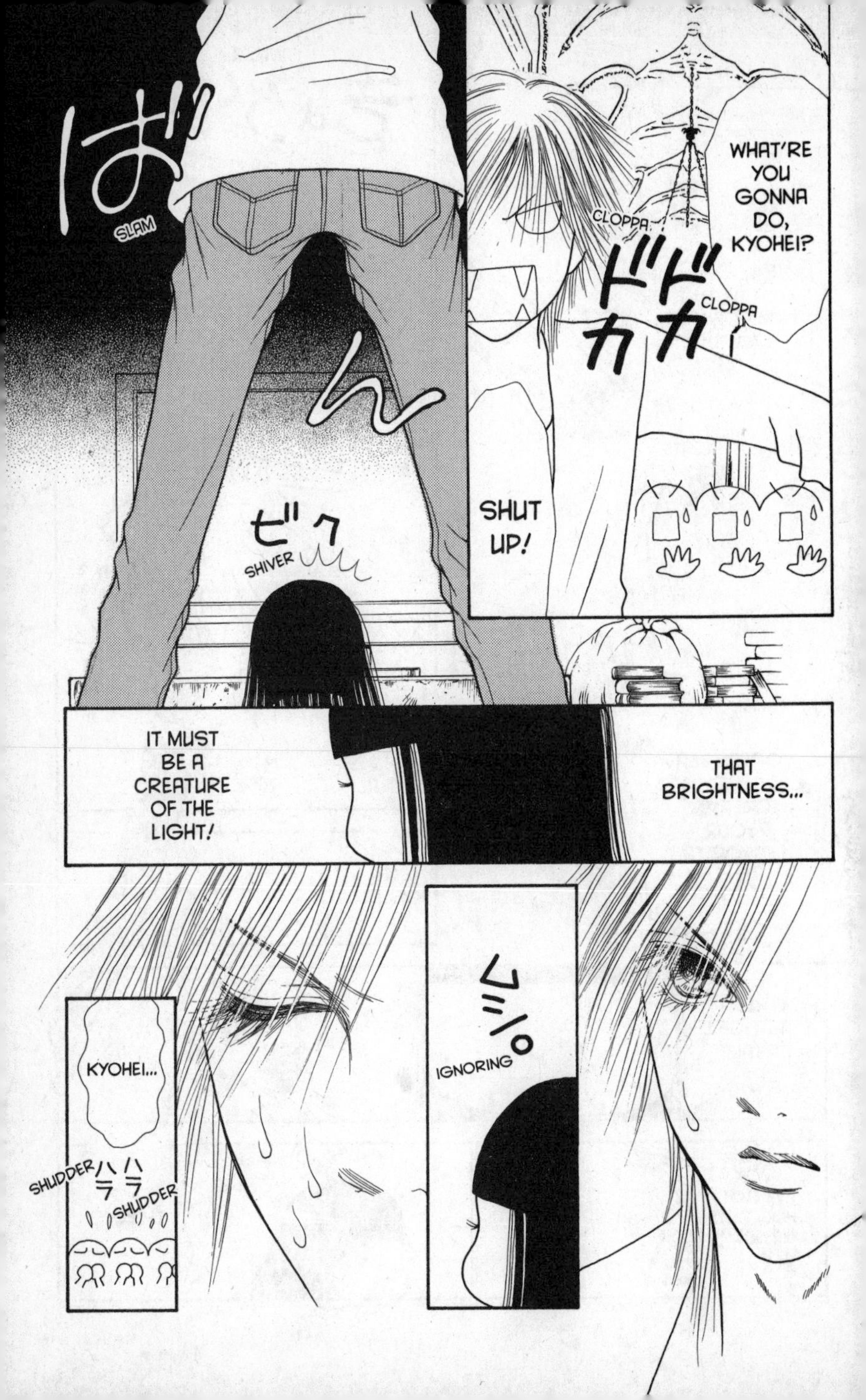
WHAT'RE YOU GONNA DO, KYOHEI?
CLOPPA
ドドカカ
CLOPPA
SHUT UP!
ばん
SLAM
ビク
SHIVER
THAT BRIGHTNESS...
IT MUST BE A CREATURE OF THE LIGHT!
ムシ
IGNORING
KYOHEI...
ハラハラ
SHUDDER
SHUDDER

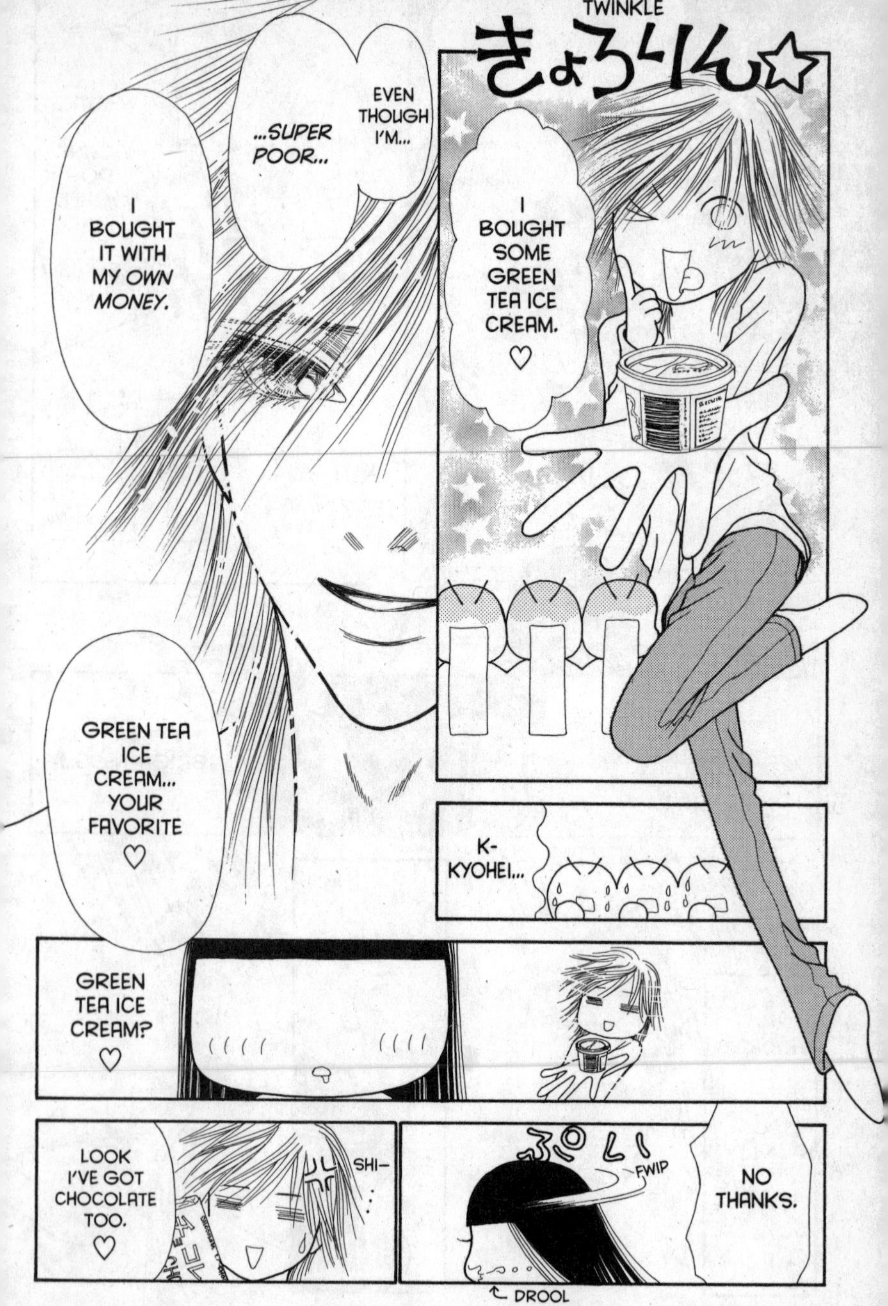
TWINKLE
きょろりん☆
I BOUGHT SOME GREEN TEA ICE CREAM. ♡
K-KYOHEI...
EVEN THOUGH I'M...
...SUPER POOR...
I BOUGHT IT WITH MY *OWN MONEY*.
GREEN TEA ICE CREAM... YOUR FAVORITE ♡
GREEN TEA ICE CREAM? ♡
NO THANKS.
FWIP
DROOL
SHI-
LOOK I'VE GOT CHOCOLATE TOO. ♡

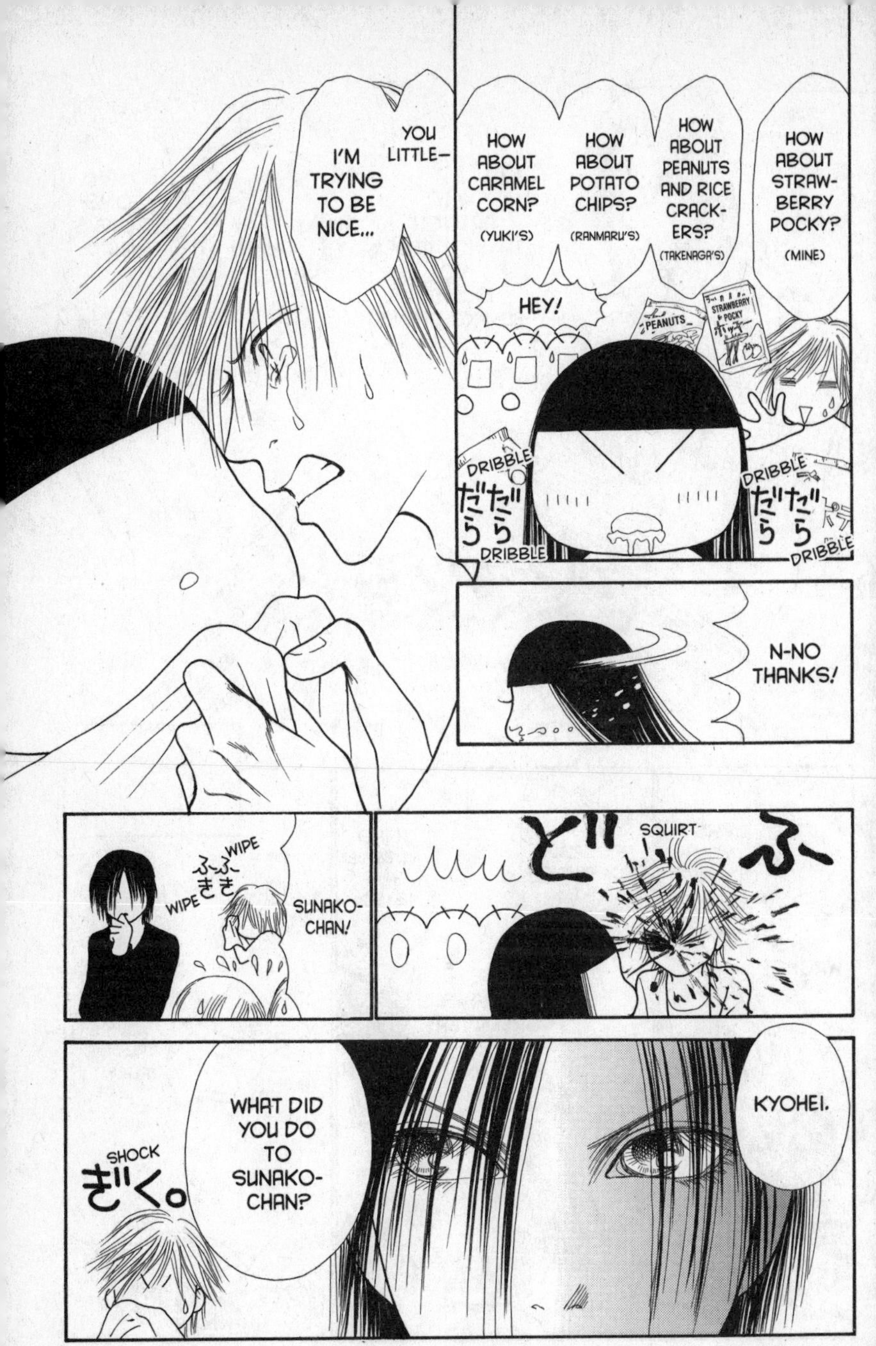
HOW ABOUT STRAWBERRY POCKY?
(MINE)
HOW ABOUT PEANUTS AND RICE CRACKERS?
(TAKENAGA'S)
HOW ABOUT POTATO CHIPS?
(RANMARU'S)
HOW ABOUT CARAMEL CORN?
(YUKI'S)
STRAWBERRY POCKY
PEANUTS
HEY!
だらだら
DRIBBLE DRIBBLE
だらだら
DRIBBLE DRIBBLE
N-NO THANKS!
YOU LITTLE—
I'M TRYING TO BE NICE...
どふ
SQUIRT
SUNAKO-CHAN!
ふきふき
WIPE WIPE
KYOHEI.
WHAT DID YOU DO TO SUNAKO-CHAN?
ぎくっ
SHOCK

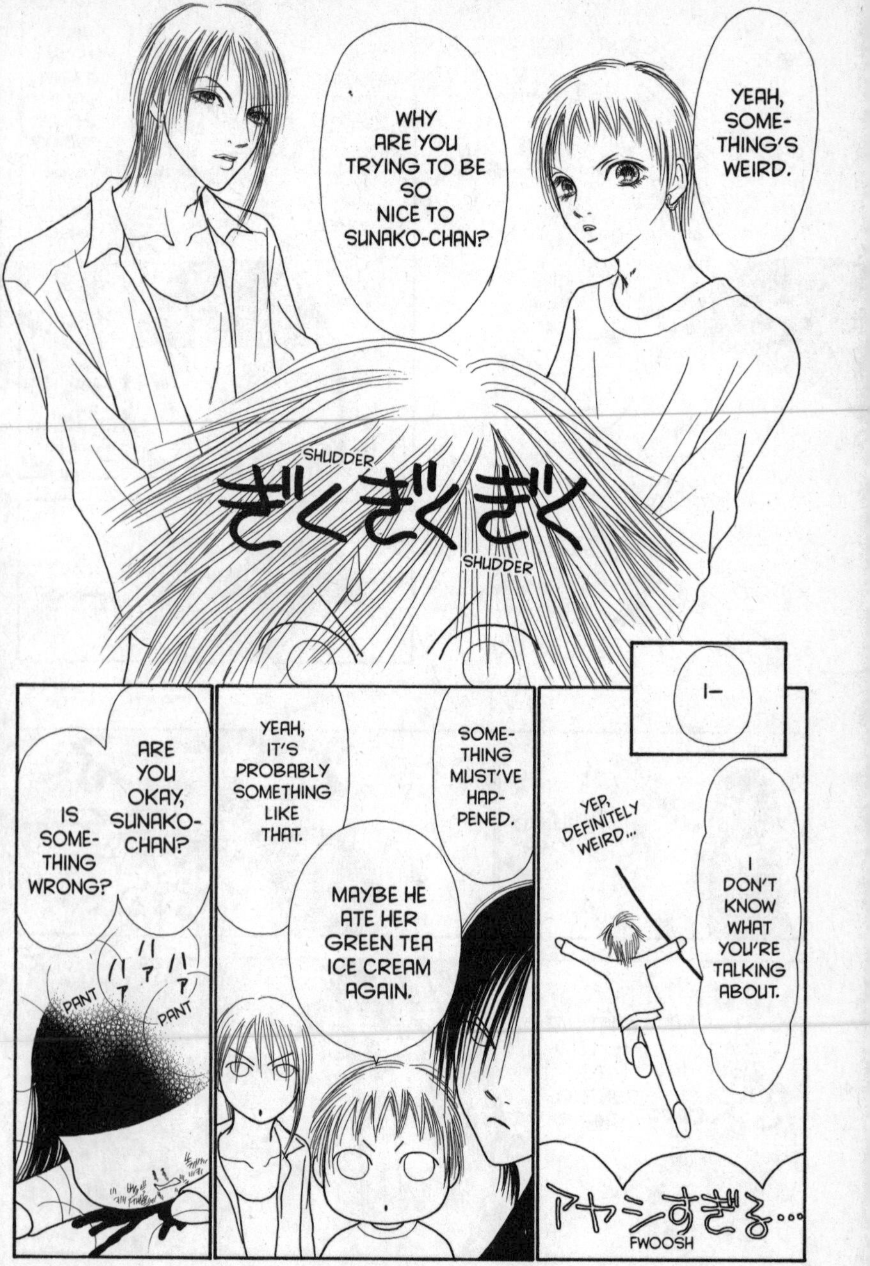
WHY ARE YOU TRYING TO BE SO NICE TO SUNAKO-CHAN?
YEAH, SOME-THING'S WEIRD.
ぎくぎくぎく
SHUDDER
SHUDDER
I–
I DON'T KNOW WHAT YOU'RE TALKING ABOUT.
YEP, DEFINITELY WEIRD...
アヤシすぎる…
FWOOSH
SOME-THING MUST'VE HAP-PENED.
YEAH, IT'S PROBABLY SOMETHING LIKE THAT.
MAYBE HE ATE HER GREEN TEA ICE CREAM AGAIN.
ARE YOU OKAY, SUNAKO-CHAN?
IS SOME-THING WRONG?
ハァハァハァ
PANT
PANT

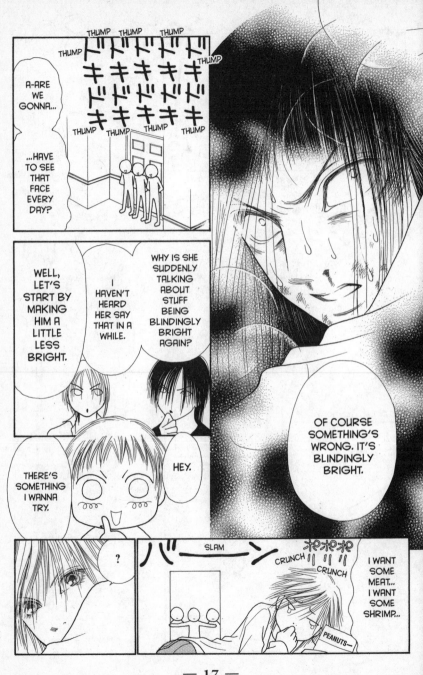

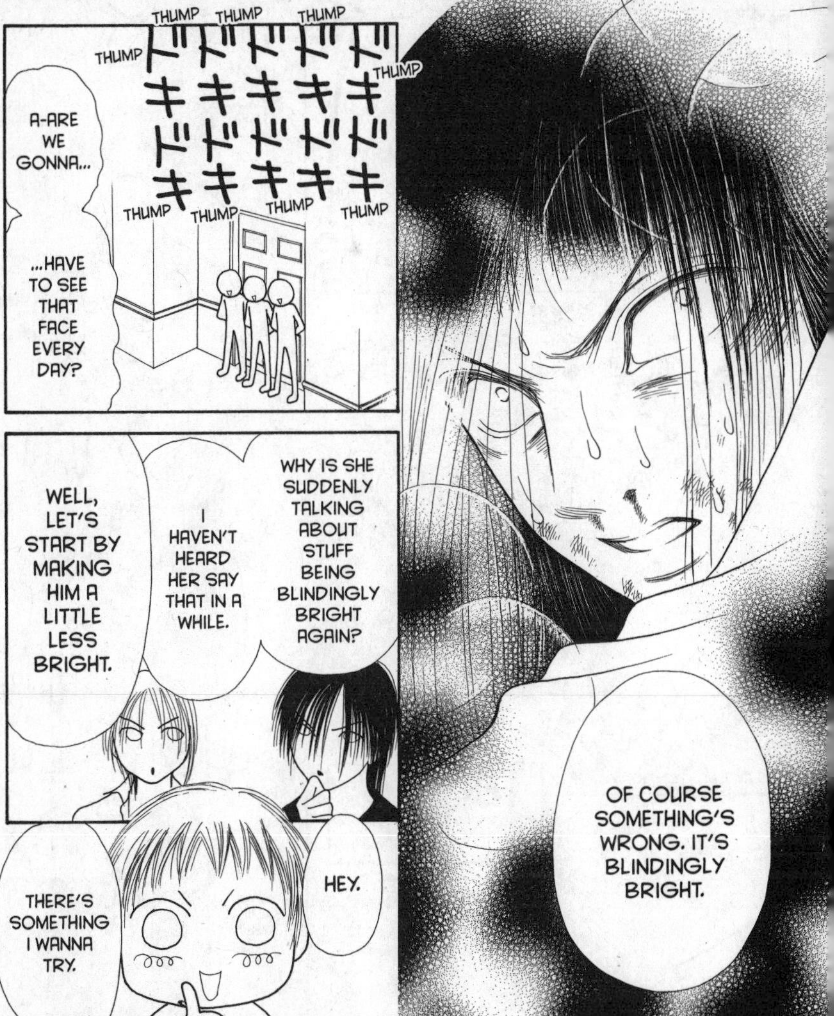
OF COURSE SOMETHING'S WRONG. IT'S BLINDINGLY BRIGHT.
THUMP THUMP THUMP THUMP THUMP
ドドドドド
キキキキキ
ドドドドド
キキキキキ
THUMP THUMP THUMP THUMP
A-ARE WE GONNA...
...HAVE TO SEE THAT FACE EVERY DAY?
WHY IS SHE SUDDENLY TALKING ABOUT STUFF BEING BLINDINGLY BRIGHT AGAIN?
I HAVEN'T HEARD HER SAY THAT IN A WHILE.
WELL, LET'S START BY MAKING HIM A LITTLE LESS BRIGHT.
HEY.
THERE'S SOMETHING I WANNA TRY.
バーン
SLAM
ポリポリポリ
CRUNCH CRUNCH
I WANT SOME MEAT... I WANT SOME SHRIMP...
PEANUTS—
?

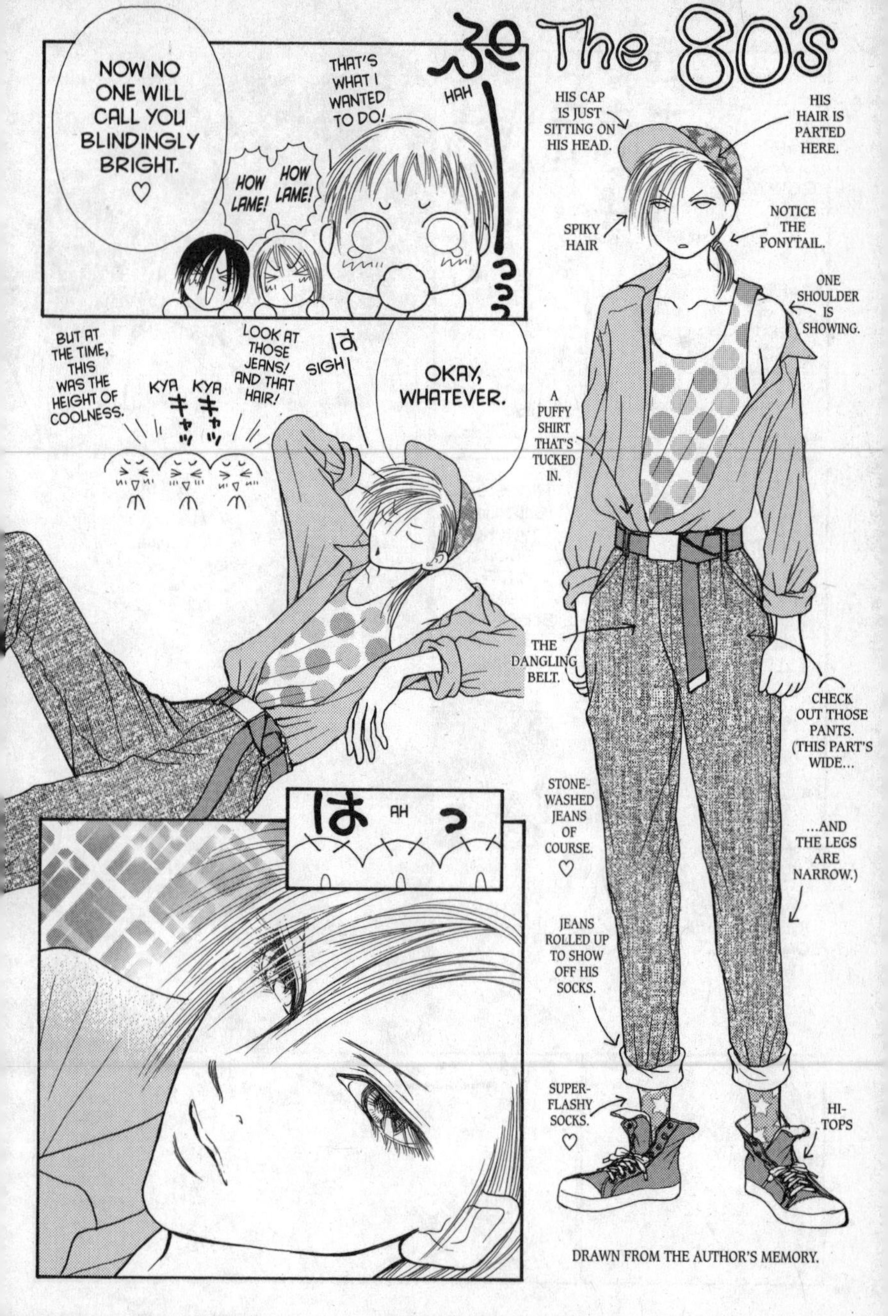

The 80's
HIS HAIR IS PARTED HERE.
HIS CAP IS JUST SITTING ON HIS HEAD.
NOTICE THE PONYTAIL.
SPIKY HAIR
ONE SHOULDER IS SHOWING.
A PUFFY SHIRT THAT'S TUCKED IN.
CHECK OUT THOSE PANTS. (THIS PART'S WIDE...
THE DANGLING BELT.
...AND THE LEGS ARE NARROW.)
STONE-WASHED JEANS OF COURSE. ♡
JEANS ROLLED UP TO SHOW OFF HIS SOCKS.
HI-TOPS
SUPER-FLASHY SOCKS. ♡
DRAWN FROM THE AUTHOR'S MEMORY.
ふ HAH
THAT'S WHAT I WANTED TO DO!
HOW LAME!
HOW LAME!
NOW NO ONE WILL CALL YOU BLINDINGLY BRIGHT. ♡
OKAY, WHATEVER.
は SIGH
LOOK AT THOSE JEANS! AND THAT HAIR!
KYA キャッ
KYA キャッ
BUT AT THE TIME, THIS WAS THE HEIGHT OF COOLNESS.
はっ AH

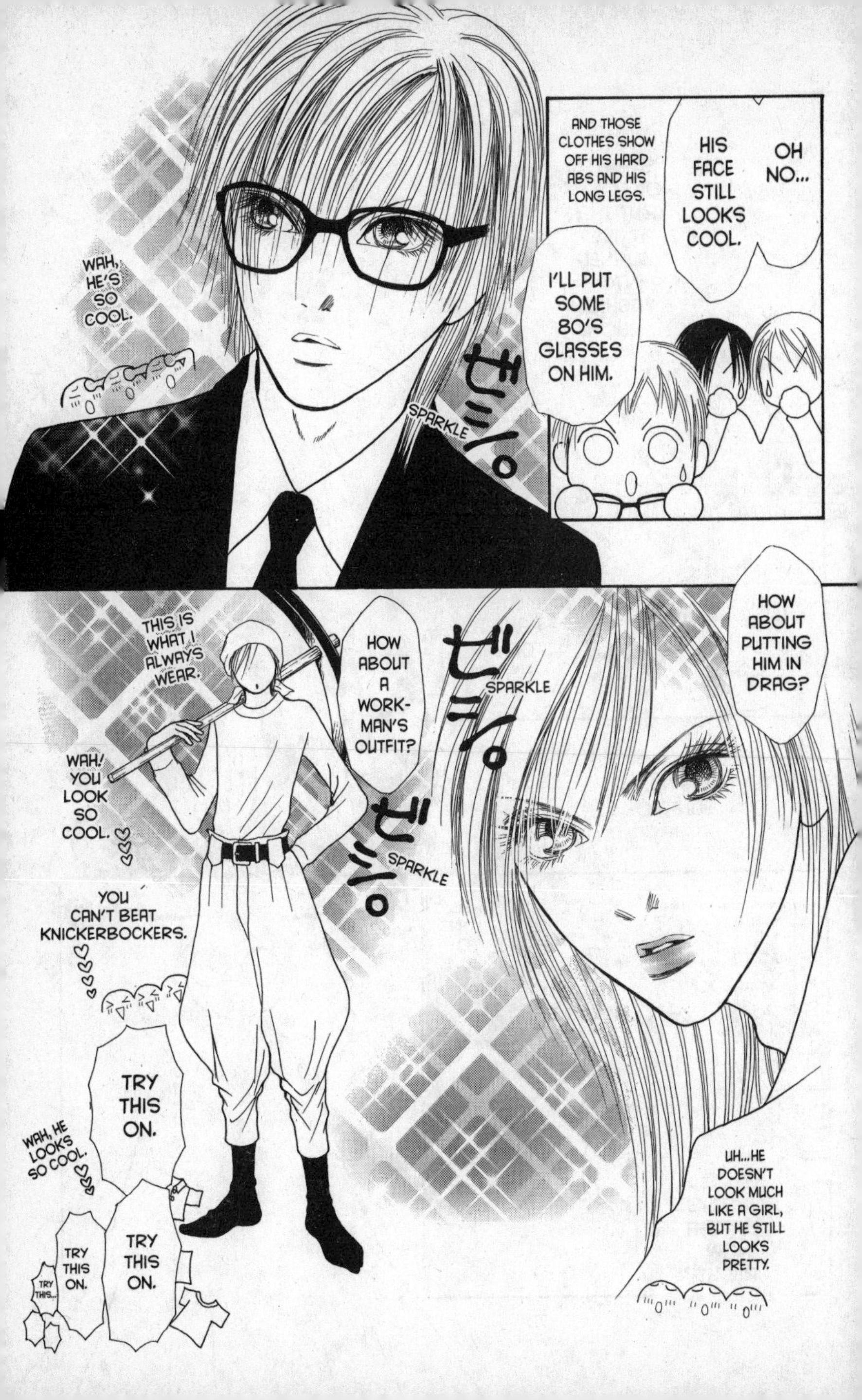
OH NO...
HIS FACE STILL LOOKS COOL.
AND THOSE CLOTHES SHOW OFF HIS HARD ABS AND HIS LONG LEGS.
I'LL PUT SOME 80'S GLASSES ON HIM.
SPARKLE
WAH, HE'S SO COOL.
HOW ABOUT PUTTING HIM IN DRAG?
SPARKLE
UH...HE DOESN'T LOOK MUCH LIKE A GIRL, BUT HE STILL LOOKS PRETTY.
HOW ABOUT A WORK-MAN'S OUTFIT?
SPARKLE
THIS IS WHAT I ALWAYS WEAR.
WAH! YOU LOOK SO COOL.
YOU CAN'T BEAT KNICKERBOCKERS.
TRY THIS ON.
WAH, HE LOOKS SO COOL.
TRY THIS ON.
TRY THIS ON.
TRY THIS...

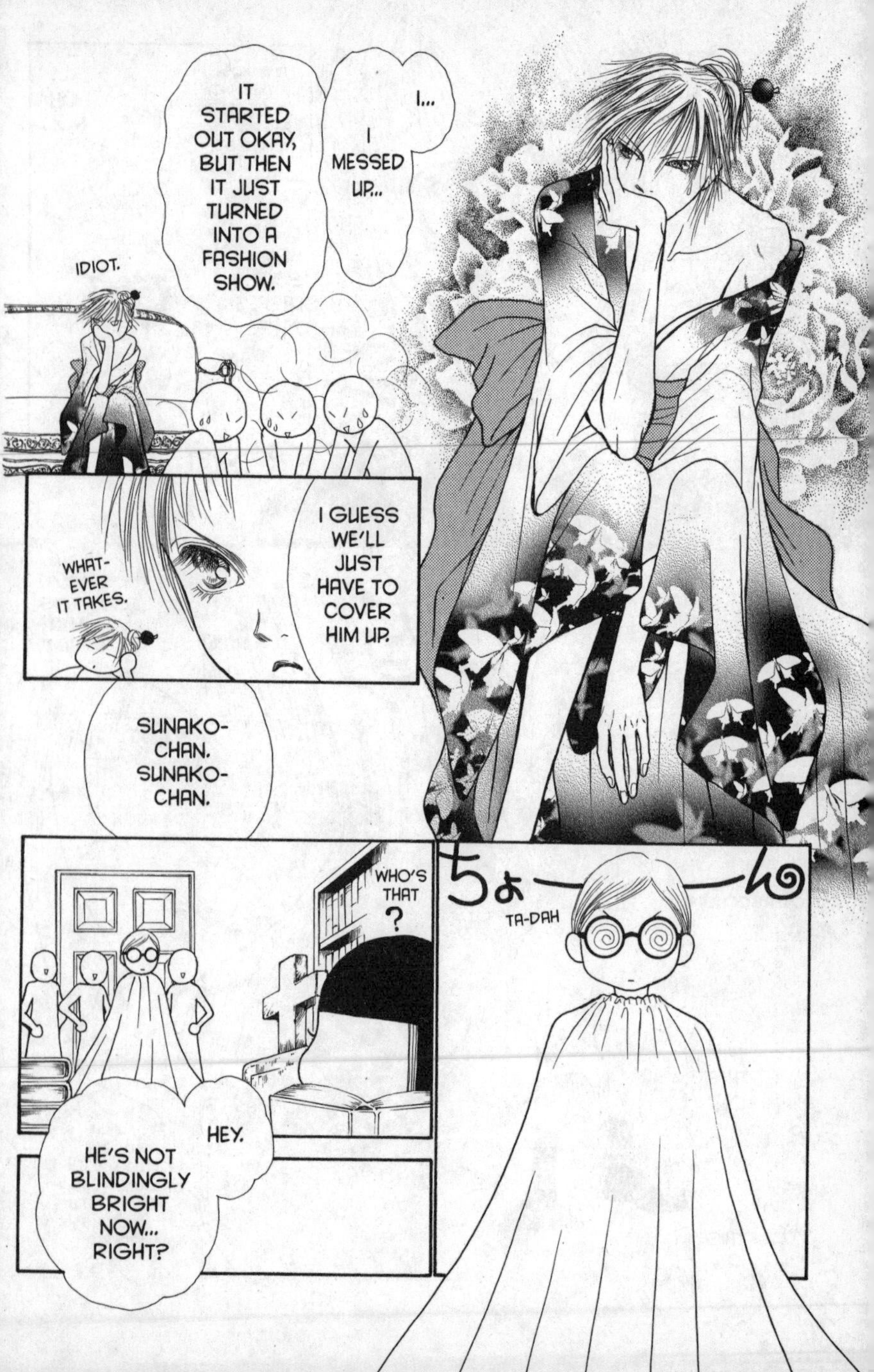
I...
I MESSED UP...
IT STARTED OUT OKAY, BUT THEN IT JUST TURNED INTO A FASHION SHOW.
IDIOT.
I GUESS WE'LL JUST HAVE TO COVER HIM UP.
WHAT-EVER IT TAKES.
SUNAKO-CHAN. SUNAKO-CHAN.
ちょーーん
TA-DAH
WHO'S THAT?
HEY.
HE'S NOT BLINDINGLY BRIGHT NOW... RIGHT?

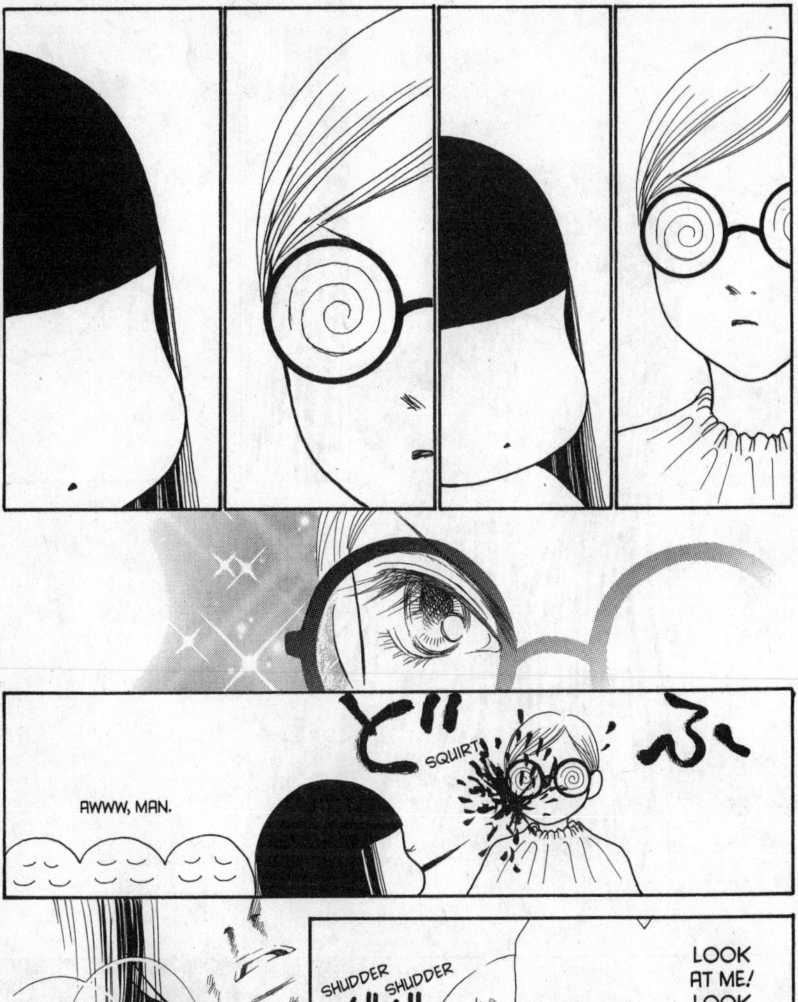

どふ
SQUIRT
AWWW, MAN.
LOOK AT ME! LOOK AT ME! I DID EVERYTHING I COULD.
WHAT'S YOUR PROBLEM?
SHUDDER SHUDDER
がくがく
GUSH GUSH
どくどく
WHAT'S MY PROBLEM?

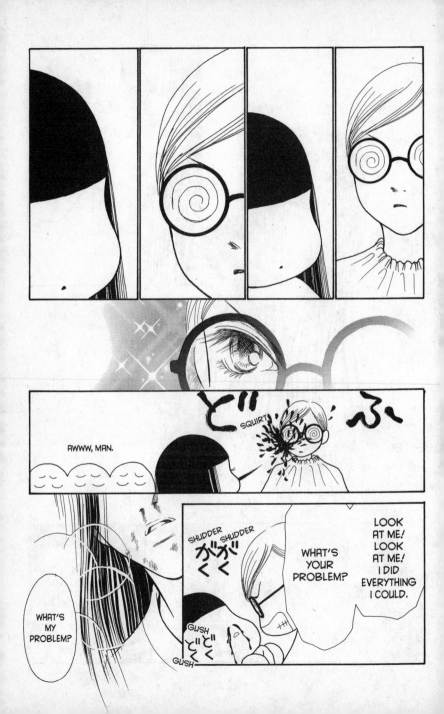

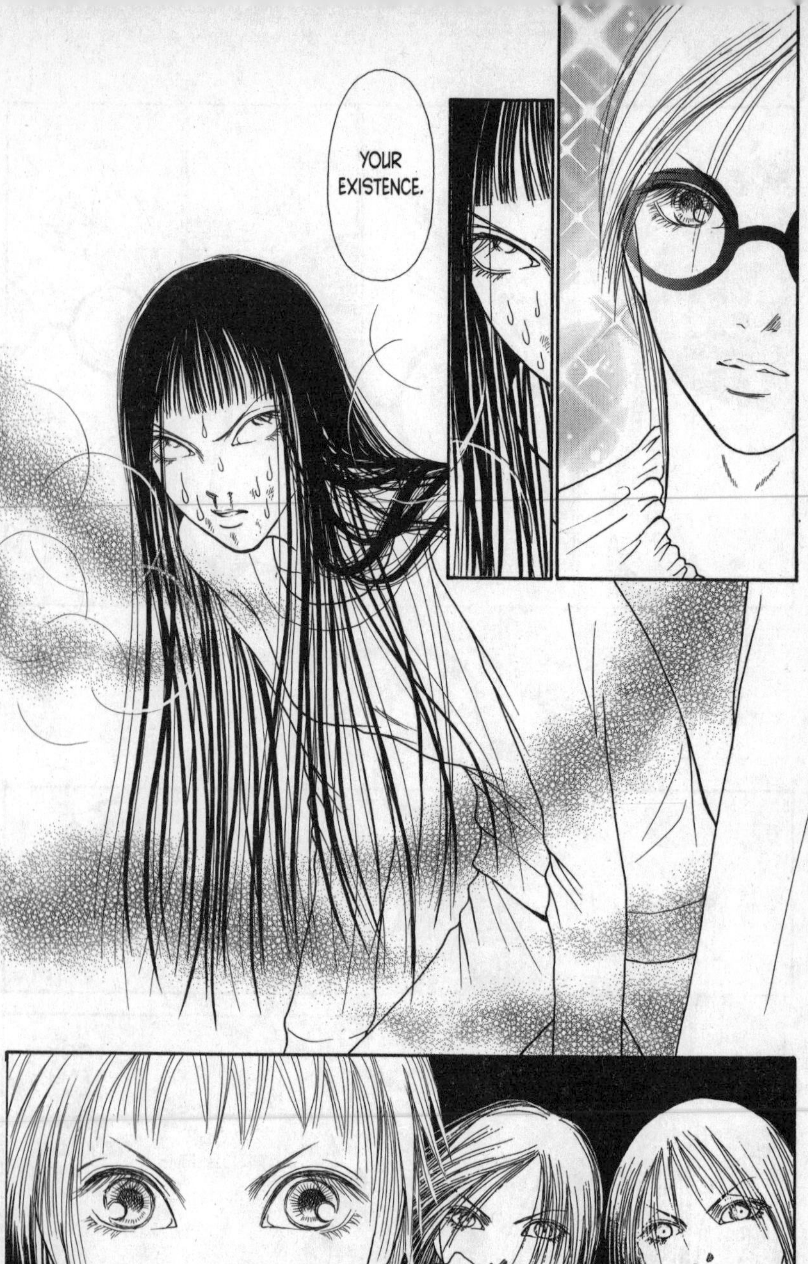
YOUR EXISTENCE.

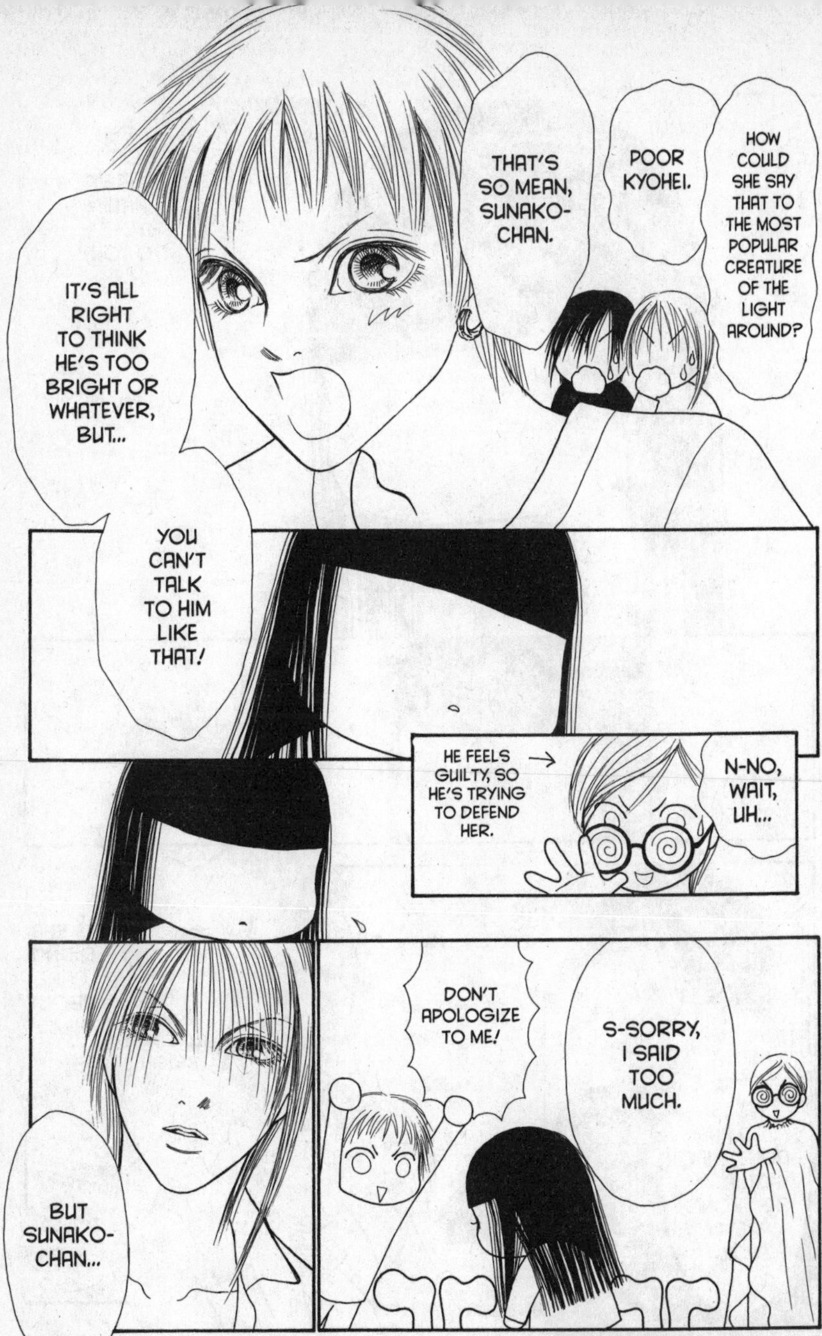
HOW COULD SHE SAY THAT TO THE MOST POPULAR CREATURE OF THE LIGHT AROUND?
POOR KYOHEI.
THAT'S SO MEAN, SUNAKO-CHAN.
IT'S ALL RIGHT TO THINK HE'S TOO BRIGHT OR WHATEVER, BUT...
YOU CAN'T TALK TO HIM LIKE THAT!
N-NO, WAIT, UH...
HE FEELS GUILTY, SO HE'S TRYING TO DEFEND HER. →
S-SORRY, I SAID TOO MUCH.
DON'T APOLOGIZE TO ME!
BUT SUNAKO-CHAN...

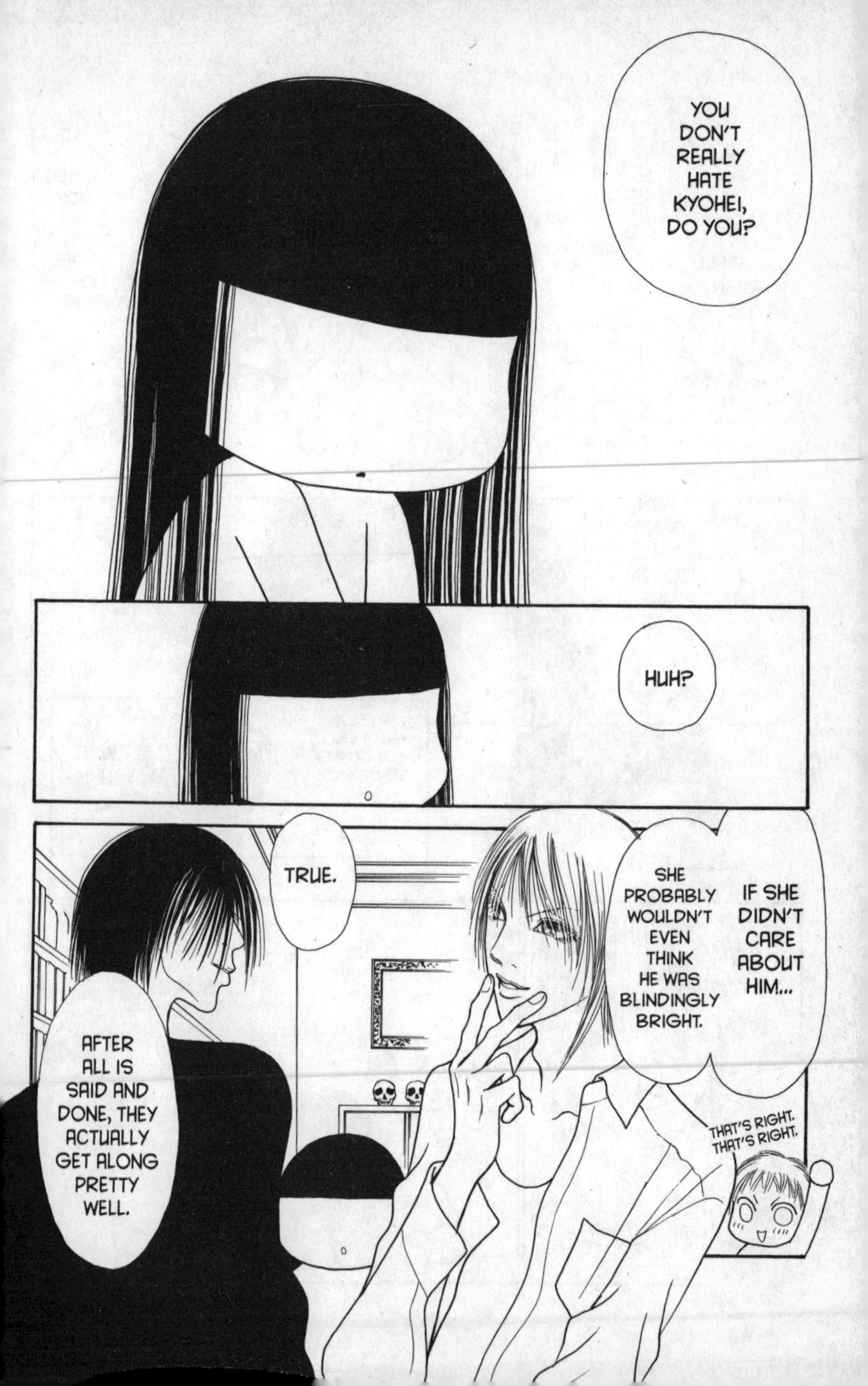
YOU DON'T REALLY HATE KYOHEI, DO YOU?
HUH?
IF SHE DIDN'T CARE ABOUT HIM... SHE PROBABLY WOULDN'T EVEN THINK HE WAS BLINDINGLY BRIGHT.
TRUE.
AFTER ALL IS SAID AND DONE, THEY ACTUALLY GET ALONG PRETTY WELL.
THAT'S RIGHT. THAT'S RIGHT.

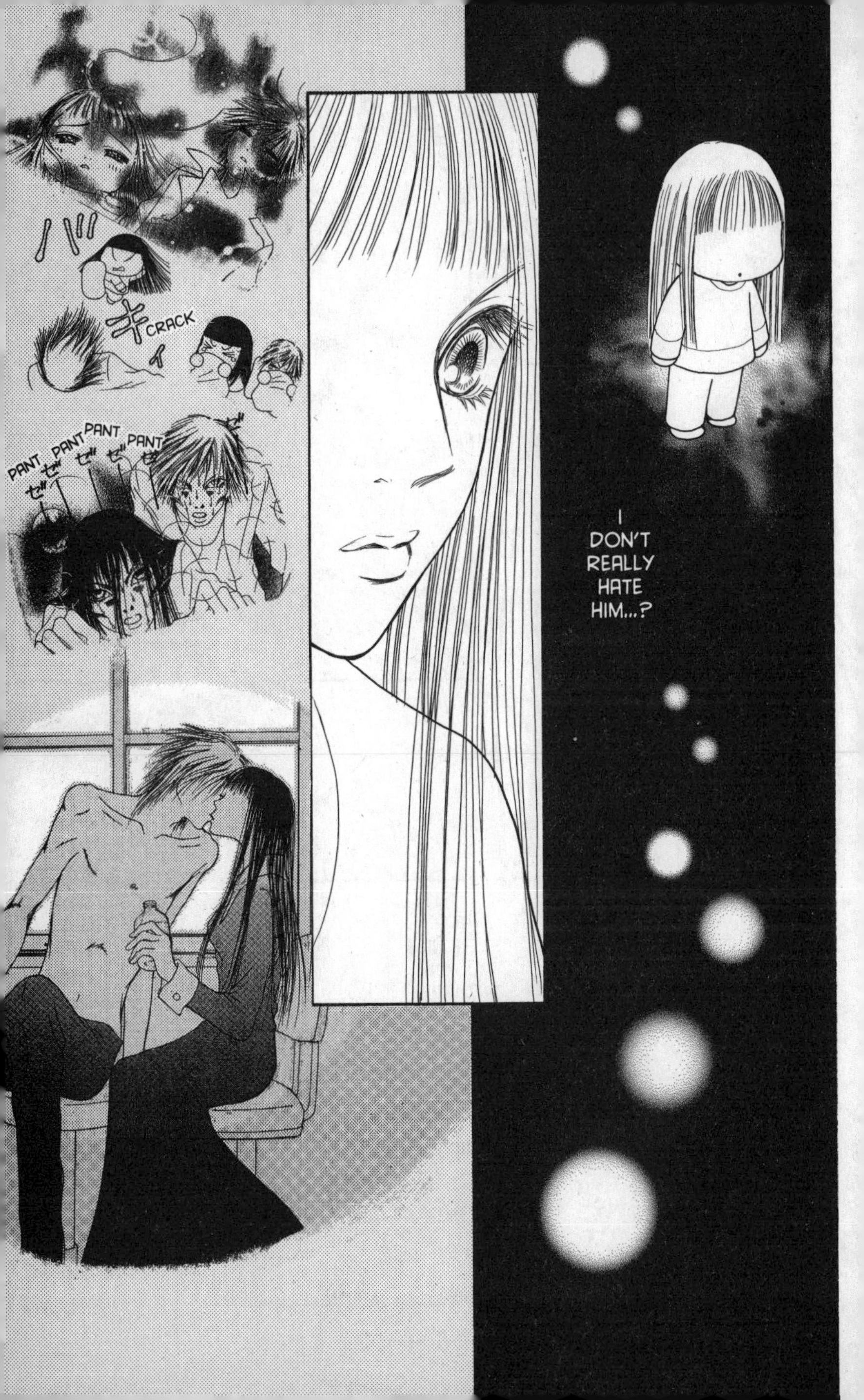
I DON'T REALLY HATE HIM...?
CRACK
PANT
PANT
PANT
PANT

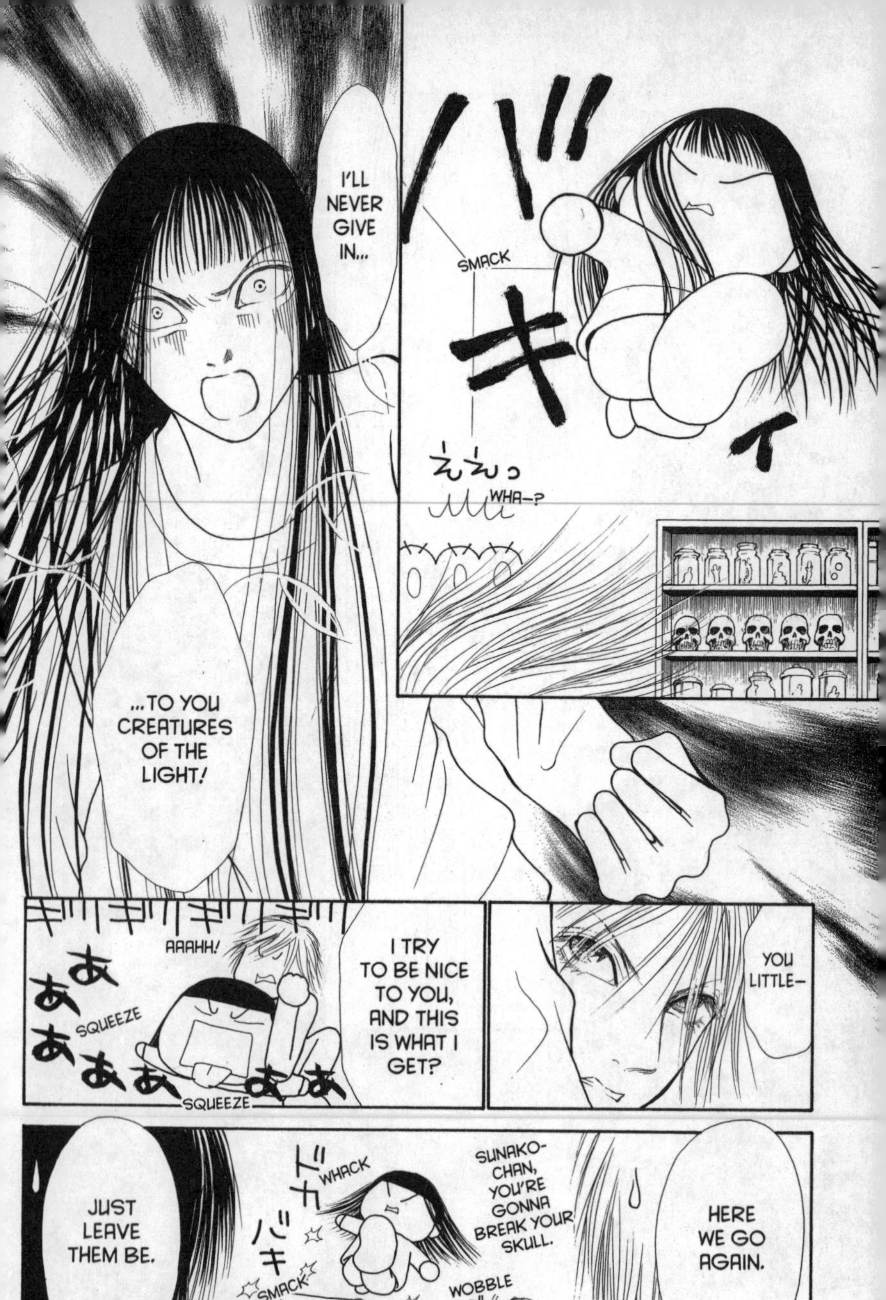
バキィ
SMACK
ええっ
WHA-?
I'LL NEVER GIVE IN...
...TO YOU CREATURES OF THE LIGHT!
YOU LITTLE-
I TRY TO BE NICE TO YOU, AND THIS IS WHAT I GET?
AAAHH!
SQUEEZE
SQUEEZE
HERE WE GO AGAIN.
SUNAKO-CHAN, YOU'RE GONNA BREAK YOUR SKULL.
WHACK
SMACK
WOBBLE
WOBBLE
JUST LEAVE THEM BE.

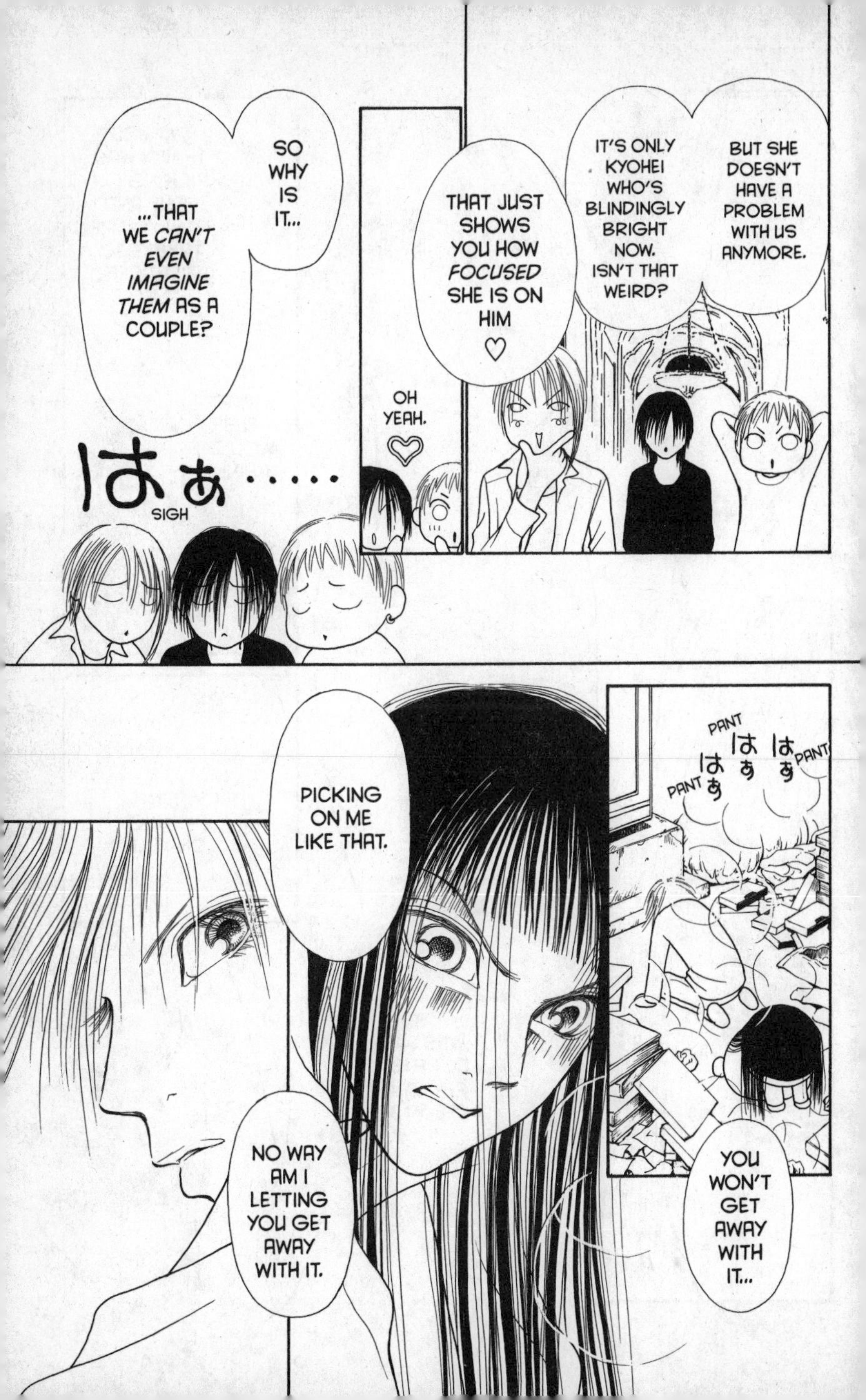

BUT SHE DOESN'T HAVE A PROBLEM WITH US ANYMORE.
IT'S ONLY KYOHEI WHO'S BLINDINGLY BRIGHT NOW. ISN'T THAT WEIRD?
THAT JUST SHOWS YOU HOW *FOCUSED* SHE IS ON HIM ♡
OH YEAH. ♡
SO WHY IS IT...
...THAT WE *CAN'T* EVEN IMAGINE *THEM* AS A COUPLE?
はぁ・・・・・
SIGH
はぁはぁはぁ
PANT PANT PANT
YOU WON'T GET AWAY WITH IT...
PICKING ON ME LIKE THAT.
NO WAY AM I LETTING YOU GET AWAY WITH IT.

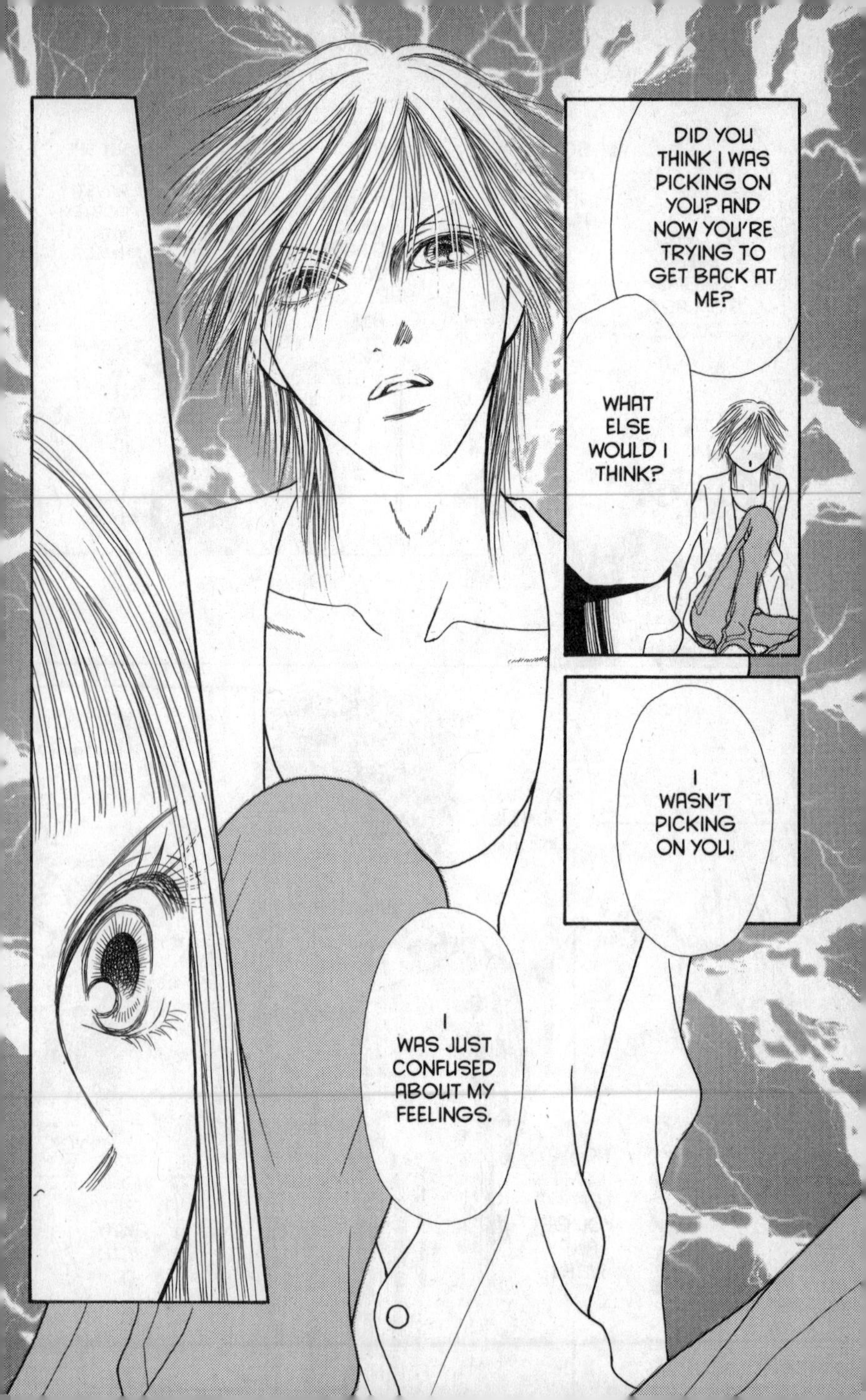
DID YOU THINK I WAS PICKING ON YOU? AND NOW YOU'RE TRYING TO GET BACK AT ME?
WHAT ELSE WOULD I THINK?
I WASN'T PICKING ON YOU.
I WAS JUST CONFUSED ABOUT MY FEELINGS.

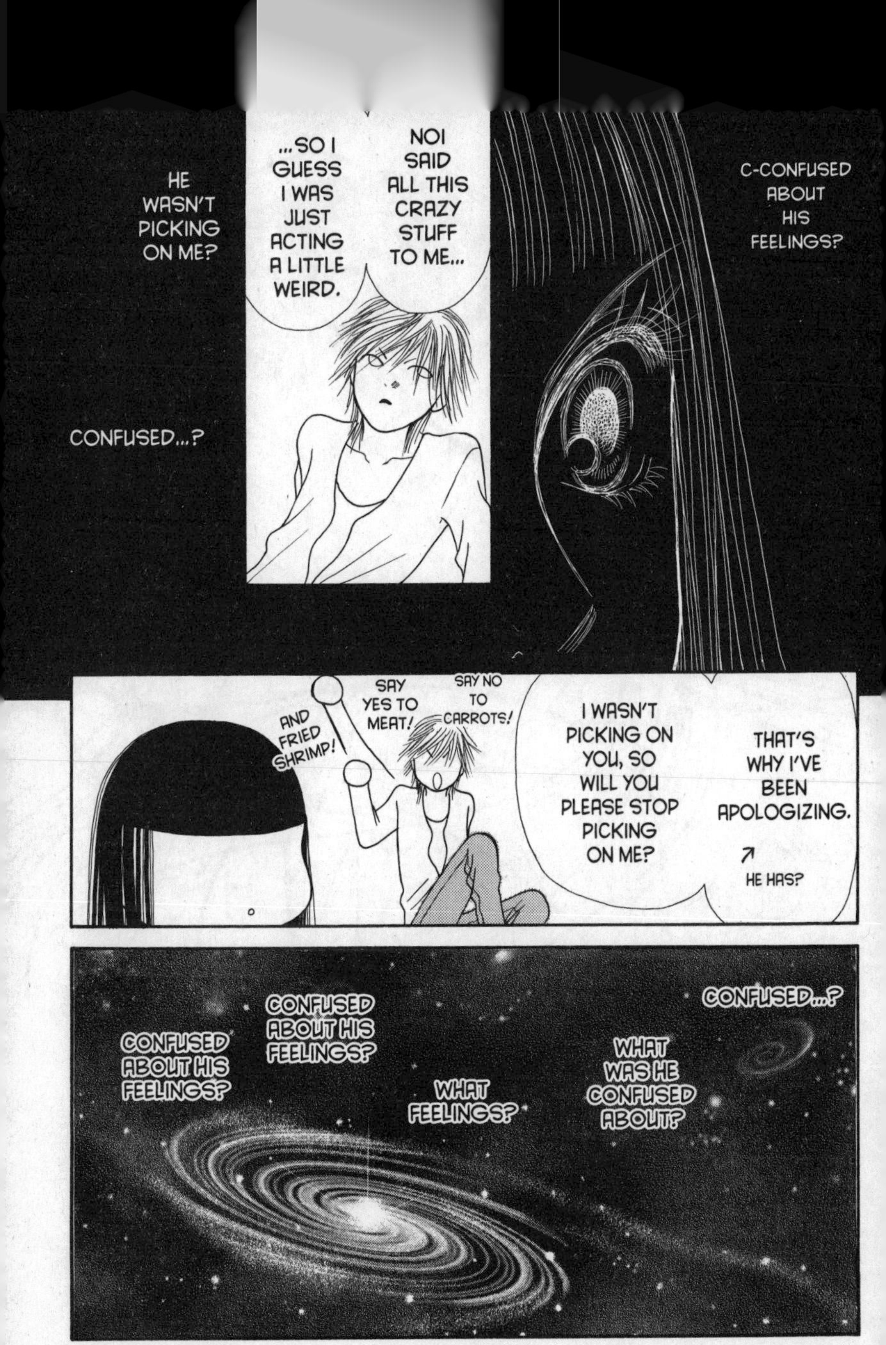

C-CONFUSED ABOUT HIS FEELINGS?
NOI SAID ALL THIS CRAZY STUFF TO ME...
...SO I GUESS I WAS JUST ACTING A LITTLE WEIRD.
HE WASN'T PICKING ON ME?
CONFUSED...?
THAT'S WHY I'VE BEEN APOLOGIZING.
HE HAS?
I WASN'T PICKING ON YOU, SO WILL YOU PLEASE STOP PICKING ON ME?
SAY NO TO CARROTS!
SAY YES TO MEAT!
AND FRIED SHRIMP!
CONFUSED...?
WHAT WAS HE CONFUSED ABOUT?
WHAT FEELINGS?
CONFUSED ABOUT HIS FEELINGS?
CONFUSED ABOUT HIS FEELINGS?

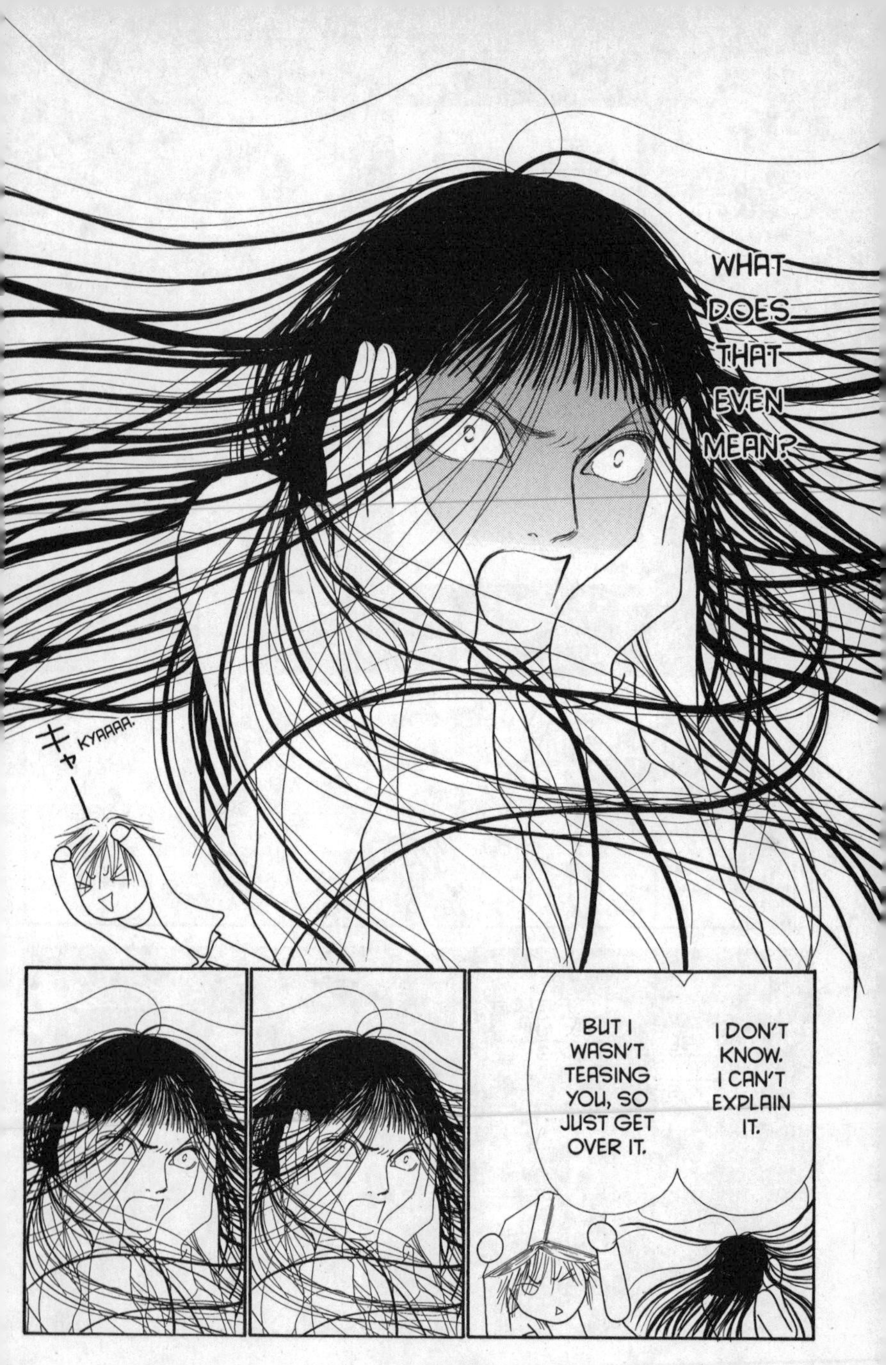
WHAT DOES THAT EVEN MEAN?
キャ KYAAAA.
I DON'T KNOW. I CAN'T EXPLAIN IT.
BUT I WASN'T TEASING YOU, SO JUST GET OVER IT.

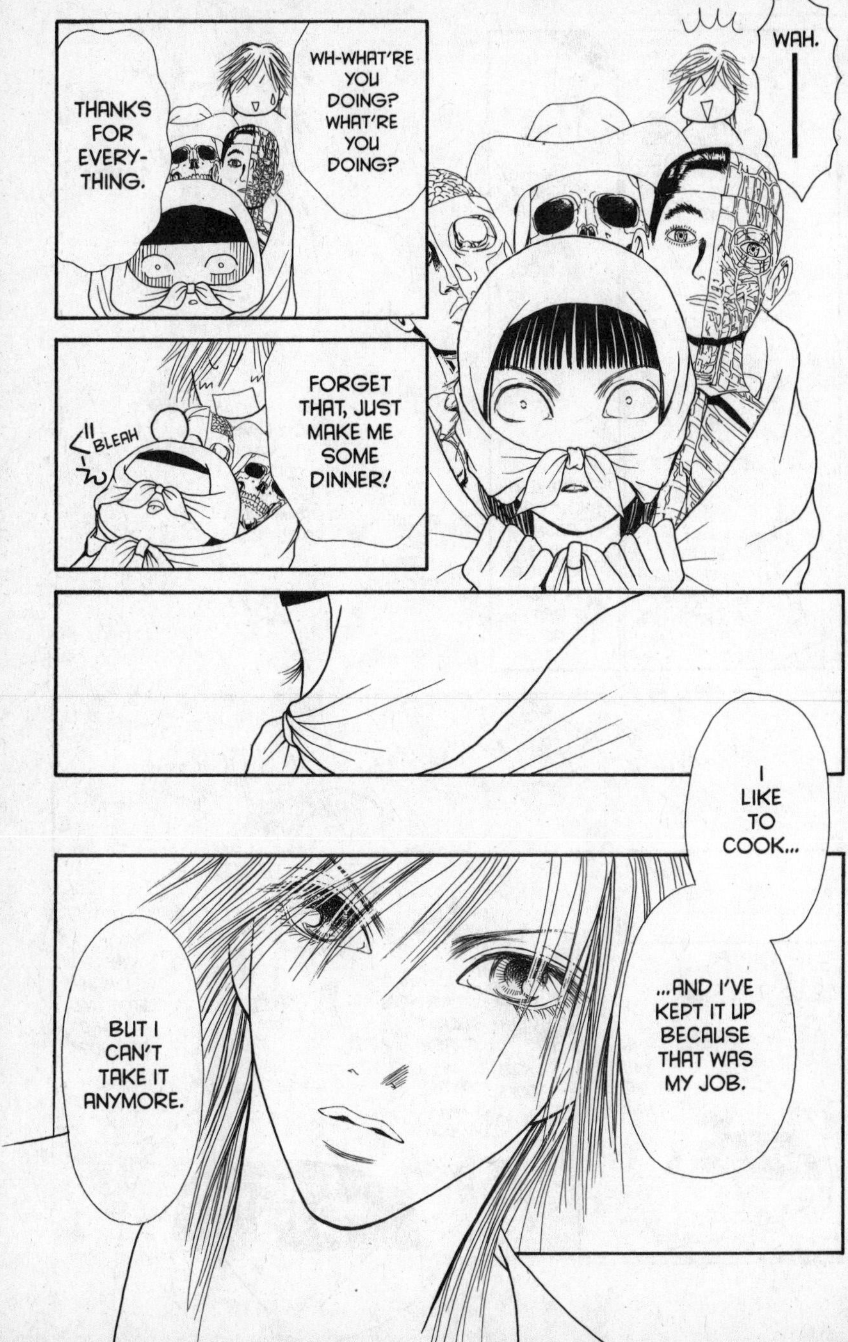
WAH.
WH-WHAT'RE YOU DOING? WHAT'RE YOU DOING?
THANKS FOR EVERY-THING.
FORGET THAT, JUST MAKE ME SOME DINNER!
BLEAH
I LIKE TO COOK...
...AND I'VE KEPT IT UP BECAUSE THAT WAS MY JOB.
BUT I CAN'T TAKE IT ANYMORE.

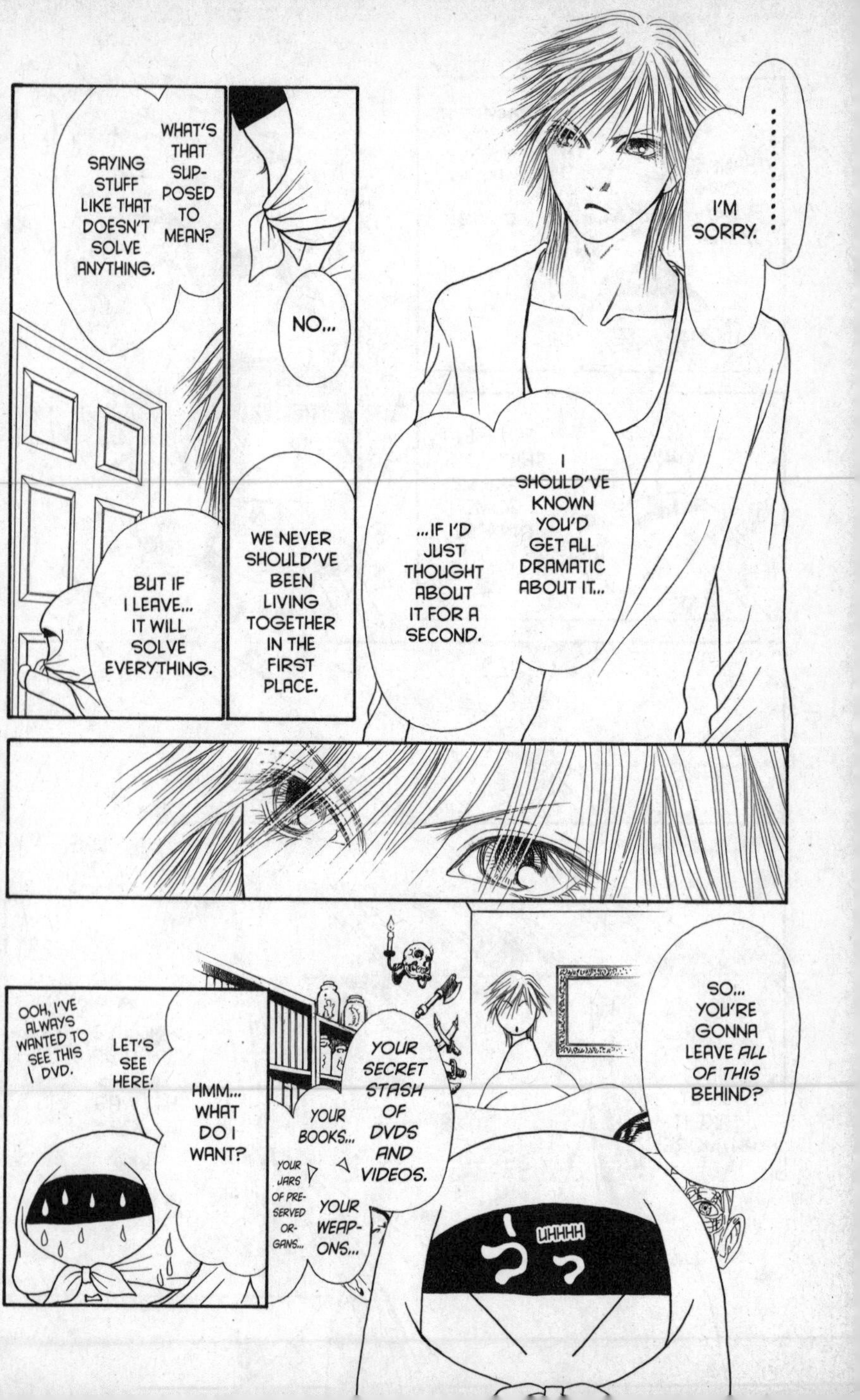
......
I'M SORRY.
I SHOULD'VE KNOWN YOU'D GET ALL DRAMATIC ABOUT IT...
...IF I'D JUST THOUGHT ABOUT IT FOR A SECOND.
NO...
WE NEVER SHOULD'VE BEEN LIVING TOGETHER IN THE FIRST PLACE.
WHAT'S THAT SUP-POSED TO MEAN?
SAYING STUFF LIKE THAT DOESN'T SOLVE ANYTHING.
BUT IF I LEAVE... IT WILL SOLVE EVERYTHING.
SO... YOU'RE GONNA LEAVE ALL OF THIS BEHIND?
うっ
UHHHH
YOUR SECRET STASH OF DVDS AND VIDEOS.
YOUR BOOKS...
YOUR WEAP-ONS...
YOUR JARS OF PRE-SERVED OR-GANS...
HMM... WHAT DO I WANT?
LET'S SEE HERE.
OOH, I'VE ALWAYS WANTED TO SEE THIS DVD.

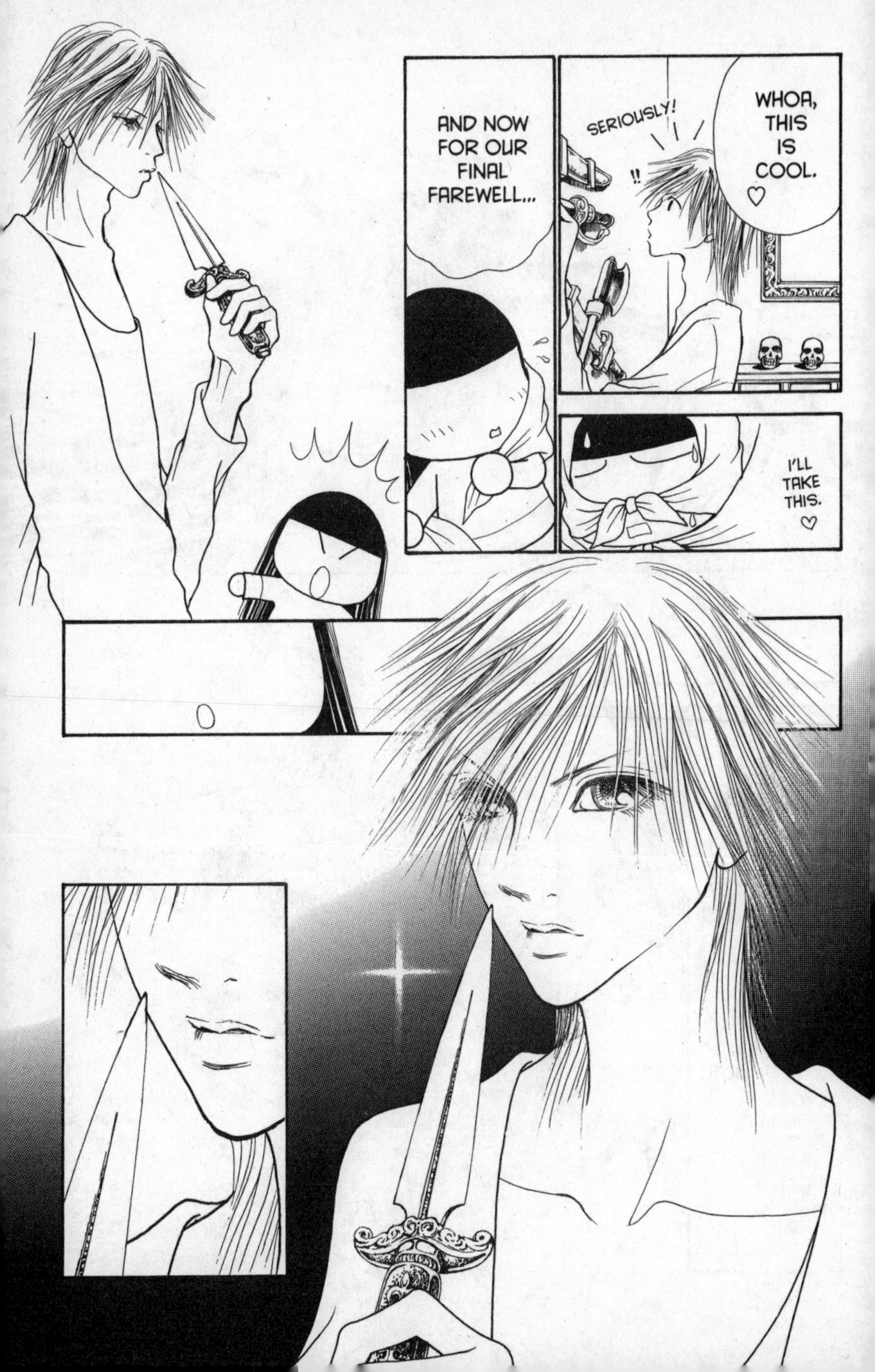
WHOA, THIS IS COOL. ♡
SERIOUSLY!
!!
AND NOW FOR OUR FINAL FAREWELL...
I'LL TAKE THIS. ♡

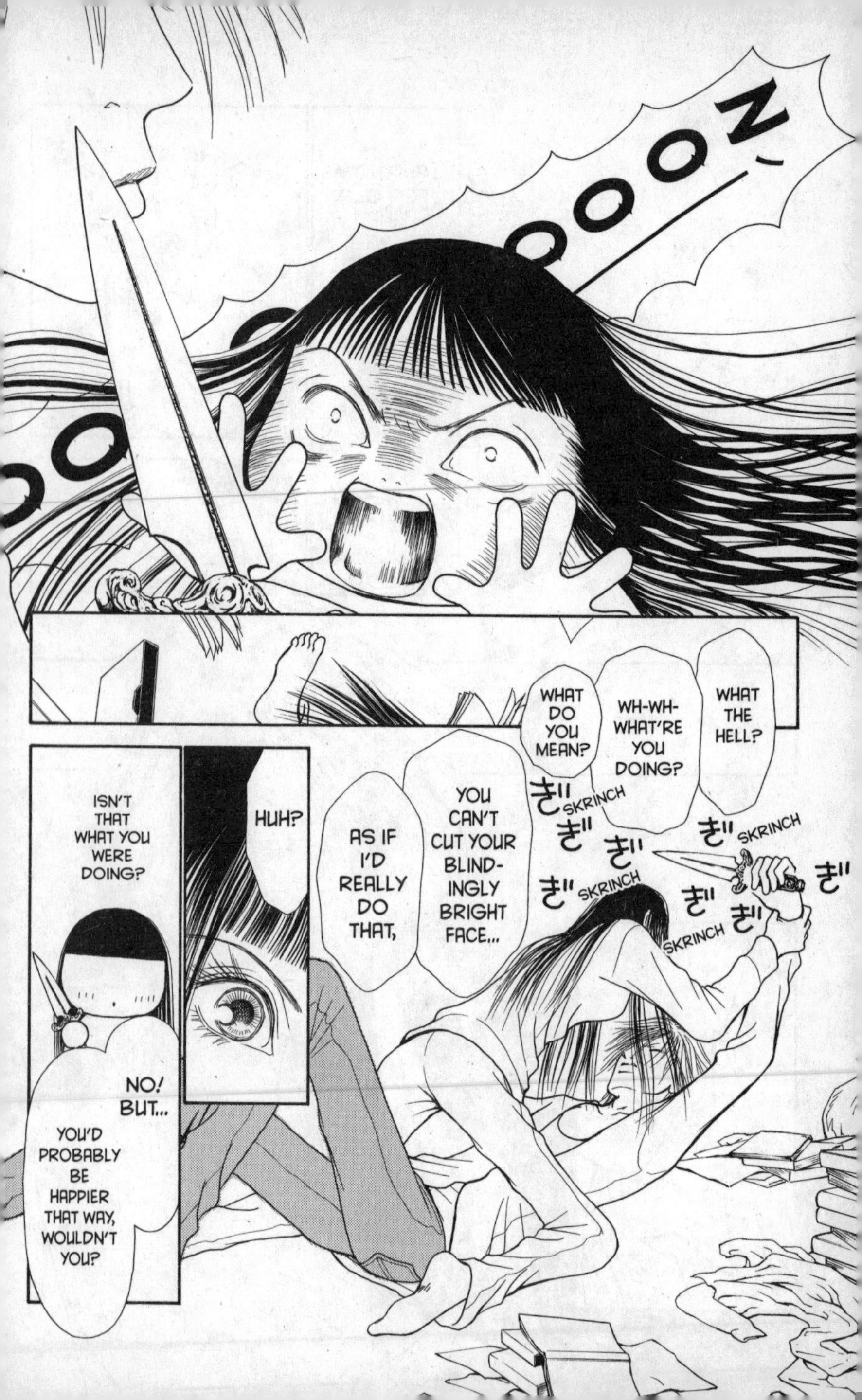
OOOOON
WHAT THE HELL?
WH-WH-WHAT'RE YOU DOING?
WHAT DO YOU MEAN?
ぎ SKRINCH
ぎ ぎ
ぎ SKRINCH
ぎ ぎ
ぎ SKRINCH
ぎ ぎ
ぎ SKRINCH
YOU CAN'T CUT YOUR BLIND-INGLY BRIGHT FACE...
AS IF I'D REALLY DO THAT,
HUH?
ISN'T THAT WHAT YOU WERE DOING?
NO! BUT...
YOU'D PROBABLY BE HAPPIER THAT WAY, WOULDN'T YOU?

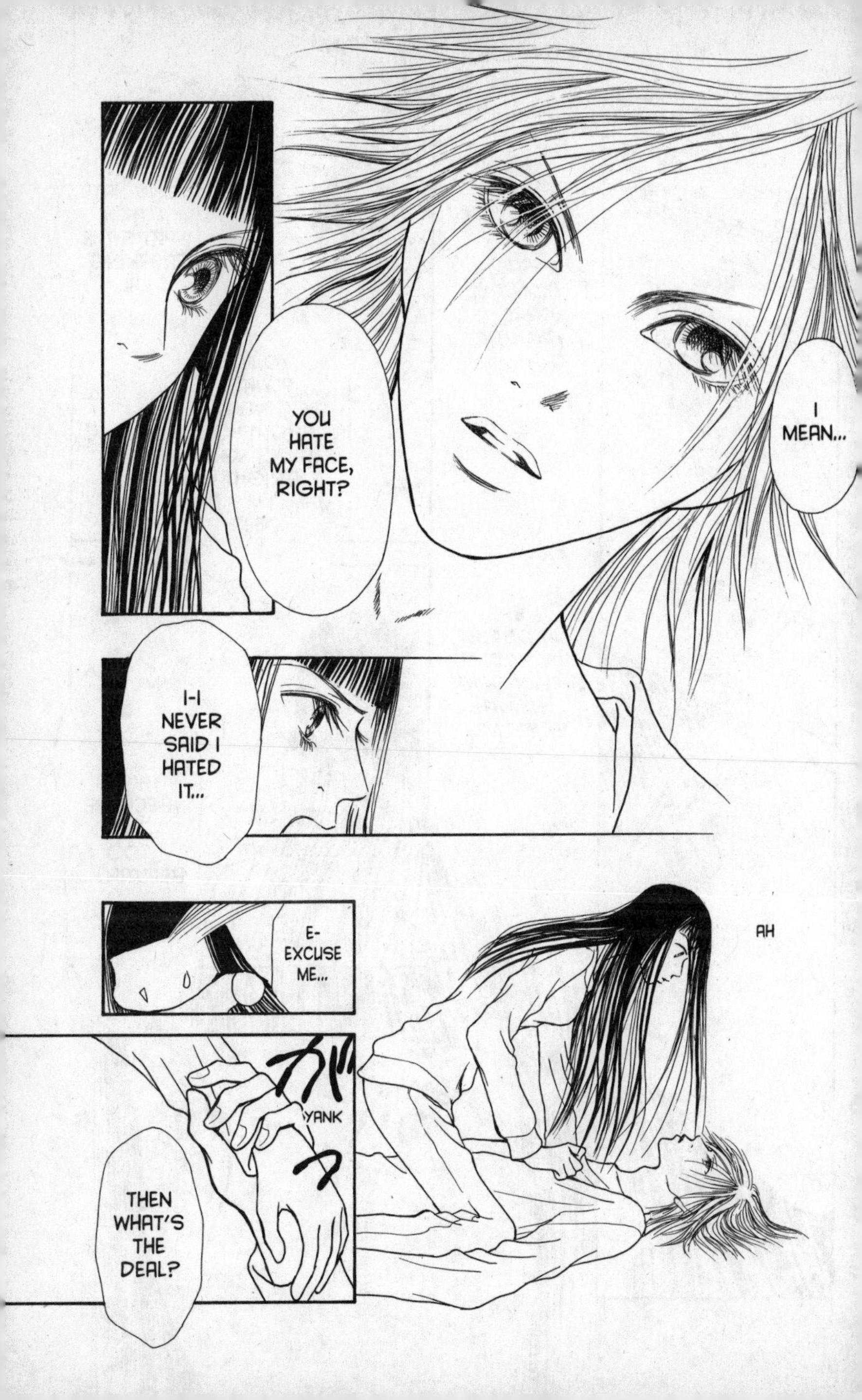
I MEAN...
YOU HATE MY FACE, RIGHT?
I-I NEVER SAID I HATED IT...
AH
E-EXCUSE ME...
YANK
THEN WHAT'S THE DEAL?

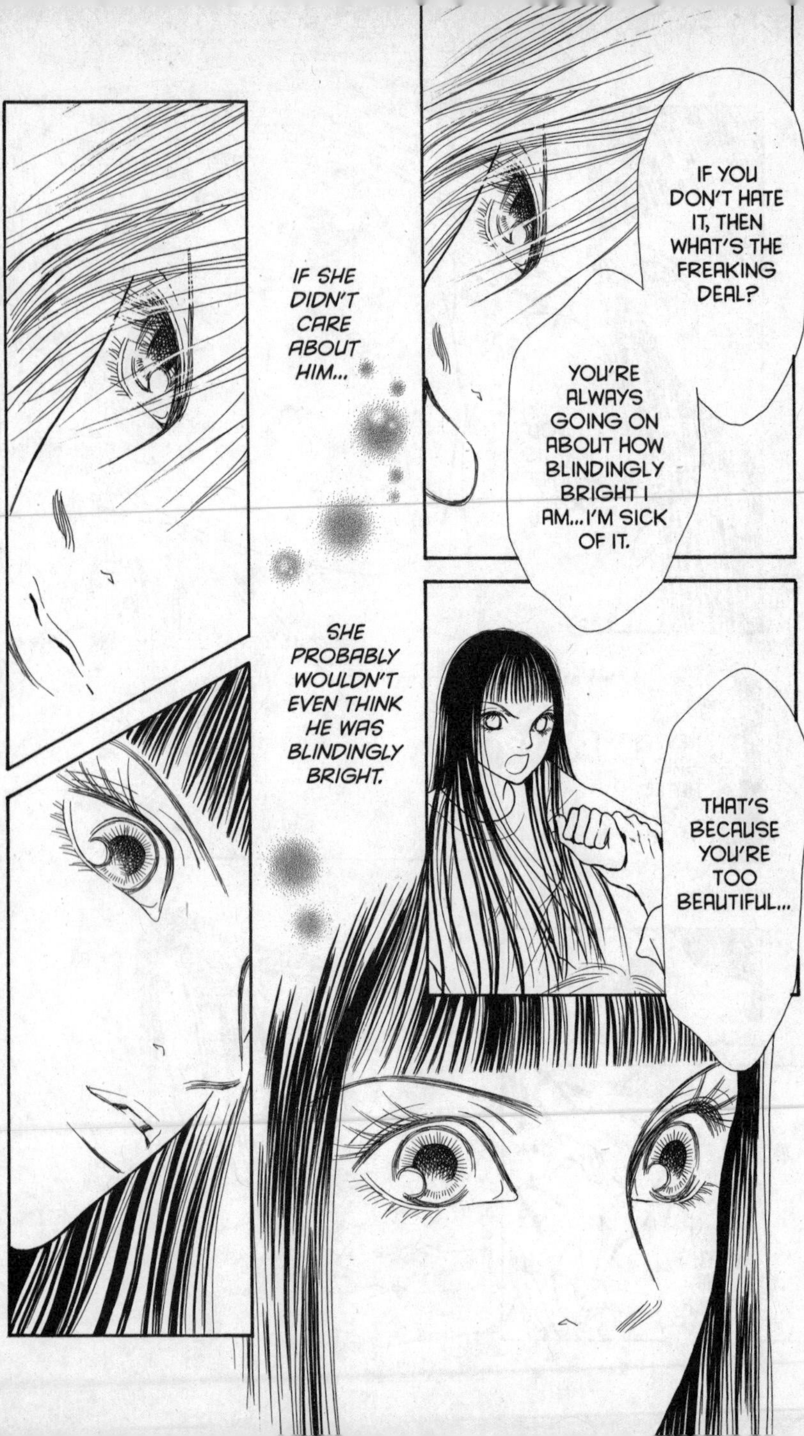
IF YOU DON'T HATE IT, THEN WHAT'S THE FREAKING DEAL?
YOU'RE ALWAYS GOING ON ABOUT HOW BLINDINGLY BRIGHT I AM...I'M SICK OF IT.
IF SHE DIDN'T CARE ABOUT HIM...
THAT'S BECAUSE YOU'RE TOO BEAUTIFUL...
SHE PROBABLY WOULDN'T EVEN THINK HE WAS BLINDINGLY BRIGHT.

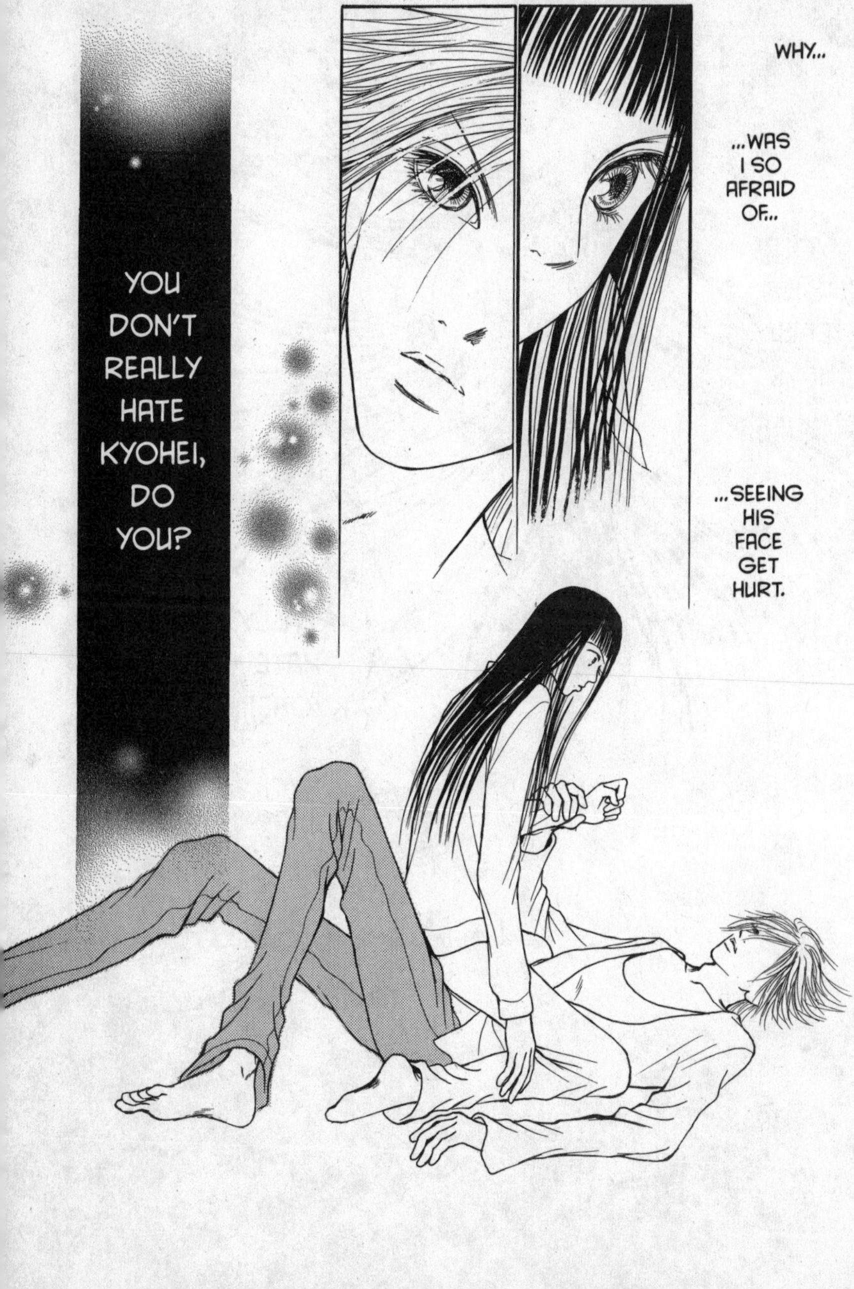
WHY...
...WAS I SO AFRAID OF...
...SEEING HIS FACE GET HURT.
YOU DON'T REALLY HATE KYOHEI, DO YOU?

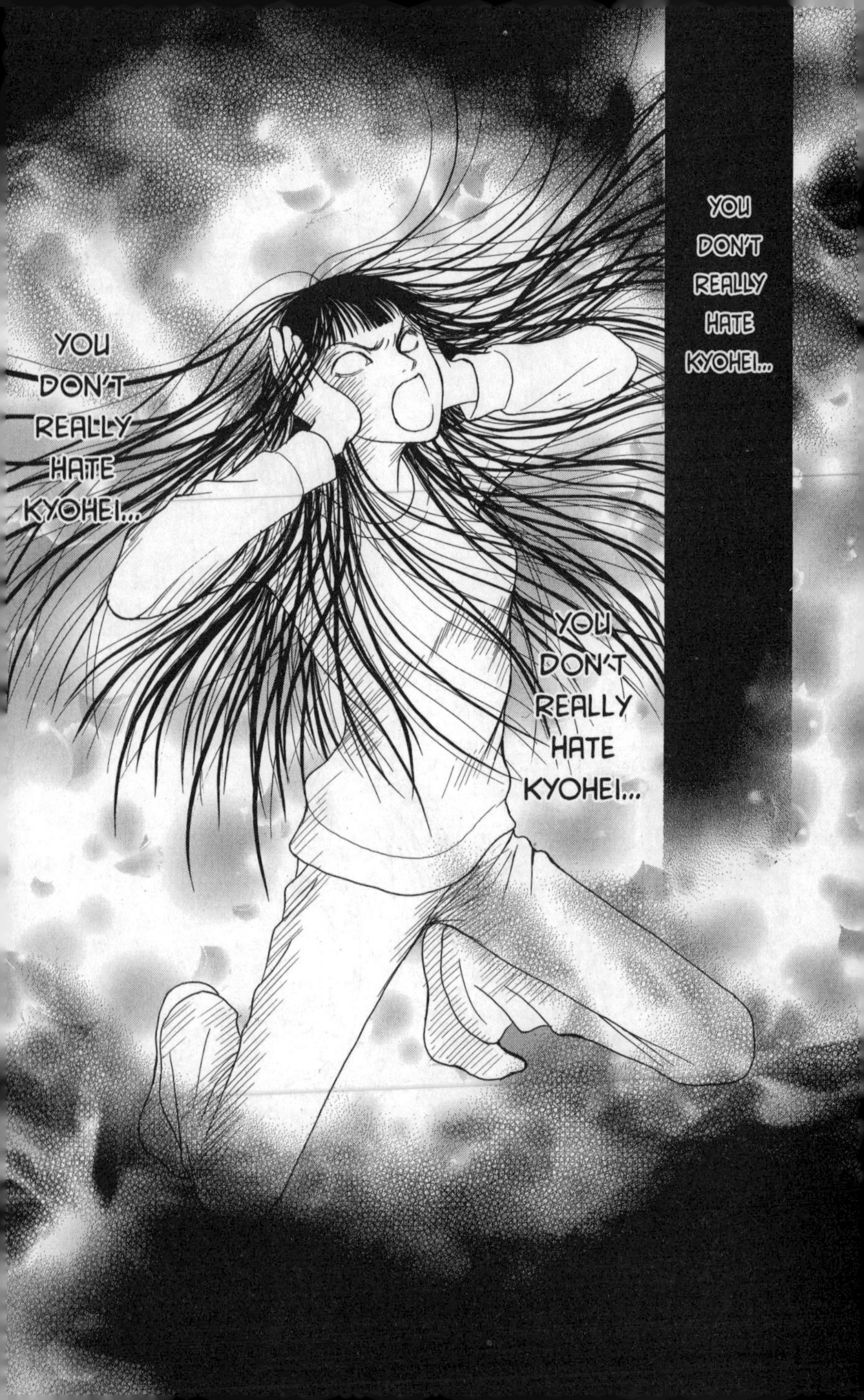
YOU DON'T REALLY HATE KYOHEI...
YOU DON'T REALLY HATE KYOHEI...
YOU DON'T REALLY HATE KYOHEI...

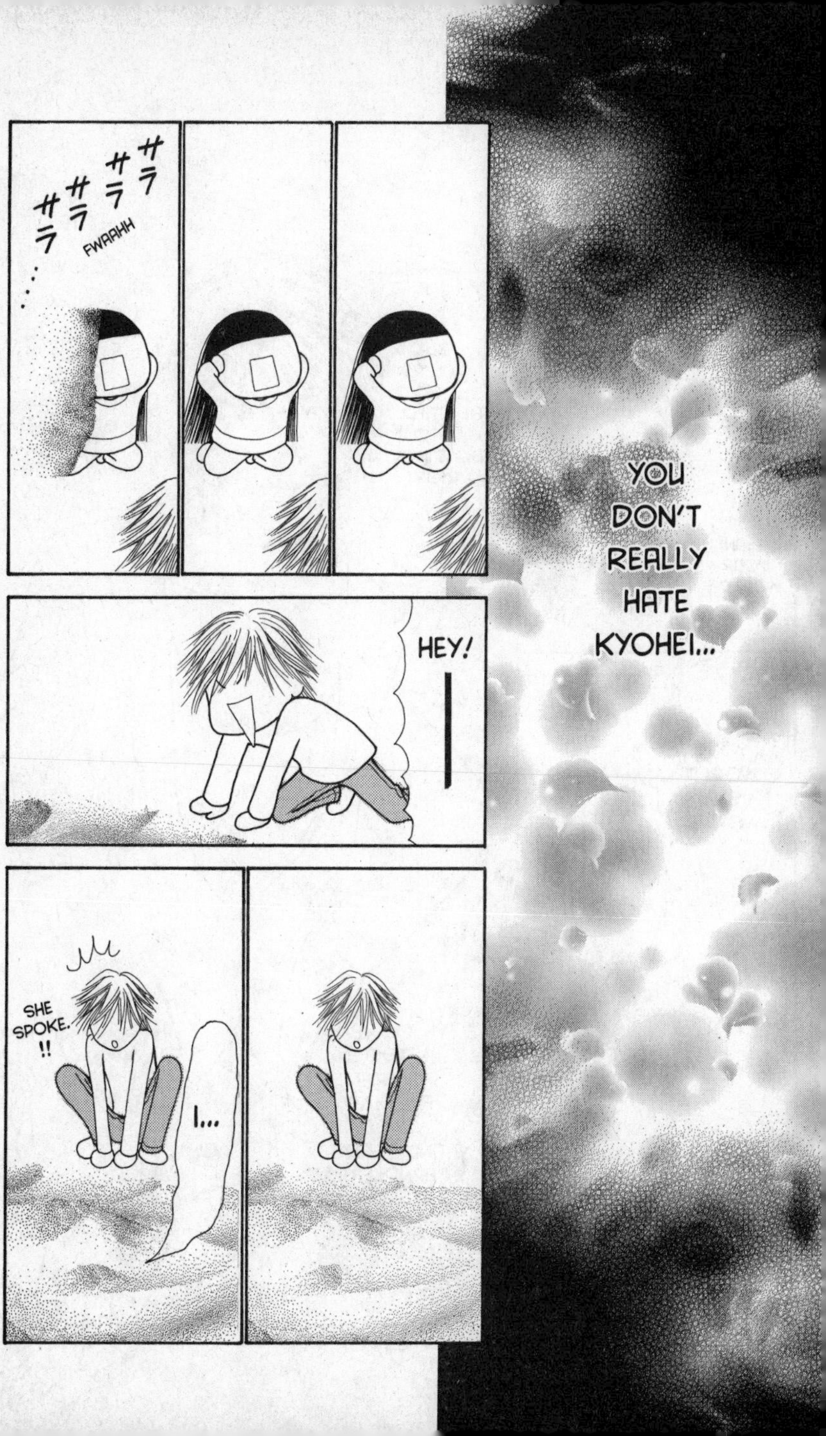

YOU DON'T REALLY HATE KYOHEI...
サラサラサラ
FWAAHH
...
HEY!
I...
SHE SPOKE. !!

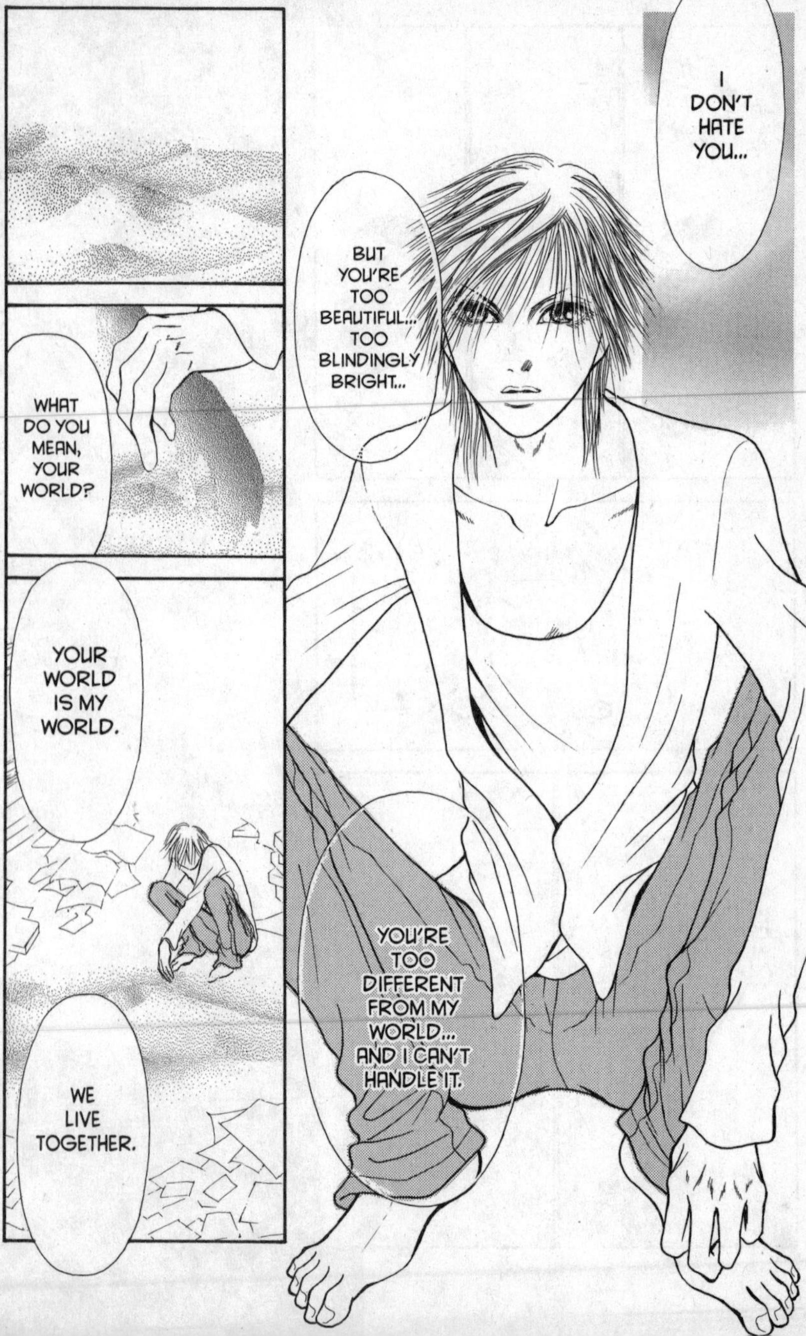

I DON'T HATE YOU...
BUT YOU'RE TOO BEAUTIFUL... TOO BLINDINGLY BRIGHT...
YOU'RE TOO DIFFERENT FROM MY WORLD... AND I CAN'T HANDLE IT.
WHAT DO YOU MEAN, YOUR WORLD?
YOUR WORLD IS MY WORLD.
WE LIVE TOGETHER.

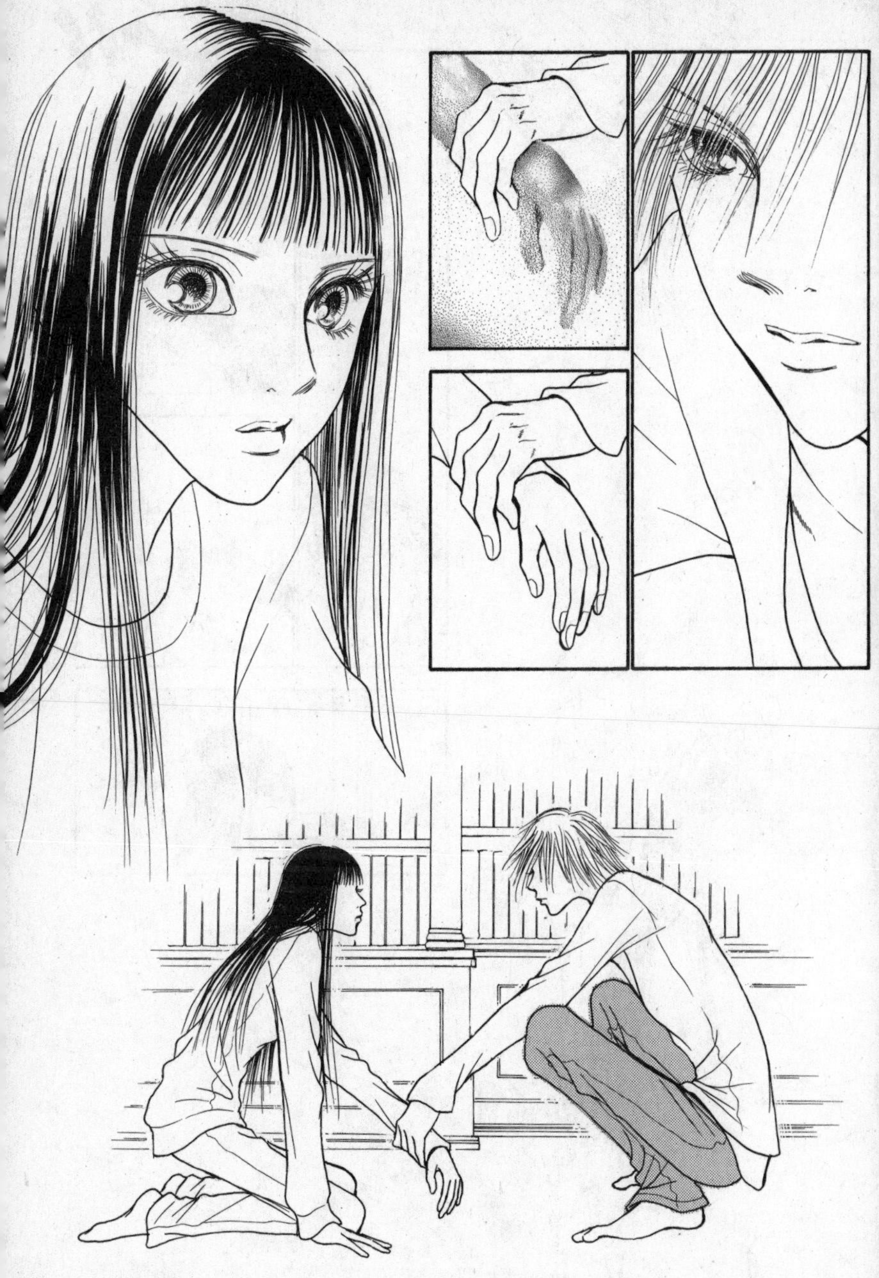

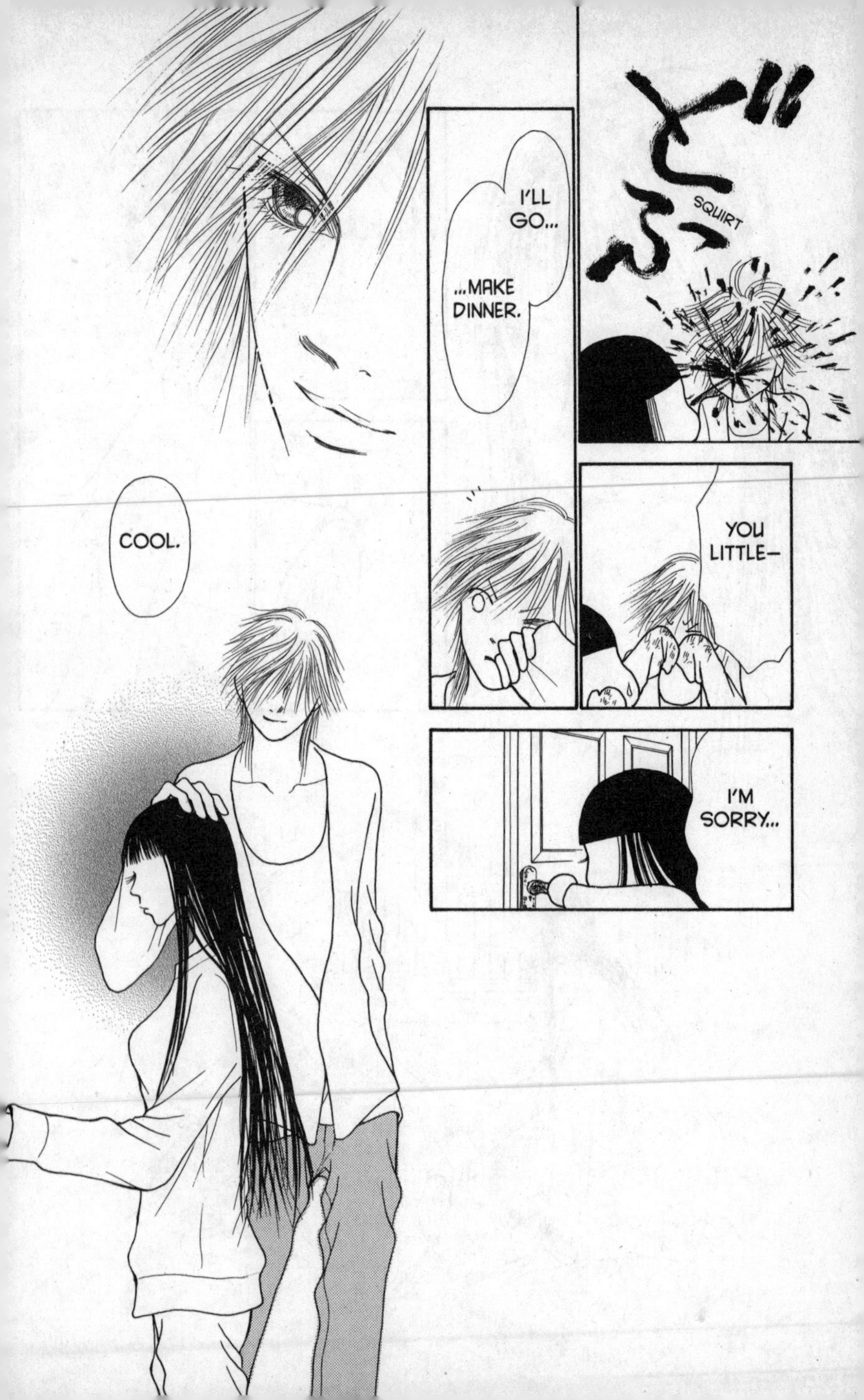
SQUIRT
YOU LITTLE—
I'LL GO...
...MAKE DINNER.
I'M SORRY...
COOL.

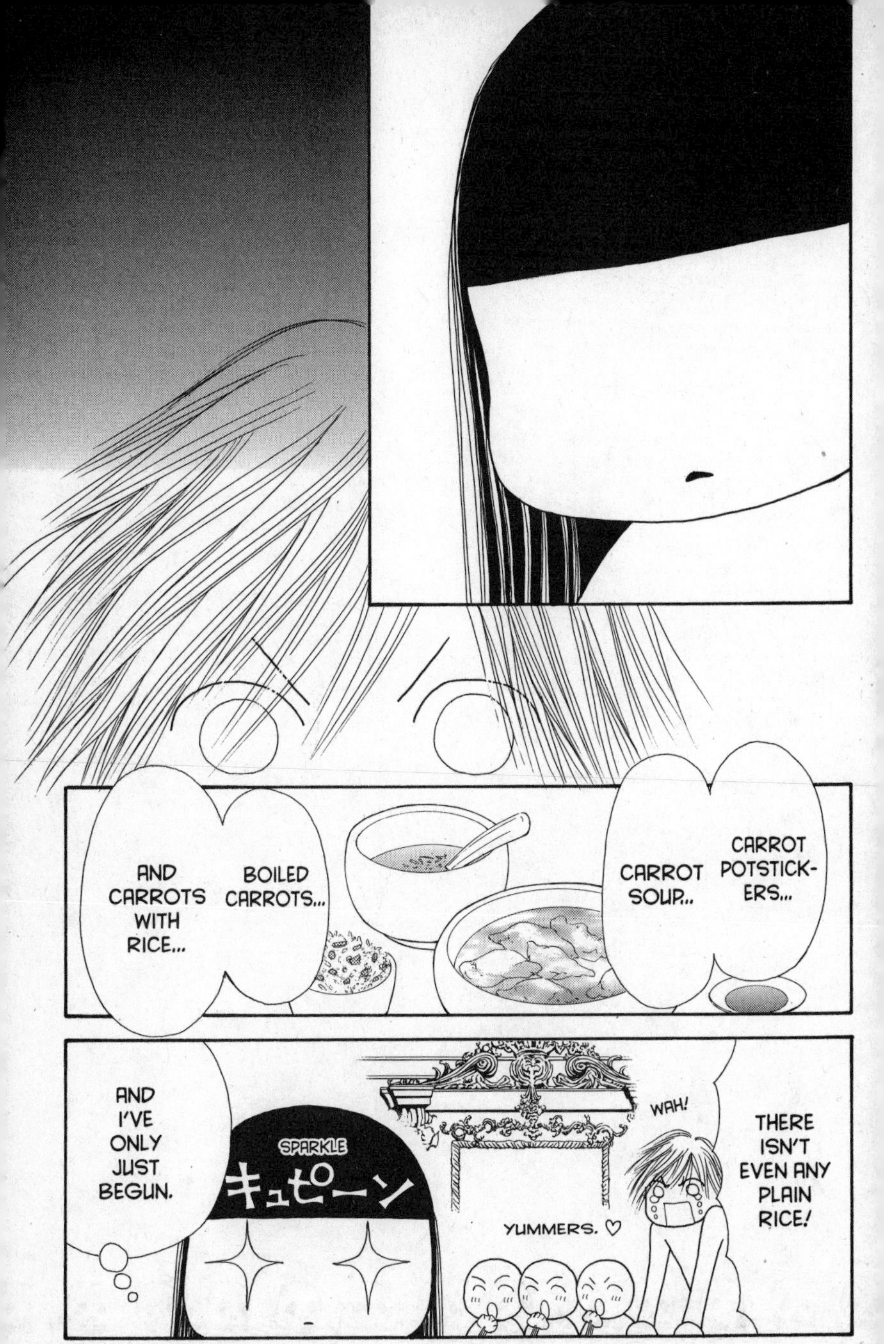
CARROT POTSTICKERS...
CARROT SOUP...
BOILED CARROTS...
AND CARROTS WITH RICE...
THERE ISN'T EVEN ANY PLAIN RICE!
WAH!
YUMMERS. ♡
SPARKLE
キュピーン
AND I'VE ONLY JUST BEGUN.

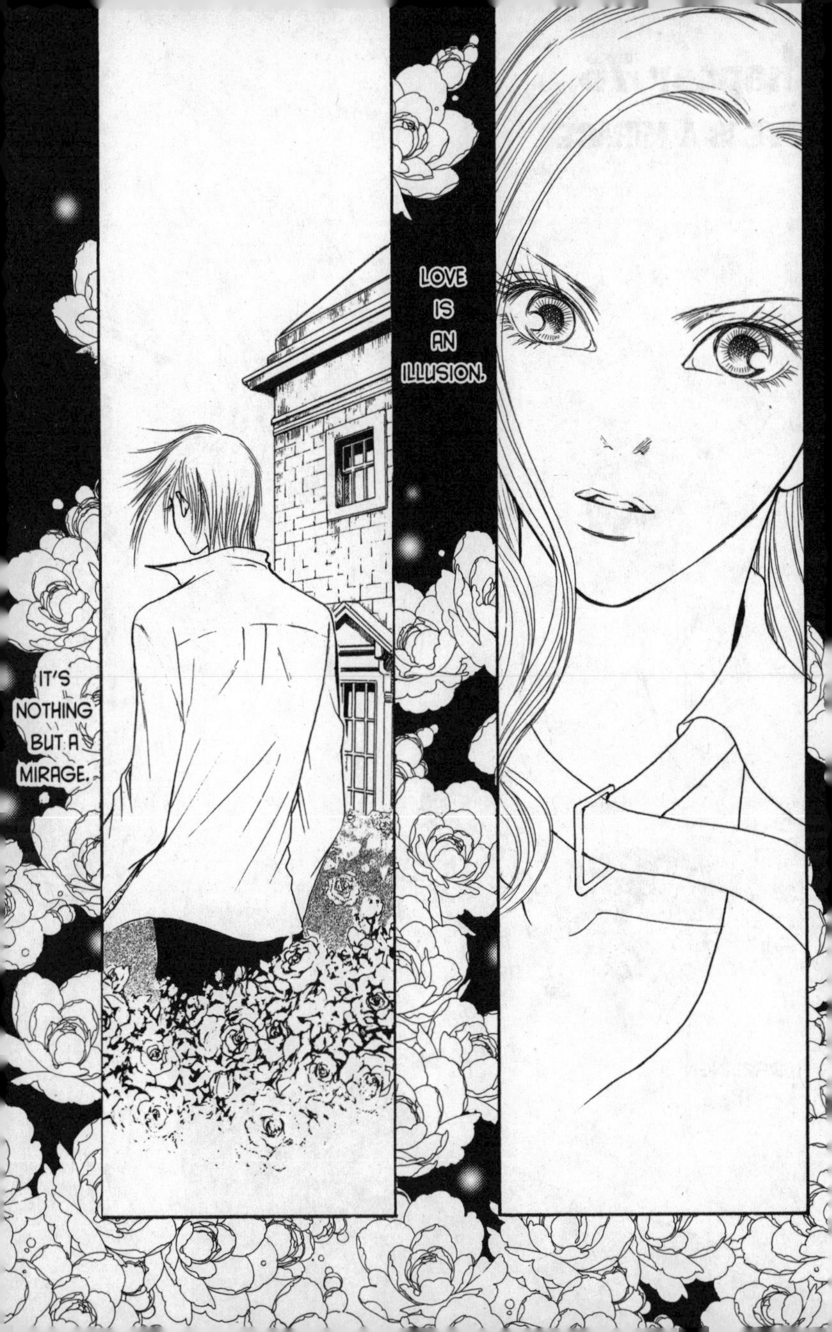
LOVE IS AN ILLUSION.
IT'S NOTHING BUT A MIRAGE.

Chapter 76

LOVE IS A MIRAGE

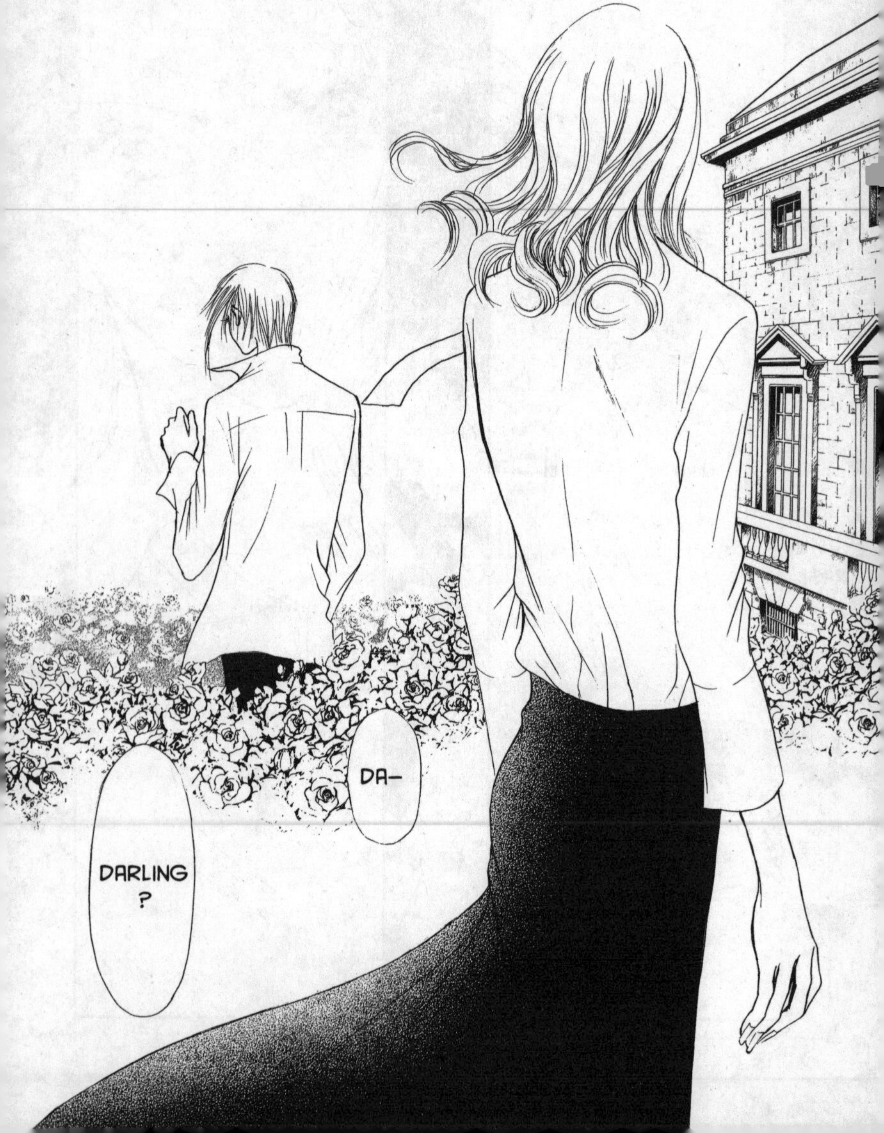
DA-
DARLING
?

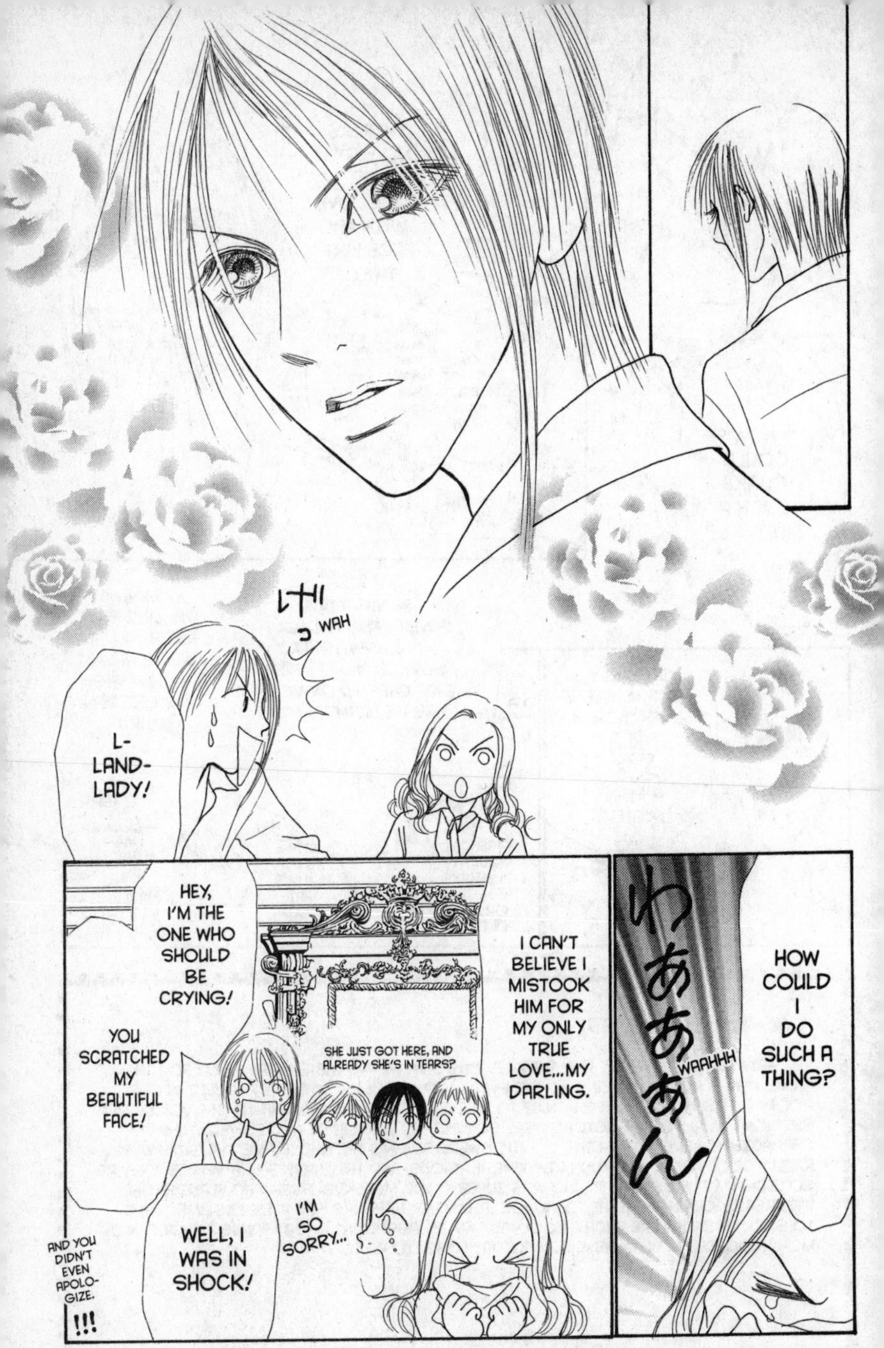
WAH
L-LANDLADY!
わあああん
WAAHHH
HOW COULD I DO SUCH A THING?
I CAN'T BELIEVE I MISTOOK HIM FOR MY ONLY TRUE LOVE...MY DARLING.
HEY, I'M THE ONE WHO SHOULD BE CRYING!
YOU SCRATCHED MY BEAUTIFUL FACE!
SHE JUST GOT HERE, AND ALREADY SHE'S IN TEARS?
I'M SO SORRY...
WELL, I WAS IN SHOCK!
AND YOU DIDN'T EVEN APOLOGIZE.
!!!

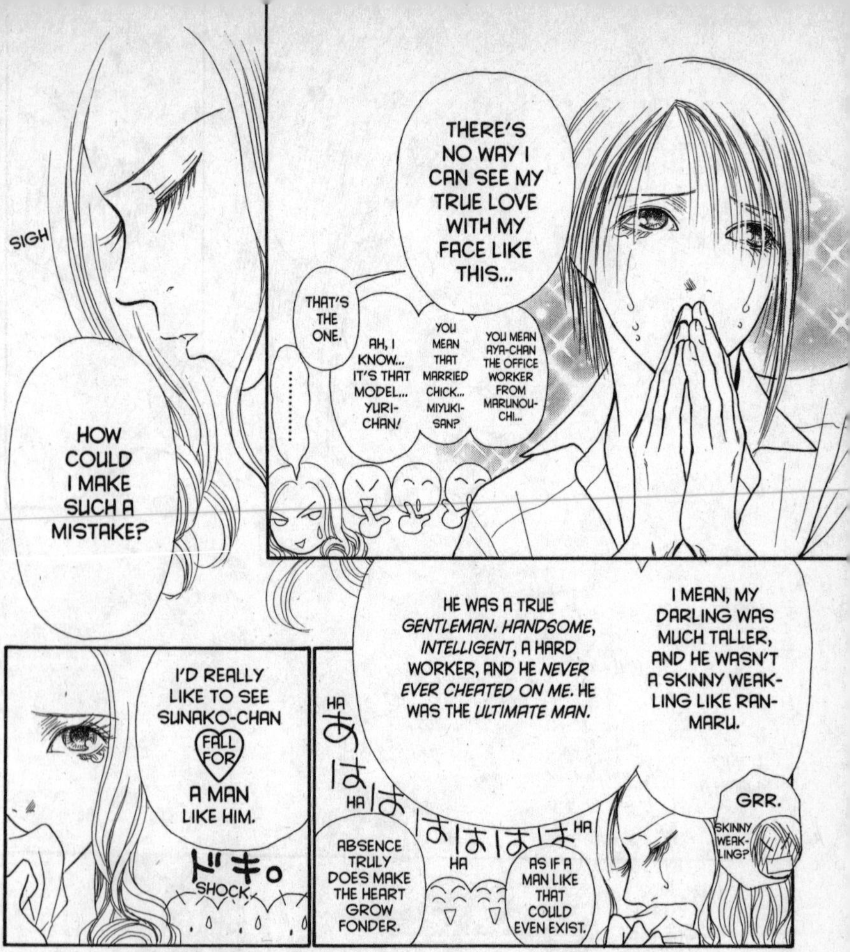
THERE'S NO WAY I CAN SEE MY TRUE LOVE WITH MY FACE LIKE THIS...
YOU MEAN AYA-CHAN THE OFFICE WORKER FROM MARUNOU-CHI...
YOU MEAN THAT MARRIED CHICK... MIYUKI-SAN?
AH, I KNOW... IT'S THAT MODEL... YURI-CHAN!
THAT'S THE ONE.
......
SIGH
HOW COULD I MAKE SUCH A MISTAKE?
I MEAN, MY DARLING WAS MUCH TALLER, AND HE WASN'T A SKINNY WEAK-LING LIKE RAN-MARU.
HE WAS A TRUE *GENTLEMAN. HANDSOME, INTELLIGENT*, A HARD WORKER, AND HE *NEVER EVER CHEATED ON ME*. HE WAS THE *ULTIMATE MAN*.
GRR.
SKINNY WEAK-LING?
あ HA は HA ははははは HA HA
AS IF A MAN LIKE THAT COULD EVEN EXIST.
ABSENCE TRULY DOES MAKE THE HEART GROW FONDER.
I'D REALLY LIKE TO SEE SUNAKO-CHAN FALL FOR A MAN LIKE HIM.
ドキ。
SHOCK

BEHIND THE SCENES

BETWEEN THIS EPISODE AND THE PREVIOUS ONE, WE HAD A BIG WRAP PARTY FOR THE ANIME. IT WAS REALLY AMAZING TO SEE EVERYBODY INVOLVED WITH THE PROJECT IN ONE ROOM. EVERYBODY WAS REALLY NICE TO ME EVEN THOUGH I ONLY WENT TO ONE VOICE-OVER SESSION. ♡ ALL OF THE ACTORS WERE SO KIND. ♡ THE GIRLS WHO PLAYED THE MAIN CHARACTERS WERE SUPER-CUTE. ♡ THEY WERE SMILING THE WHOLE TIME. THE GUYS WERE REALLY COOL TOO... AND FUNNY. THEY'RE HILARIOUS, AND THEY HAVE GREAT VOICES. THEY'RE SO LUCKY. ♡ EVERYONE REALLY WAS SUPER-COOL. MORIKUBO-SAN WHO PLAYS KYOHEI WAS REALLY CARING, AND HE TOTALLY HELPED ME OUT. THANKS FOR ALWAYS BEING THERE TO BACK ME UP. YOU'RE SUCH A COOL-GUY. ♡ MY ASSISTANT CHOBI-SAN IS A HUGE FAN OF MORIKUBO-SAN'S. SHE WAS GIDDY ALL DAY LONG. TO BE CONTINUED.

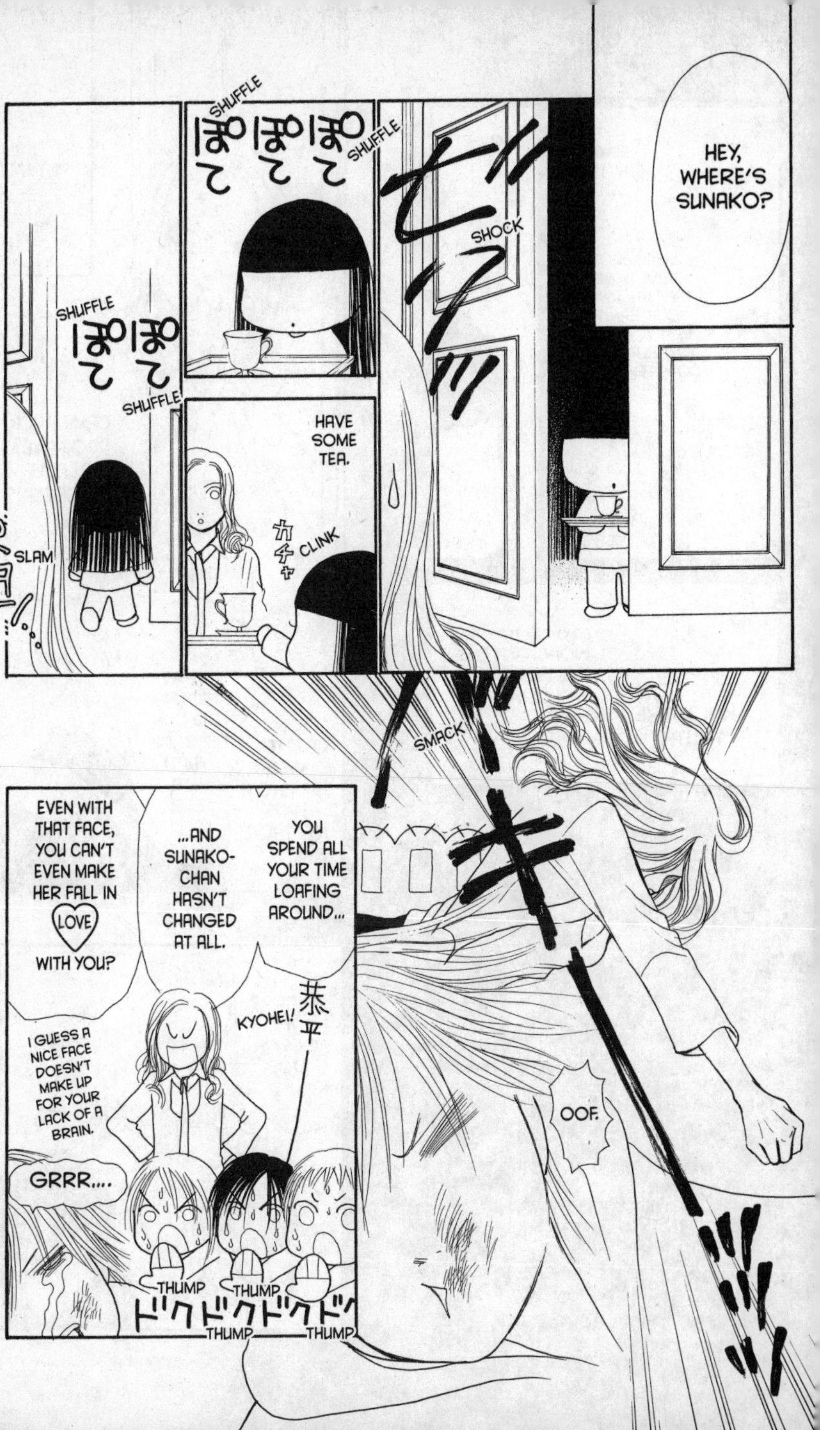
HEY, WHERE'S SUNAKO?
SHOCK
ぽてぽてぽて
SHUFFLE
SHUFFLE
HAVE SOME TEA.
カチャ
CLINK
SHUFFLE
ぽてぽて
SHUFFLE
パターン…
SLAM
SMACK
OOF.
YOU SPEND ALL YOUR TIME LOAFING AROUND...
...AND SUNAKO-CHAN HASN'T CHANGED AT ALL.
EVEN WITH THAT FACE, YOU CAN'T EVEN MAKE HER FALL IN LOVE WITH YOU?
恭平
KYOHEI!
I GUESS A NICE FACE DOESN'T MAKE UP FOR YOUR LACK OF A BRAIN.
GRRR....
ドクドクドクドク
THUMP
THUMP
THUMP
THUMP

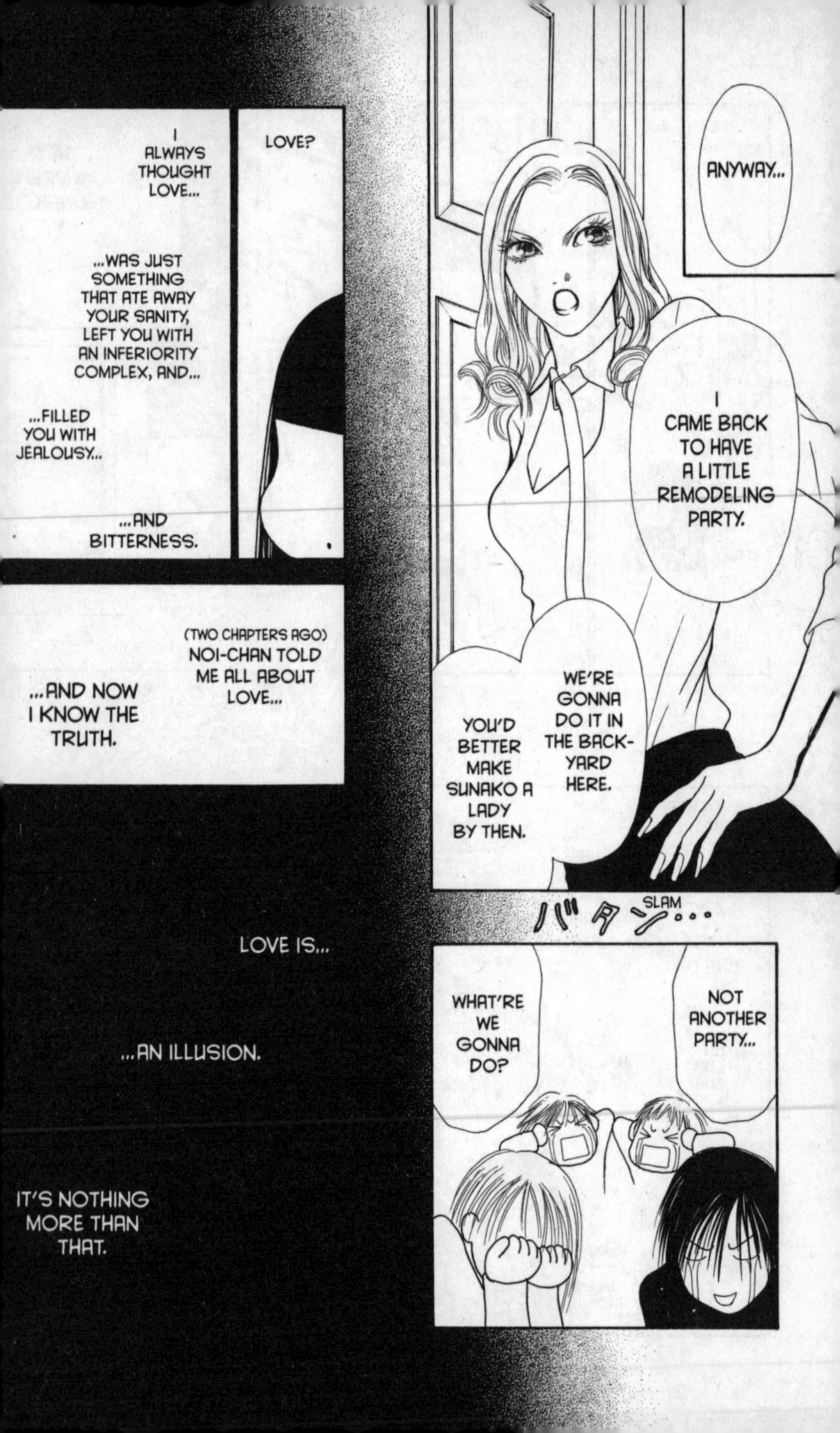

ANYWAY...
I CAME BACK TO HAVE A LITTLE REMODELING PARTY.
WE'RE GONNA DO IT IN THE BACK-YARD HERE.
YOU'D BETTER MAKE SUNAKO A LADY BY THEN.
SLAM
NOT ANOTHER PARTY...
WHAT'RE WE GONNA DO?
LOVE?
I ALWAYS THOUGHT LOVE...
...WAS JUST SOMETHING THAT ATE AWAY YOUR SANITY, LEFT YOU WITH AN INFERIORITY COMPLEX, AND...
...FILLED YOU WITH JEALOUSY...
...AND BITTERNESS.
(TWO CHAPTERS AGO) NOI-CHAN TOLD ME ALL ABOUT LOVE...
...AND NOW I KNOW THE TRUTH.
LOVE IS...
...AN ILLUSION.
IT'S NOTHING MORE THAN THAT.

ANYWAY, IT HAS NOTHING TO DO WITH ME. ♡

SO MANY PEOPLE GET HUNG UP ON LOVE WHILE LIFE PASSES THEM BY.

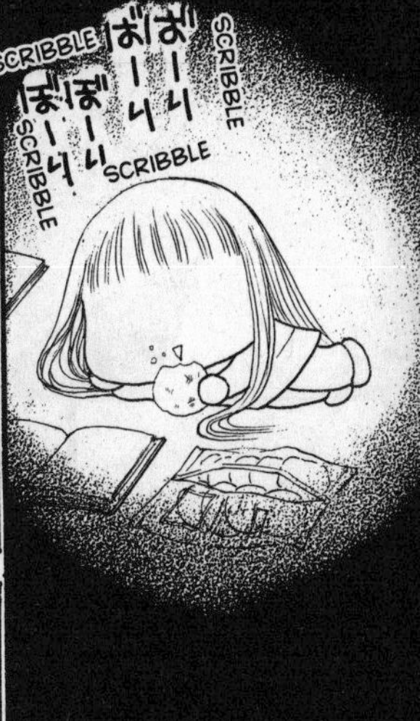
ぼーり SCRIBBLE
ぼーり SCRIBBLE
ぼーり SCRIBBLE
SCRIBBLE

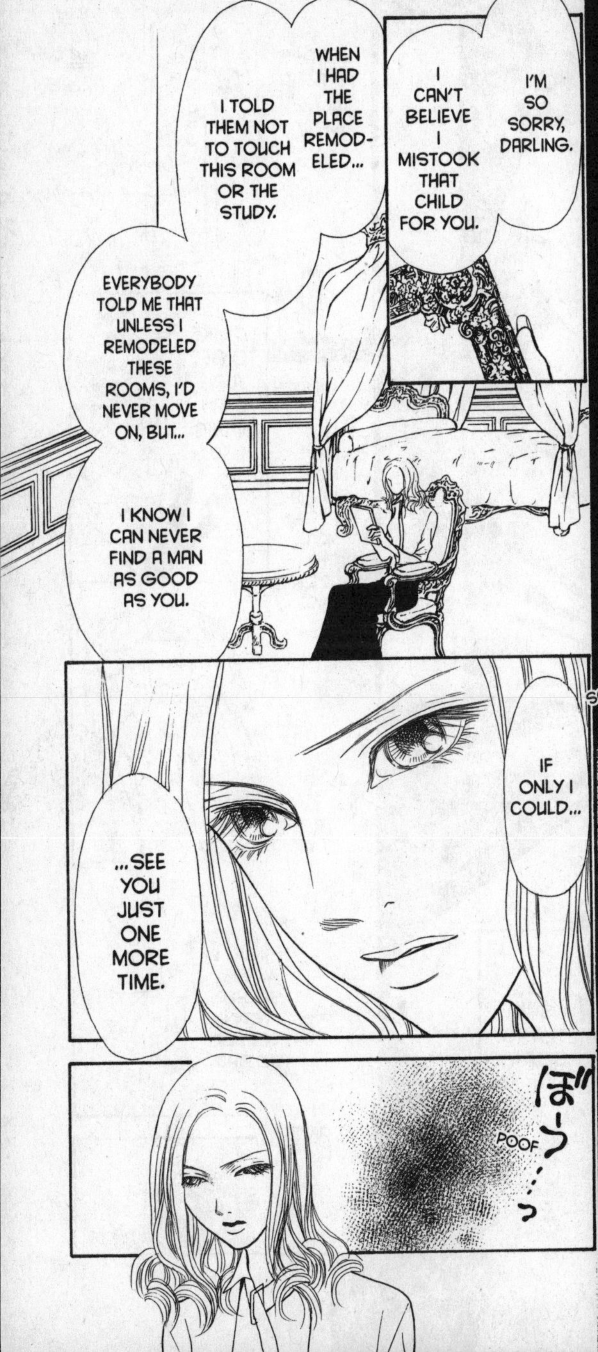
I'M SO SORRY, DARLING.
I CAN'T BELIEVE I MISTOOK THAT CHILD FOR YOU.
WHEN I HAD THE PLACE REMODELED...
I TOLD THEM NOT TO TOUCH THIS ROOM OR THE STUDY.
EVERYBODY TOLD ME THAT UNLESS I REMODELED THESE ROOMS, I'D NEVER MOVE ON, BUT...
I KNOW I CAN NEVER FIND A MAN AS GOOD AS YOU.
IF ONLY I COULD...
...SEE YOU JUST ONE MORE TIME.
ぼうっ…っ POOF

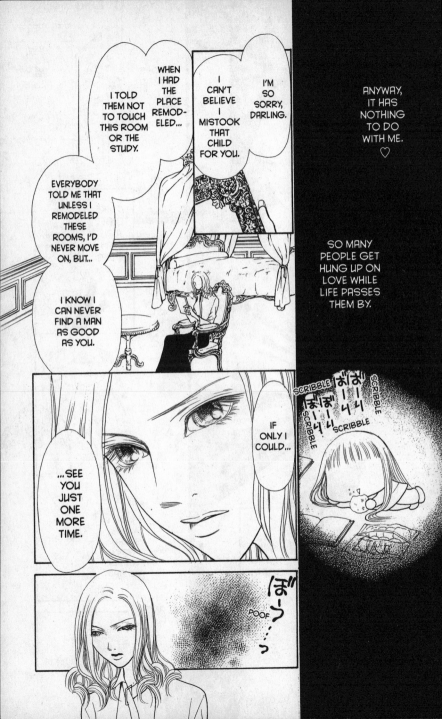

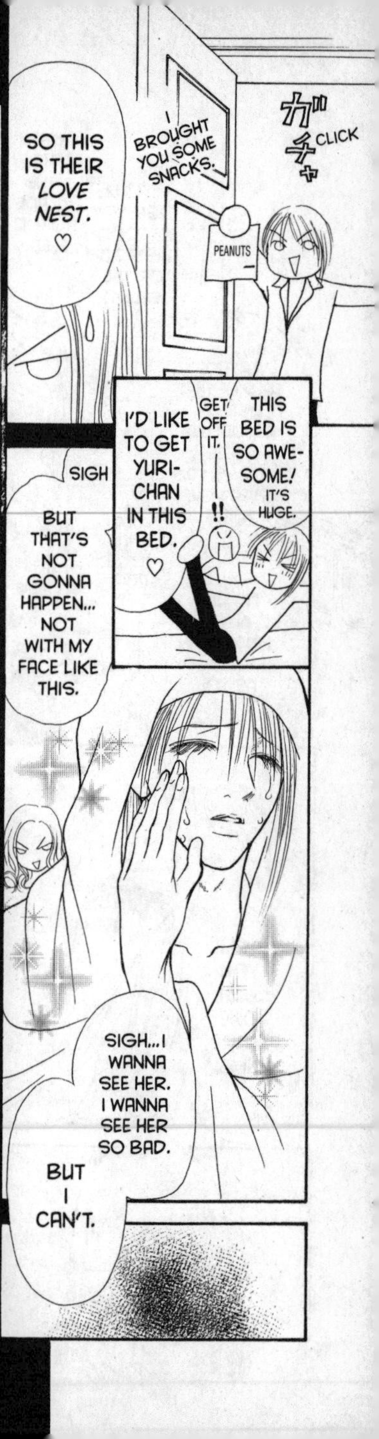
CLICK
I BROUGHT YOU SOME SNACKS.
PEANUTS
SO THIS IS THEIR *LOVE NEST.* ♡
THIS BED IS SO AWESOME! IT'S HUGE.
GET OFF IT.
!!
I'D LIKE TO GET YURI-CHAN IN THIS BED. ♡
SIGH
BUT THAT'S NOT GONNA HAPPEN... NOT WITH MY FACE LIKE THIS.
SIGH... I WANNA SEE HER. I WANNA SEE HER SO BAD.
BUT I CAN'T.
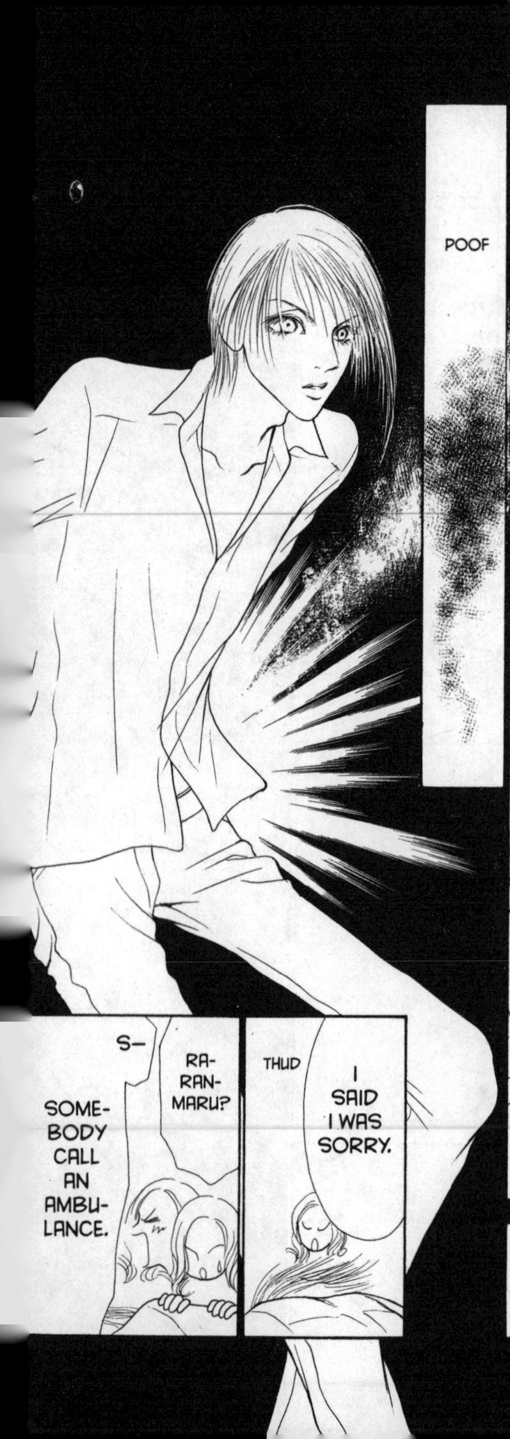
POOF
I SAID I WAS SORRY.
THUD
RA-RANMARU?
S—
SOMEBODY CALL AN AMBULANCE.

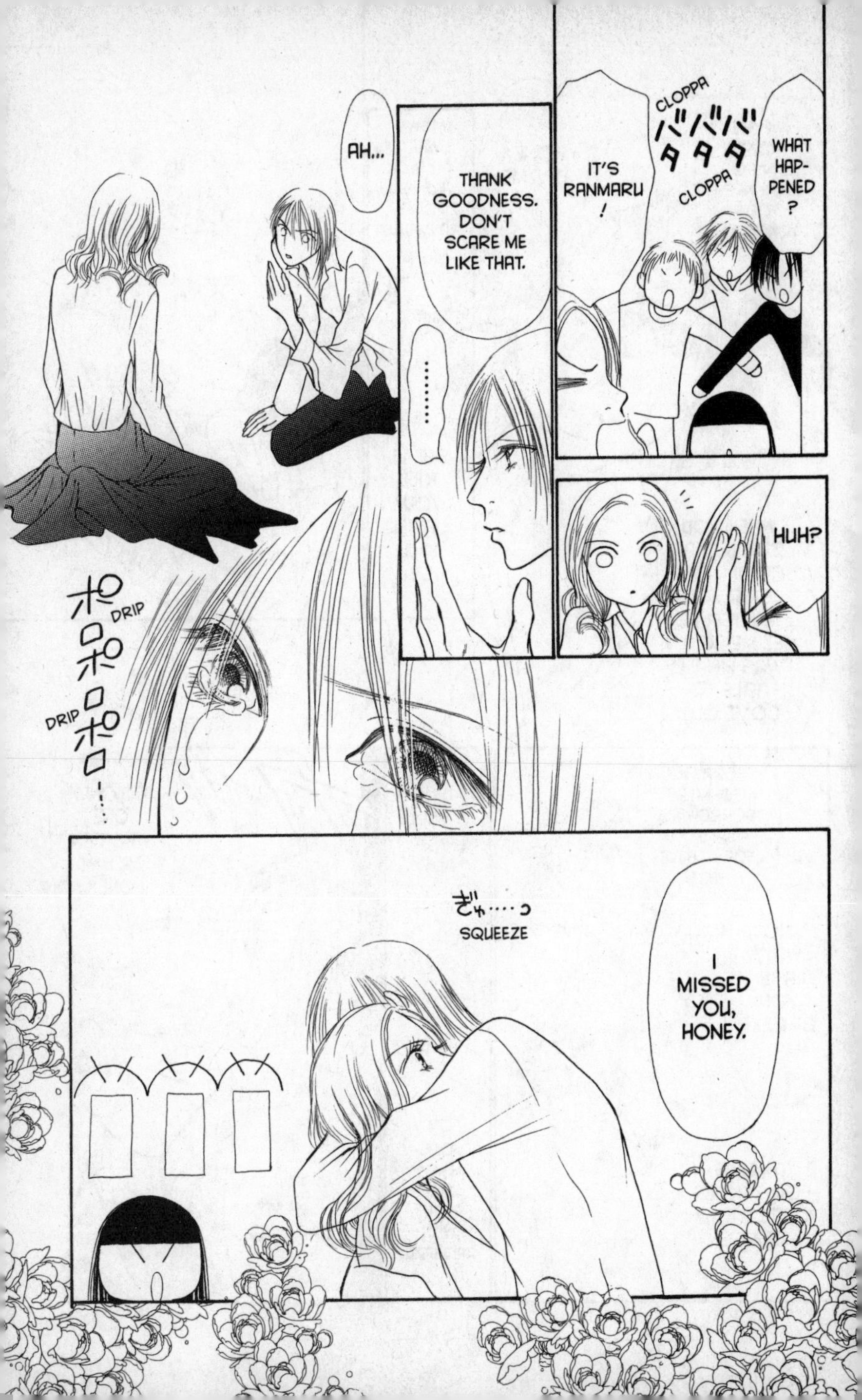

WHAT HAP-PENED?
バババ タタタ
CLOPPA
CLOPPA
IT'S RANMARU!
HUH?
THANK GOODNESS. DON'T SCARE ME LIKE THAT.
......
AH...
ポロポロポロ…
DRIP
DRIP
I MISSED YOU, HONEY.
ぎゅ…っ
SQUEEZE

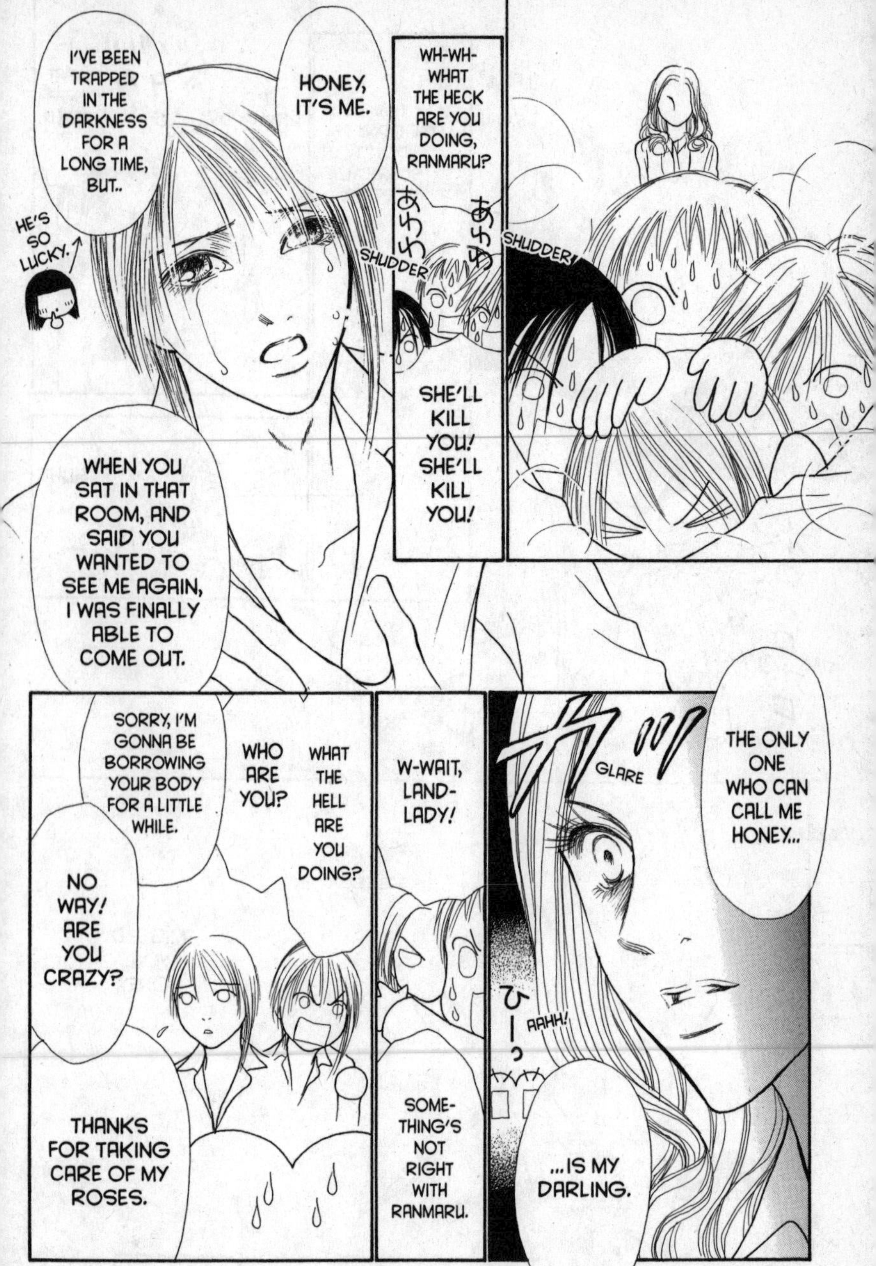
あわわ
SHUDDER!
あわわ
SHUDDER
WH-WH-WHAT THE HECK ARE YOU DOING, RANMARU?
SHE'LL KILL YOU! SHE'LL KILL YOU!
HONEY, IT'S ME.
I'VE BEEN TRAPPED IN THE DARKNESS FOR A LONG TIME, BUT..
HE'S SO LUCKY.
WHEN YOU SAT IN THAT ROOM, AND SAID YOU WANTED TO SEE ME AGAIN, I WAS FINALLY ABLE TO COME OUT.
THE ONLY ONE WHO CAN CALL ME HONEY...
カッ
GLARE
ひーっ
AAHH!
...IS MY DARLING.
W-WAIT, LANDLADY!
SOMETHING'S NOT RIGHT WITH RANMARU.
WHAT THE HELL ARE YOU DOING?
WHO ARE YOU?
SORRY, I'M GONNA BE BORROWING YOUR BODY FOR A LITTLE WHILE.
NO WAY! ARE YOU CRAZY?
THANKS FOR TAKING CARE OF MY ROSES.

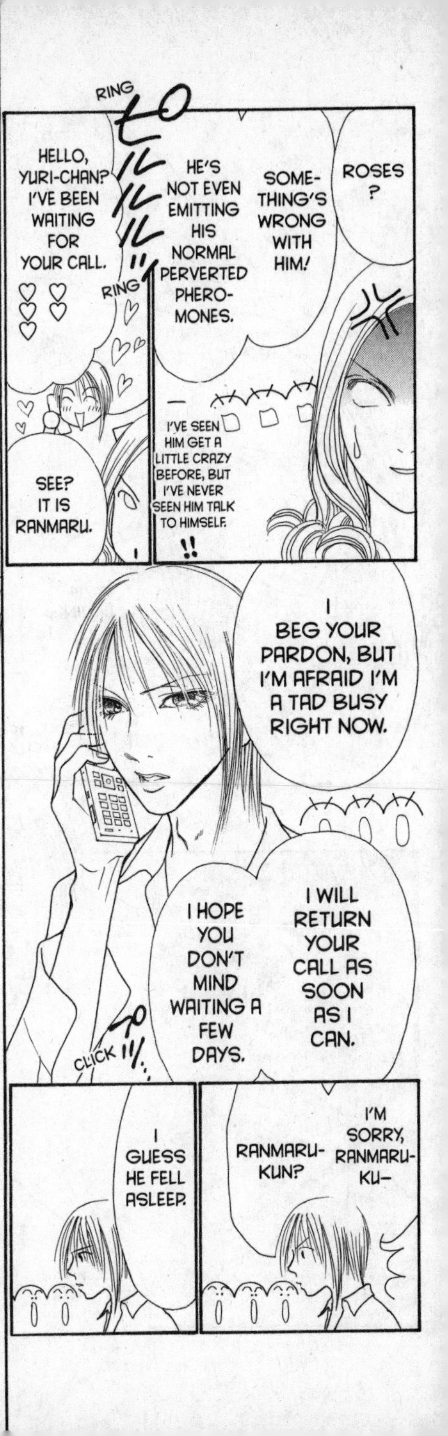
ROSES?
SOMETHING'S WRONG WITH HIM!
HE'S NOT EVEN EMITTING HIS NORMAL PERVERTED PHEROMONES.
I'VE SEEN HIM GET A LITTLE CRAZY BEFORE, BUT I'VE NEVER SEEN HIM TALK TO HIMSELF.
!!
RING
RING
HELLO, YURI-CHAN? I'VE BEEN WAITING FOR YOUR CALL.
SEE? IT IS RANMARU.
I BEG YOUR PARDON, BUT I'M AFRAID I'M A TAD BUSY RIGHT NOW.
I WILL RETURN YOUR CALL AS SOON AS I CAN.
I HOPE YOU DON'T MIND WAITING A FEW DAYS.
CLICK
I'M SORRY, RANMARU-KU-
RANMARU-KUN?
I GUESS HE FELL ASLEEP.
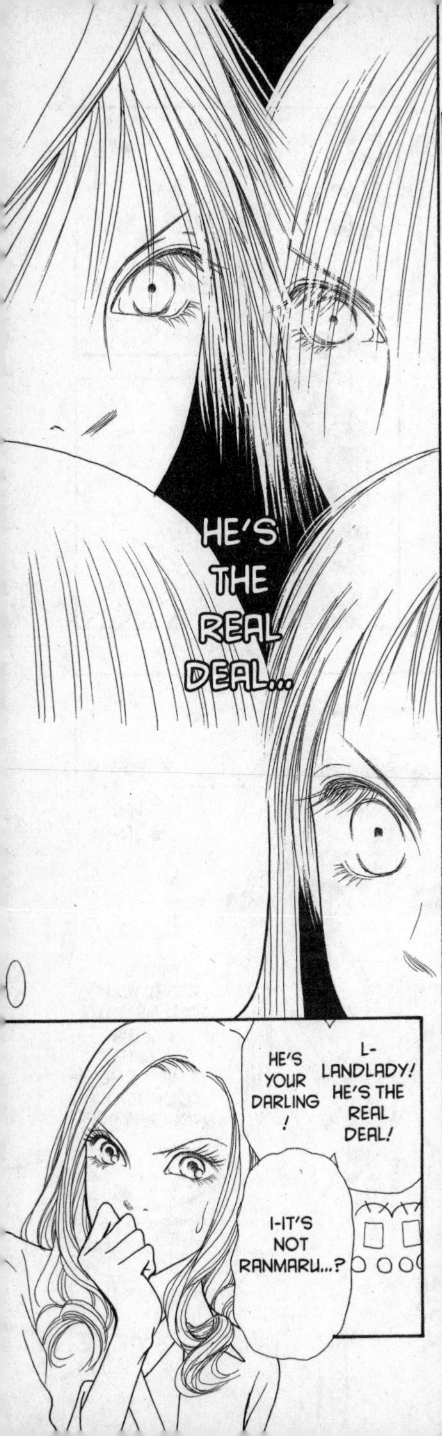
HE'S THE REAL DEAL...
L-LANDLADY! HE'S THE REAL DEAL!
HE'S YOUR DARLING!
I-IT'S NOT RANMARU...?

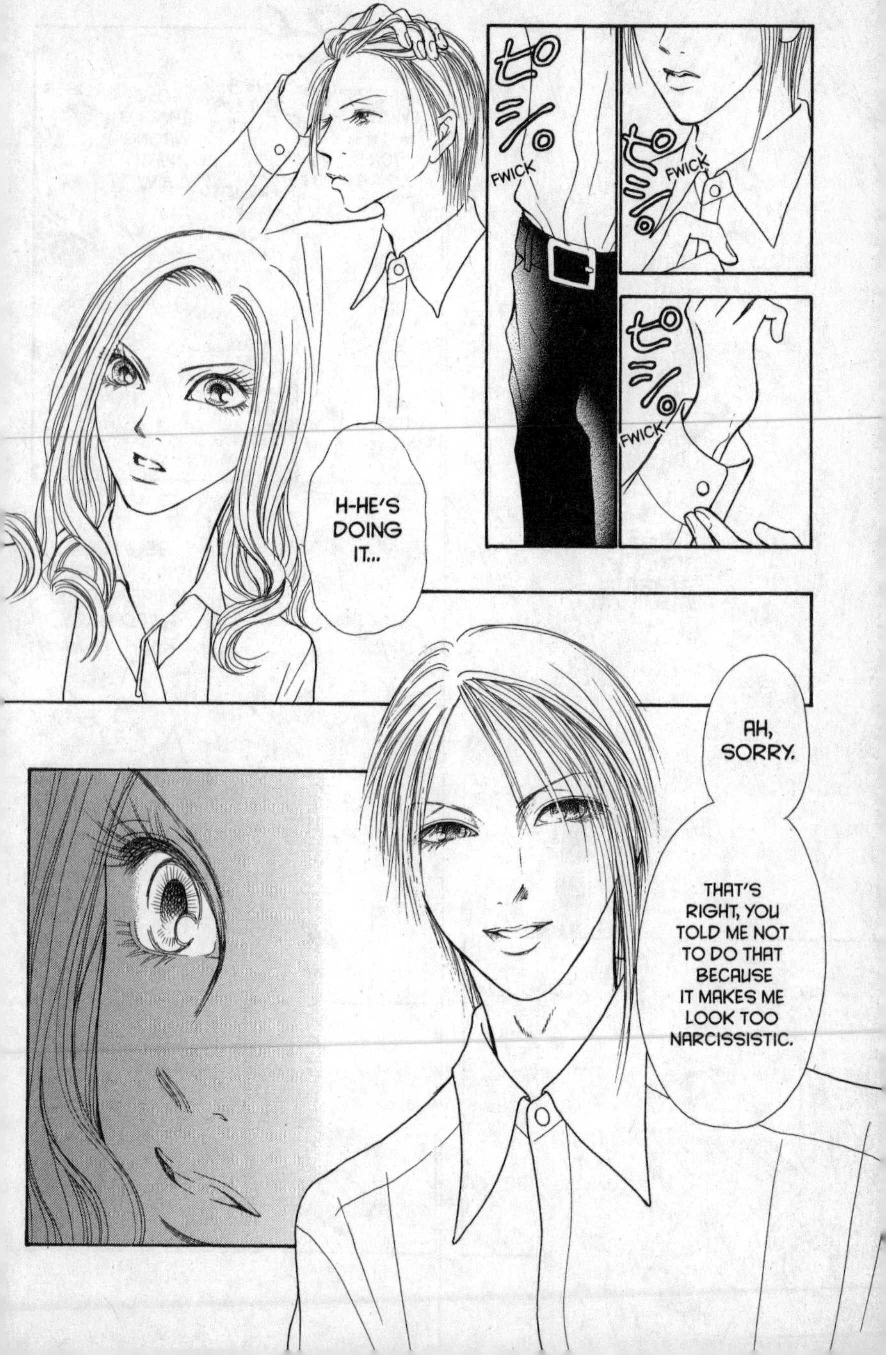
FWICK
FWICK
FWICK
H-HE'S DOING IT...
AH, SORRY.
THAT'S RIGHT, YOU TOLD ME NOT TO DO THAT BECAUSE IT MAKES ME LOOK TOO NARCISSISTIC.

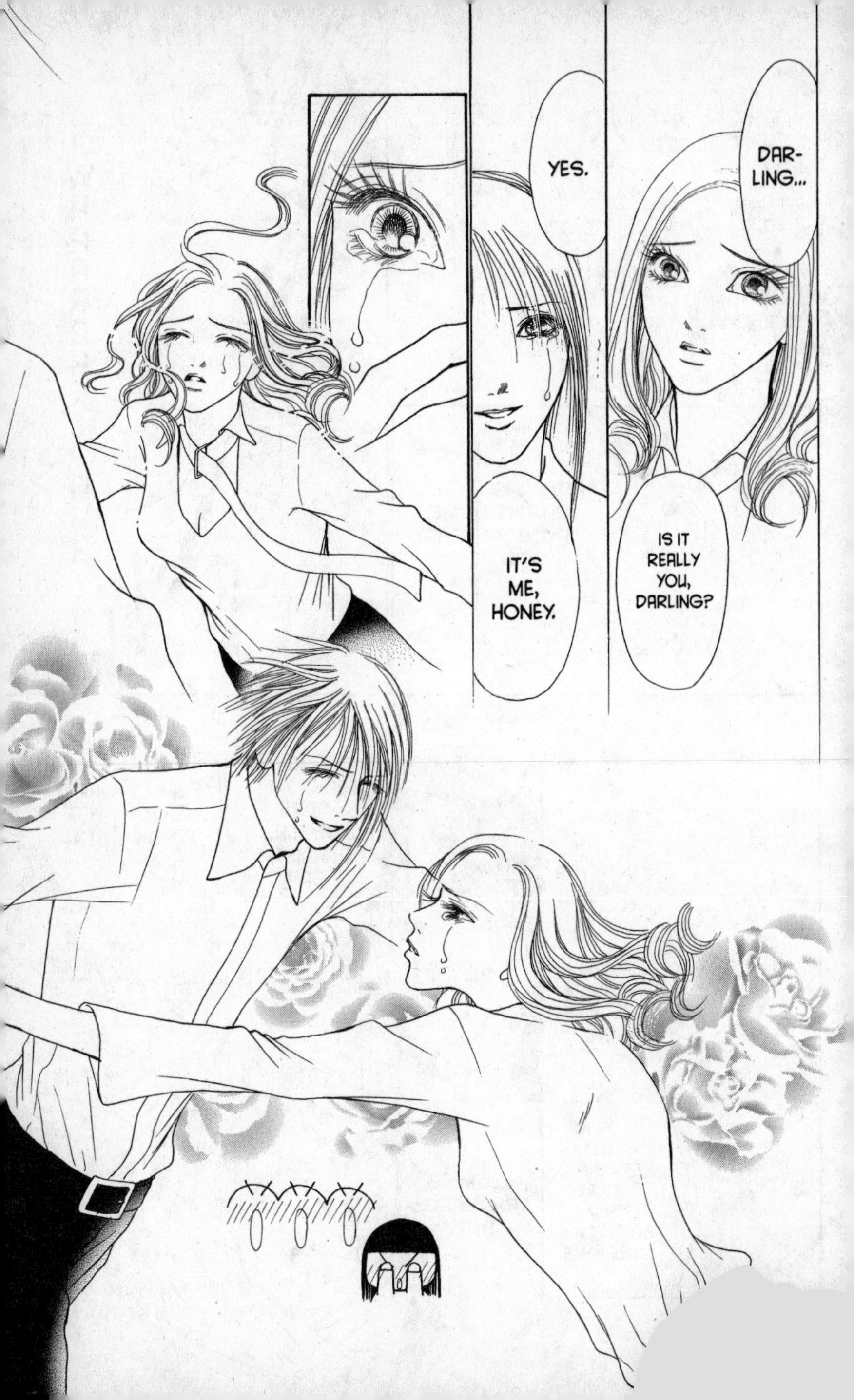
DAR-
LING...
IS IT
REALLY
YOU,
DARLING?
YES.
IT'S
ME,
HONEY.

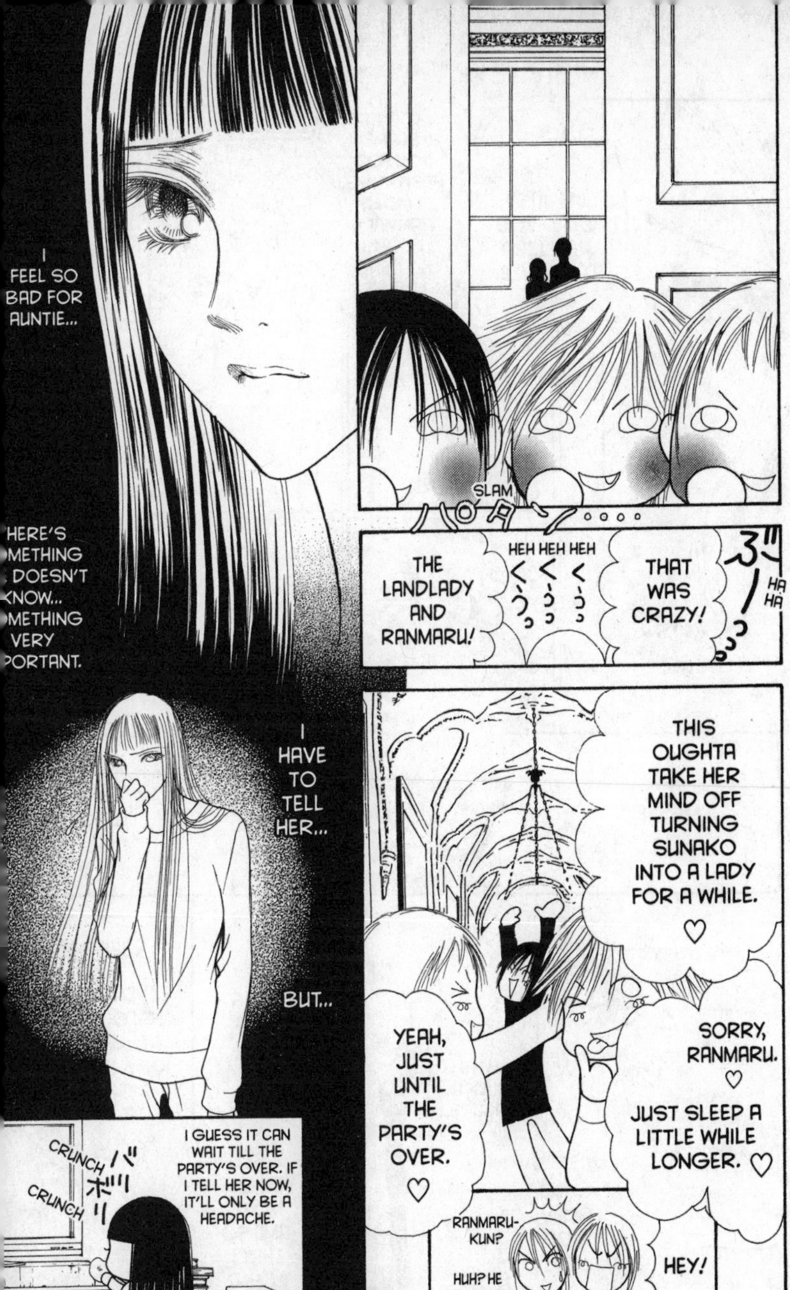

SLAM
ハタン。。。。
THE LANDLADY AND RANMARU!
HEH HEH HEH
くっくっくっ
THAT WAS CRAZY!
HA HA
ぶーっっ
THIS OUGHTA TAKE HER MIND OFF TURNING SUNAKO INTO A LADY FOR A WHILE. ♡
SORRY, RANMARU. ♡
JUST SLEEP A LITTLE WHILE LONGER. ♡
YEAH, JUST UNTIL THE PARTY'S OVER. ♡
HEY!
RANMARU-KUN?
HUH? HE FELL ASLEEP AGAIN.
I FEEL SO BAD FOR AUNTIE...
HERE'S
METHING
DOESN'T
KNOW...
METHING
VERY
PORTANT.
I HAVE TO TELL HER...
BUT...
I GUESS IT CAN WAIT TILL THE PARTY'S OVER. IF I TELL HER NOW, IT'LL ONLY BE A HEADACHE.
CRUNCH
バリ
CRUNCH
ボリ

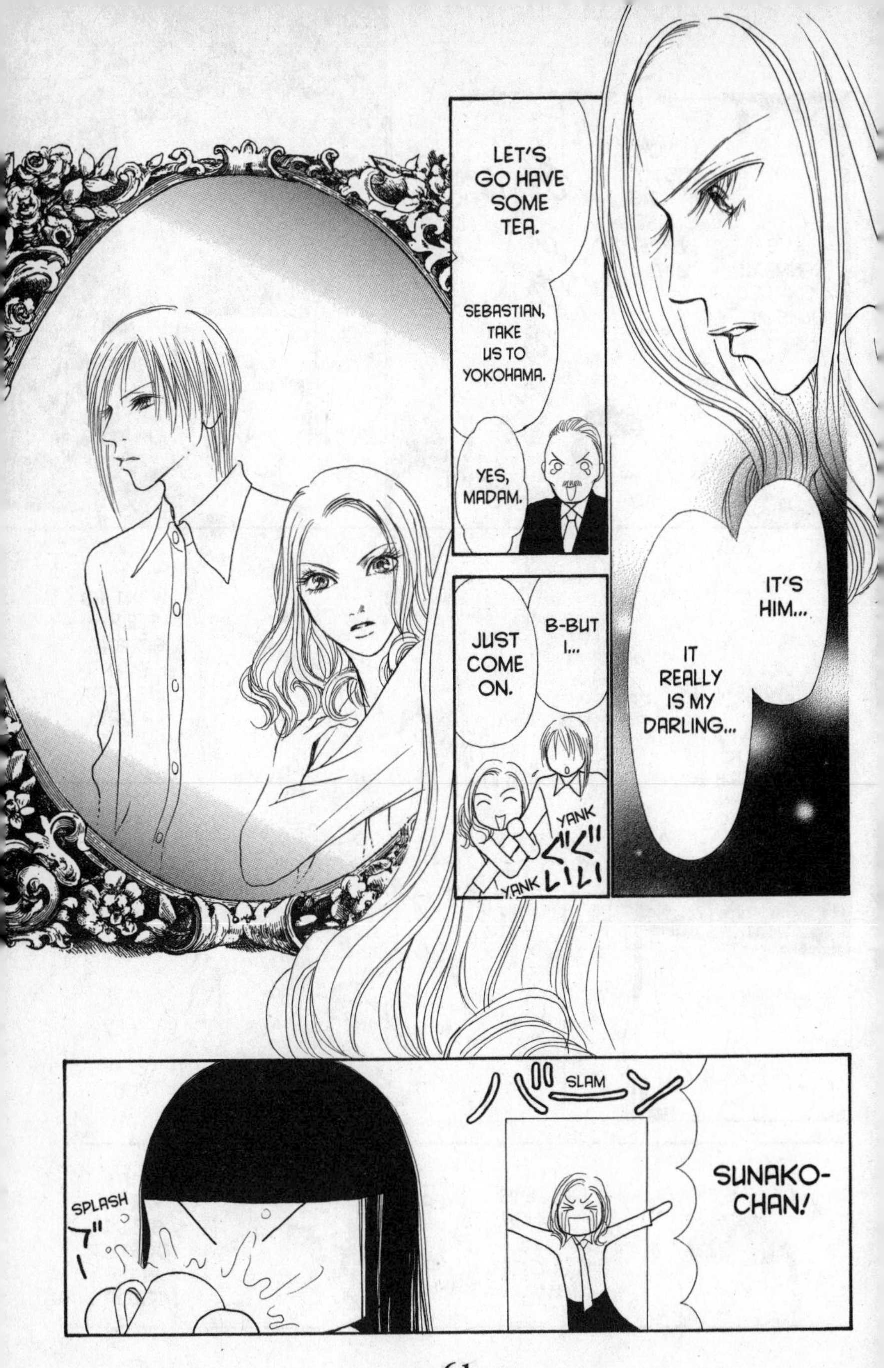
IT'S HIM...
IT REALLY IS MY DARLING...
LET'S GO HAVE SOME TEA.
SEBASTIAN, TAKE US TO YOKOHAMA.
YES, MADAM.
B-BUT I...
JUST COME ON.
YANK
YANK
SLAM
SUNAKO-CHAN!
SPLASH

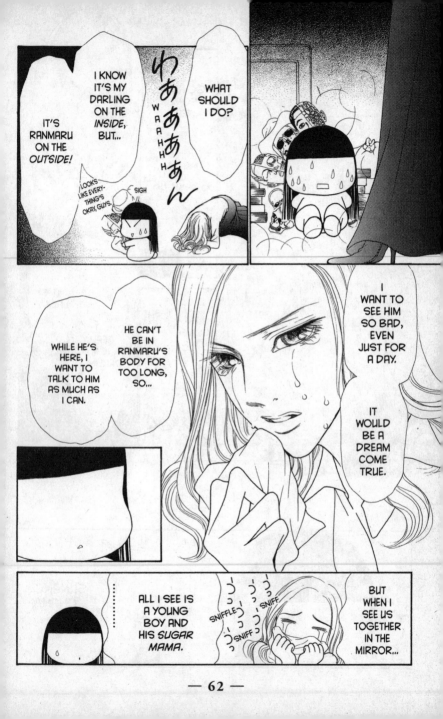

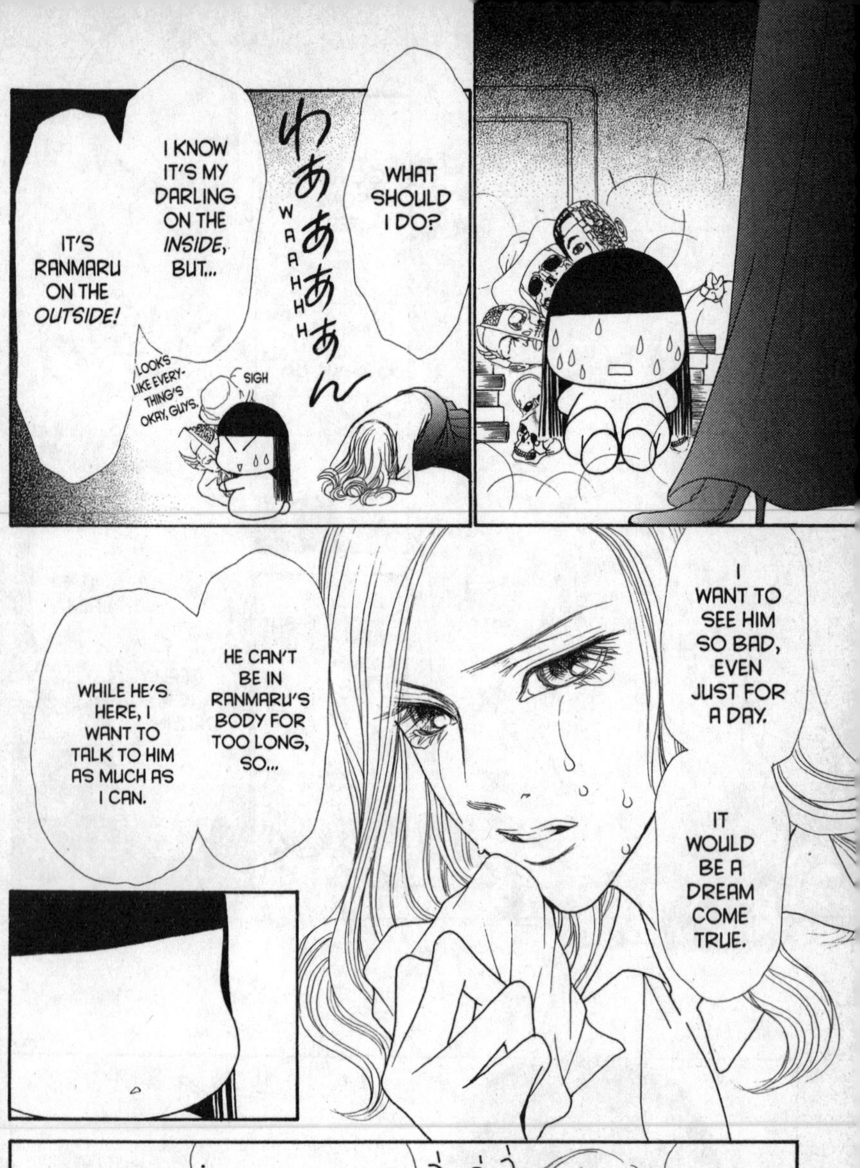
WHAT SHOULD I DO?
わあああん
WAAHHH
I KNOW IT'S MY DARLING ON THE *INSIDE*, BUT...
IT'S RANMARU ON THE *OUTSIDE!*
SIGH
LOOKS LIKE EVERY-THING'S OKAY, GUYS.
I WANT TO SEE HIM SO BAD, EVEN JUST FOR A DAY.
IT WOULD BE A DREAM COME TRUE.
HE CAN'T BE IN RANMARU'S BODY FOR TOO LONG, SO...
WHILE HE'S HERE, I WANT TO TALK TO HIM AS MUCH AS I CAN.
BUT WHEN I SEE US TOGETHER IN THE MIRROR...
SNIFF
SNIFFLE
SNIFF
ALL I SEE IS A YOUNG BOY AND HIS *SUGAR MAMA.*
......

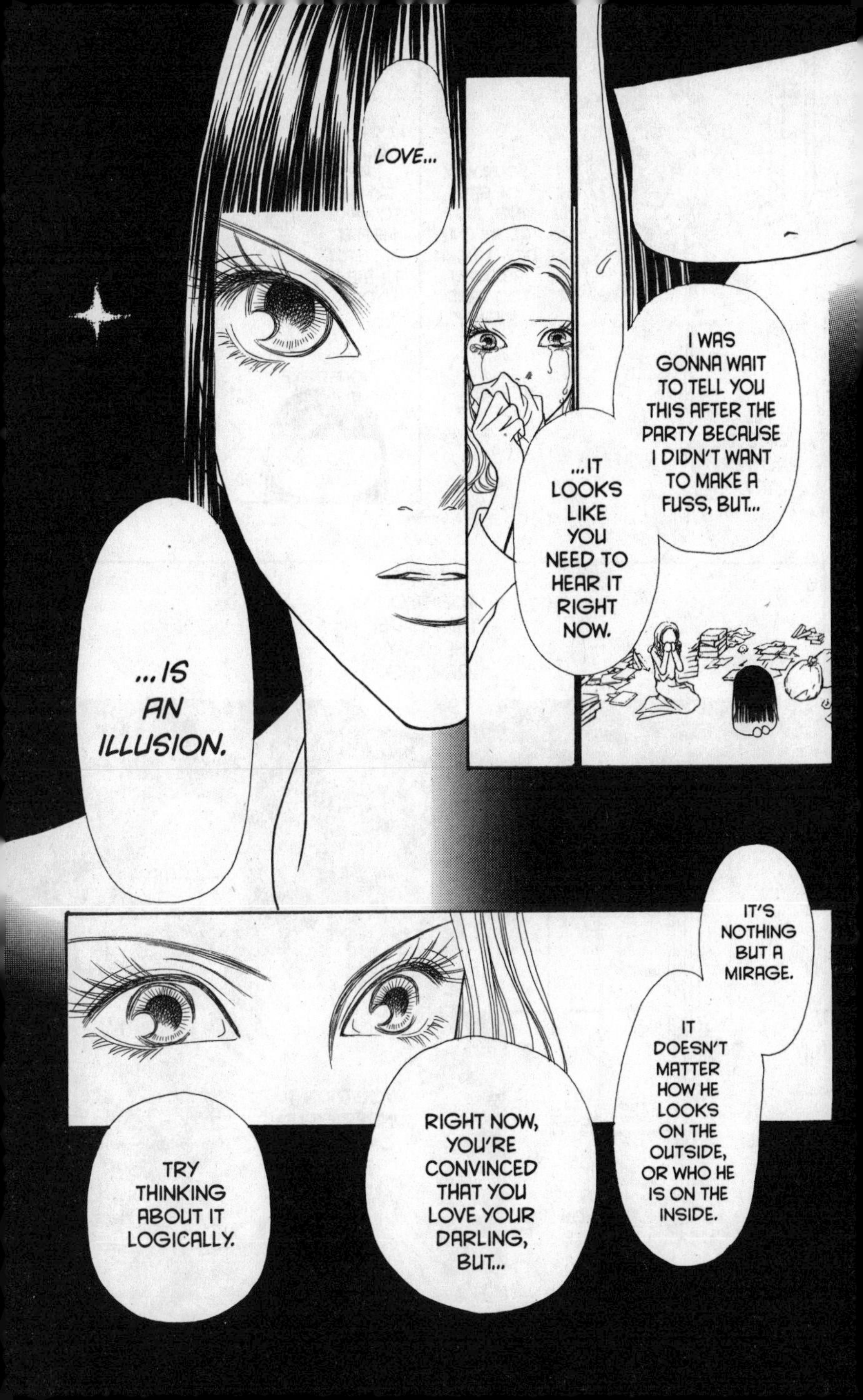

I WAS GONNA WAIT TO TELL YOU THIS AFTER THE PARTY BECAUSE I DIDN'T WANT TO MAKE A FUSS, BUT...
...IT LOOKS LIKE YOU NEED TO HEAR IT RIGHT NOW.
LOVE...
...IS AN ILLUSION.
IT'S NOTHING BUT A MIRAGE.
IT DOESN'T MATTER HOW HE LOOKS ON THE OUTSIDE, OR WHO HE IS ON THE INSIDE.
RIGHT NOW, YOU'RE CONVINCED THAT YOU LOVE YOUR DARLING, BUT...
TRY THINKING ABOUT IT LOGICALLY.

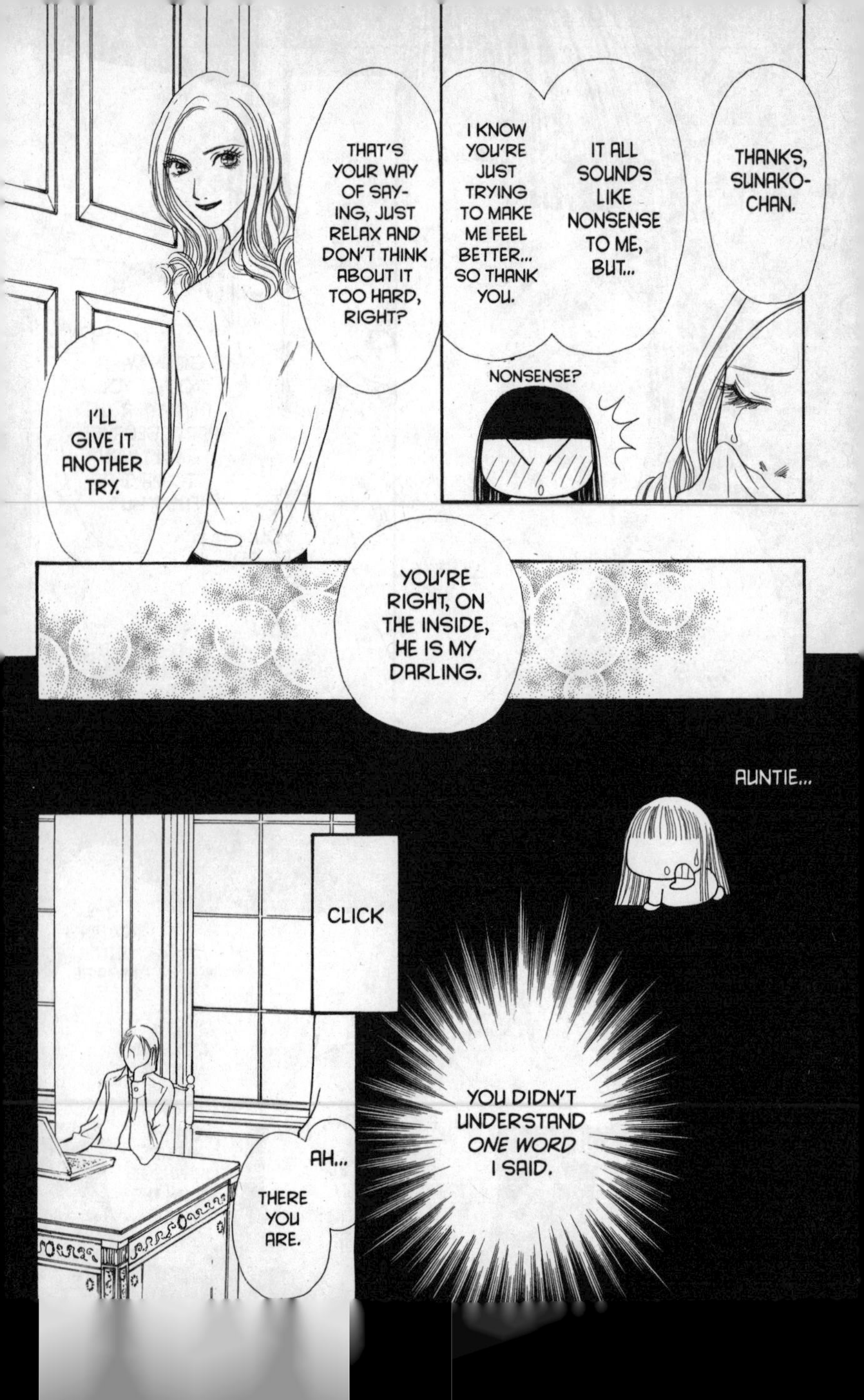
THANKS, SUNAKO-CHAN.
IT ALL SOUNDS LIKE NONSENSE TO ME, BUT...
I KNOW YOU'RE JUST TRYING TO MAKE ME FEEL BETTER... SO THANK YOU.
NONSENSE?
THAT'S YOUR WAY OF SAY-ING, JUST RELAX AND DON'T THINK ABOUT IT TOO HARD, RIGHT?
I'LL GIVE IT ANOTHER TRY.
YOU'RE RIGHT, ON THE INSIDE, HE IS MY DARLING.
AUNTIE...
YOU DIDN'T UNDERSTAND *ONE WORD* I SAID.
CLICK
AH...
THERE YOU ARE.

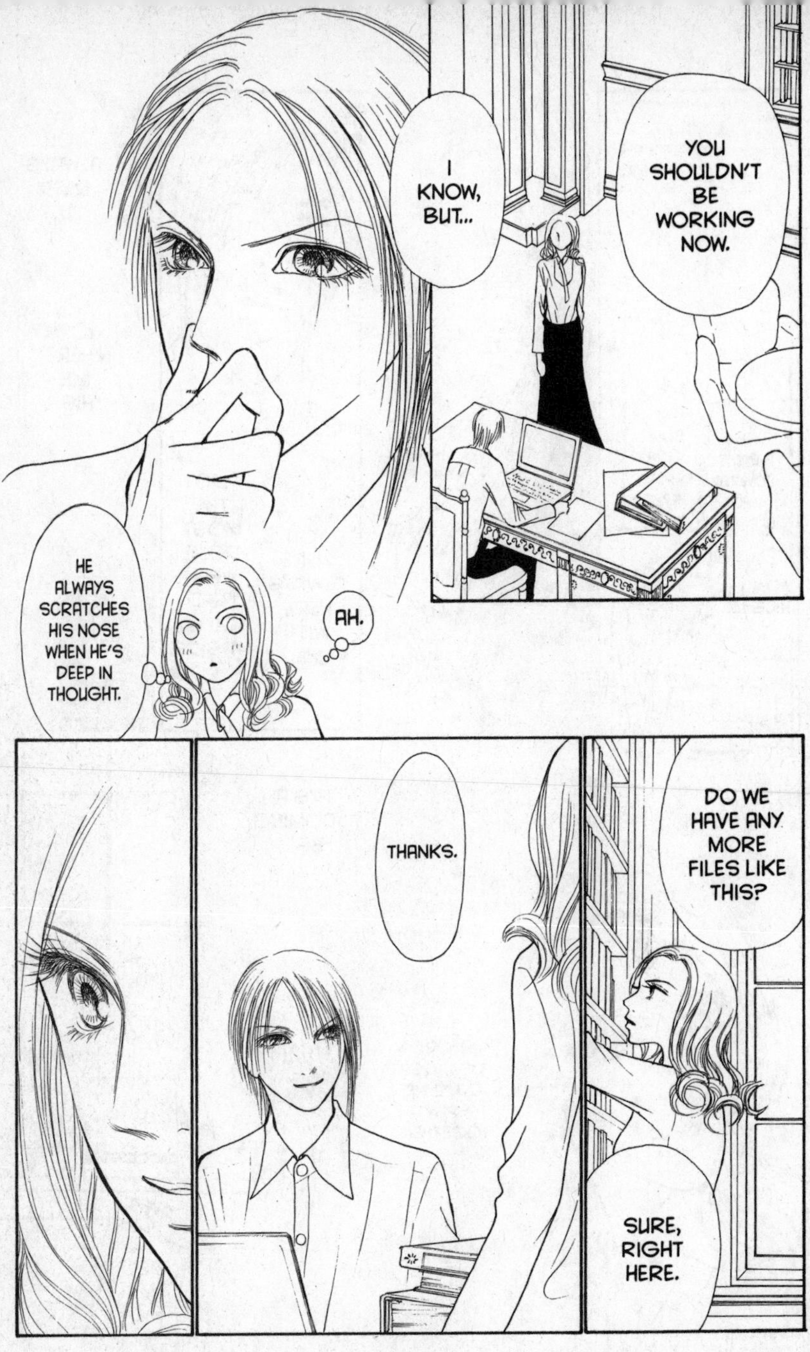
YOU SHOULDN'T BE WORKING NOW.
I KNOW, BUT...
AH.
HE ALWAYS SCRATCHES HIS NOSE WHEN HE'S DEEP IN THOUGHT.
DO WE HAVE ANY MORE FILES LIKE THIS?
SURE, RIGHT HERE.
THANKS.

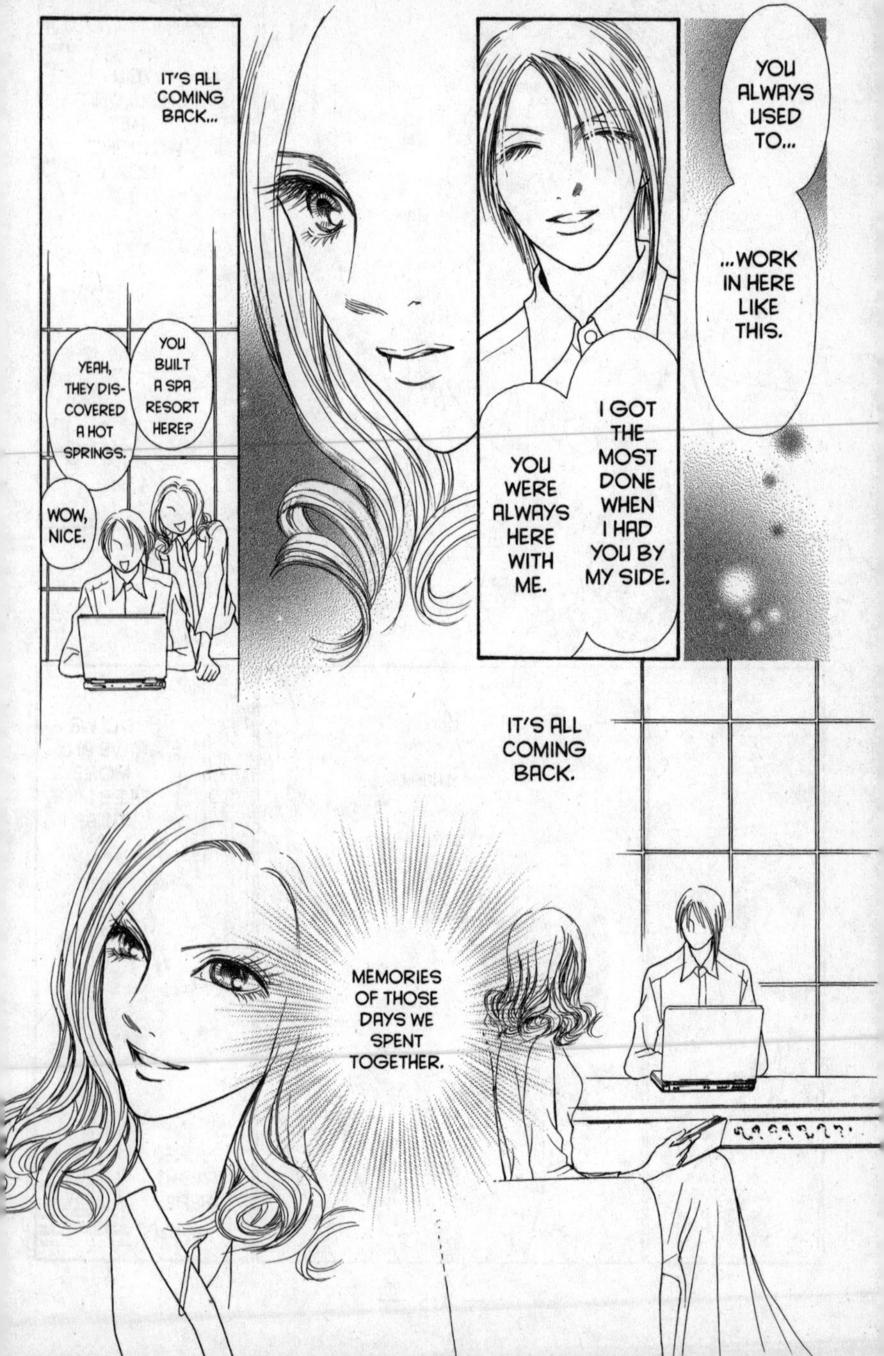

YOU ALWAYS USED TO...
...WORK IN HERE LIKE THIS.
I GOT THE MOST DONE WHEN I HAD YOU BY MY SIDE.
YOU WERE ALWAYS HERE WITH ME.
IT'S ALL COMING BACK...
YOU BUILT A SPA RESORT HERE?
YEAH, THEY DIS-COVERED A HOT SPRINGS.
WOW, NICE.
IT'S ALL COMING BACK.
MEMORIES OF THOSE DAYS WE SPENT TOGETHER.

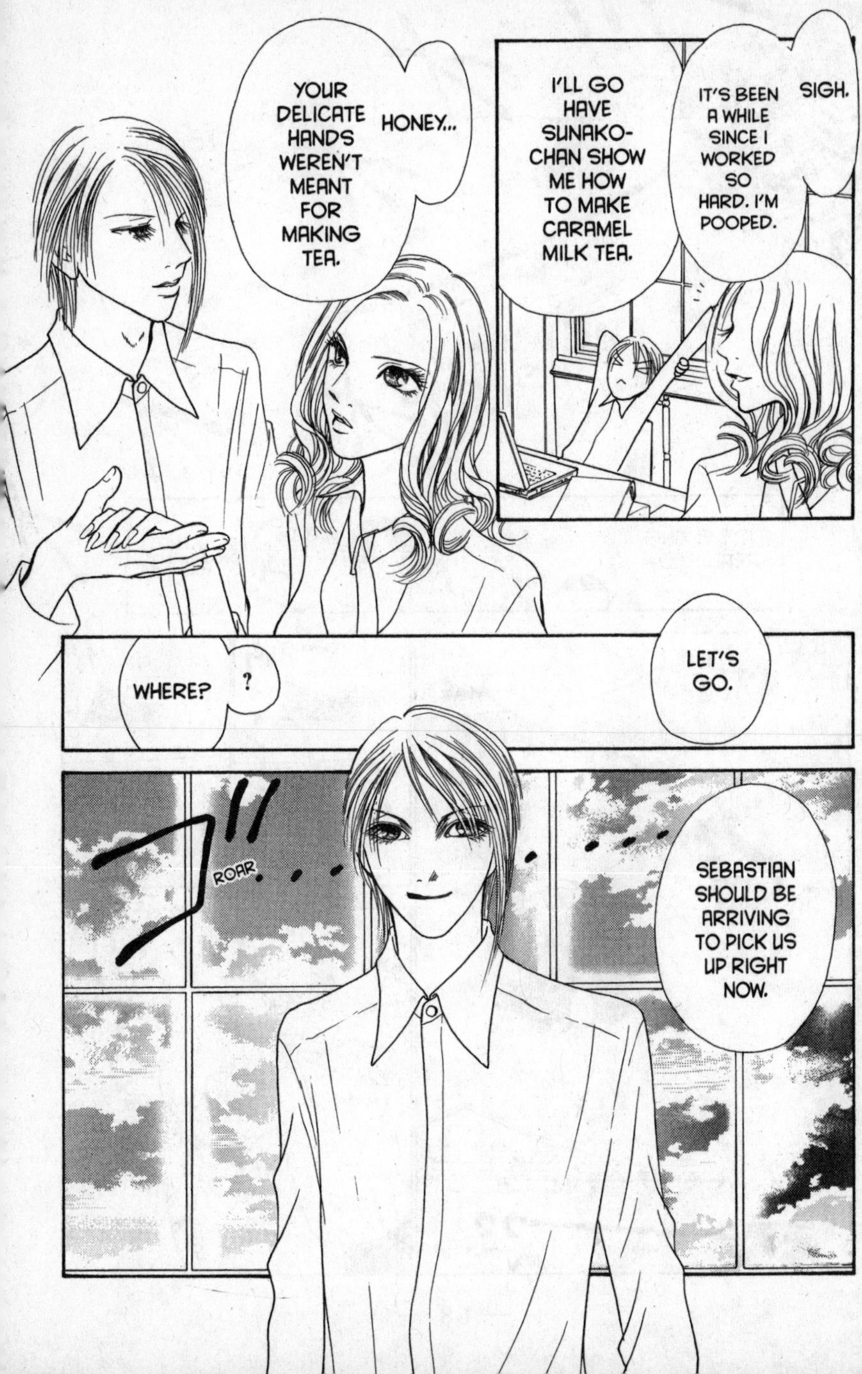
SIGH.
IT'S BEEN A WHILE SINCE I WORKED SO HARD. I'M POOPED.
I'LL GO HAVE SUNAKO-CHAN SHOW ME HOW TO MAKE CARAMEL MILK TEA.
HONEY...
YOUR DELICATE HANDS WEREN'T MEANT FOR MAKING TEA.
LET'S GO.
?
WHERE?
SEBASTIAN SHOULD BE ARRIVING TO PICK US UP RIGHT NOW.
ROAR

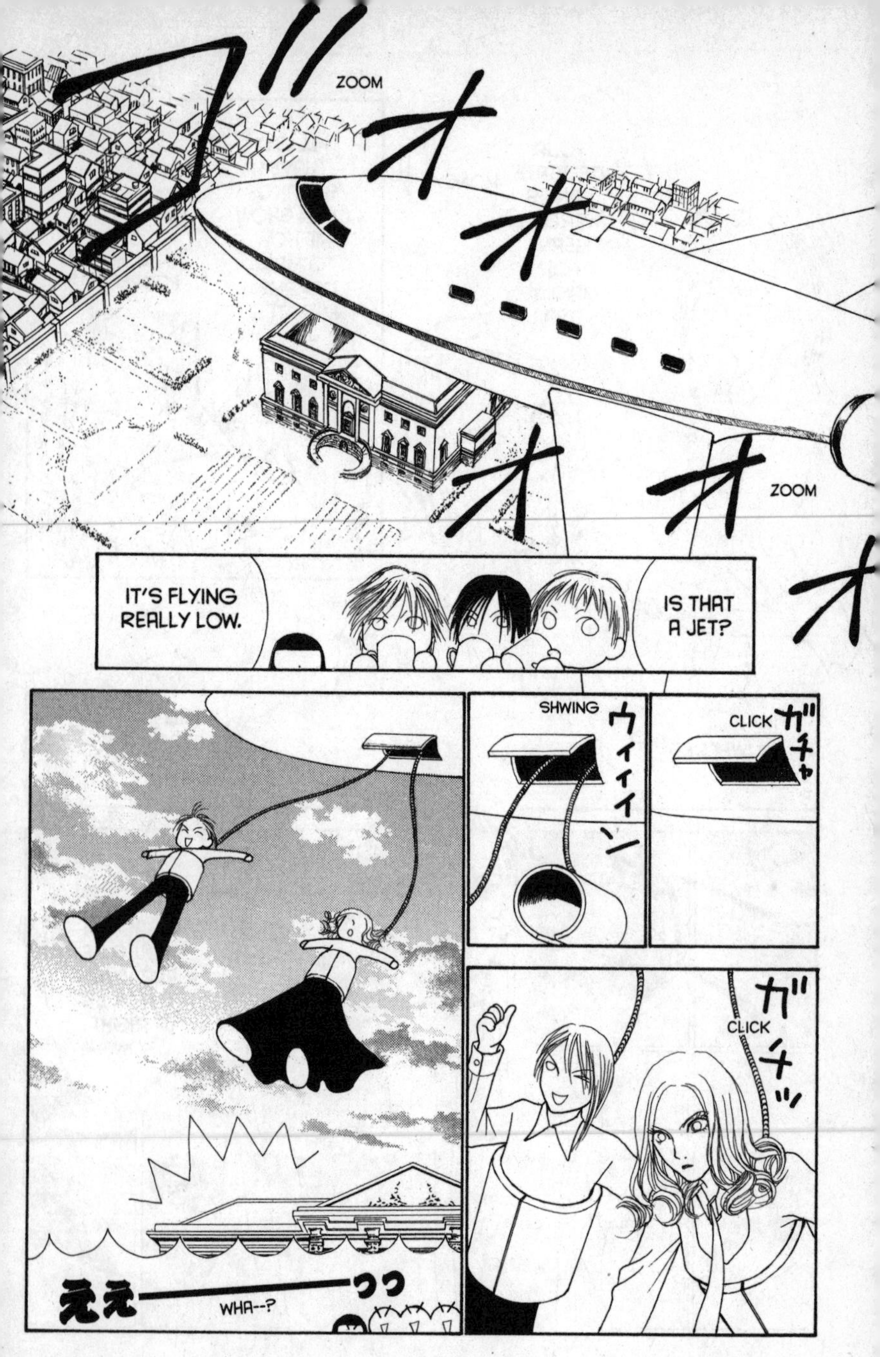
ZOOM
ZOOM
IS THAT A JET?
IT'S FLYING REALLY LOW.
ガチャ
CLICK
ウィイイン
SHWING
ガチッ
CLICK
ええーーっっ
WHA--?

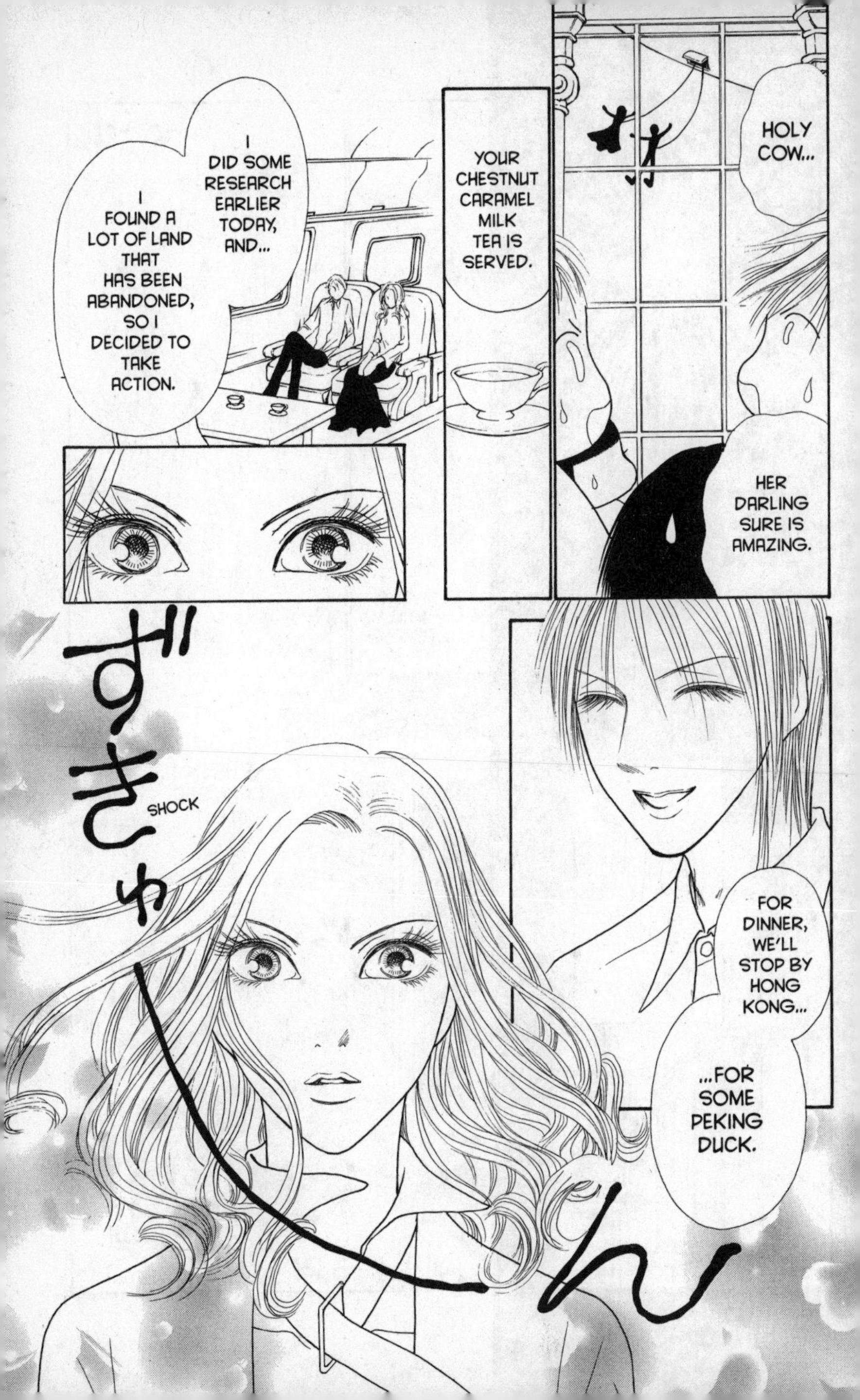
HOLY COW...
HER DARLING SURE IS AMAZING.
YOUR CHESTNUT CARAMEL MILK TEA IS SERVED.
I DID SOME RESEARCH EARLIER TODAY, AND...
I FOUND A LOT OF LAND THAT HAS BEEN ABANDONED, SO I DECIDED TO TAKE ACTION.
FOR DINNER, WE'LL STOP BY HONG KONG...
...FOR SOME PEKING DUCK.
ずきゅーん
SHOCK

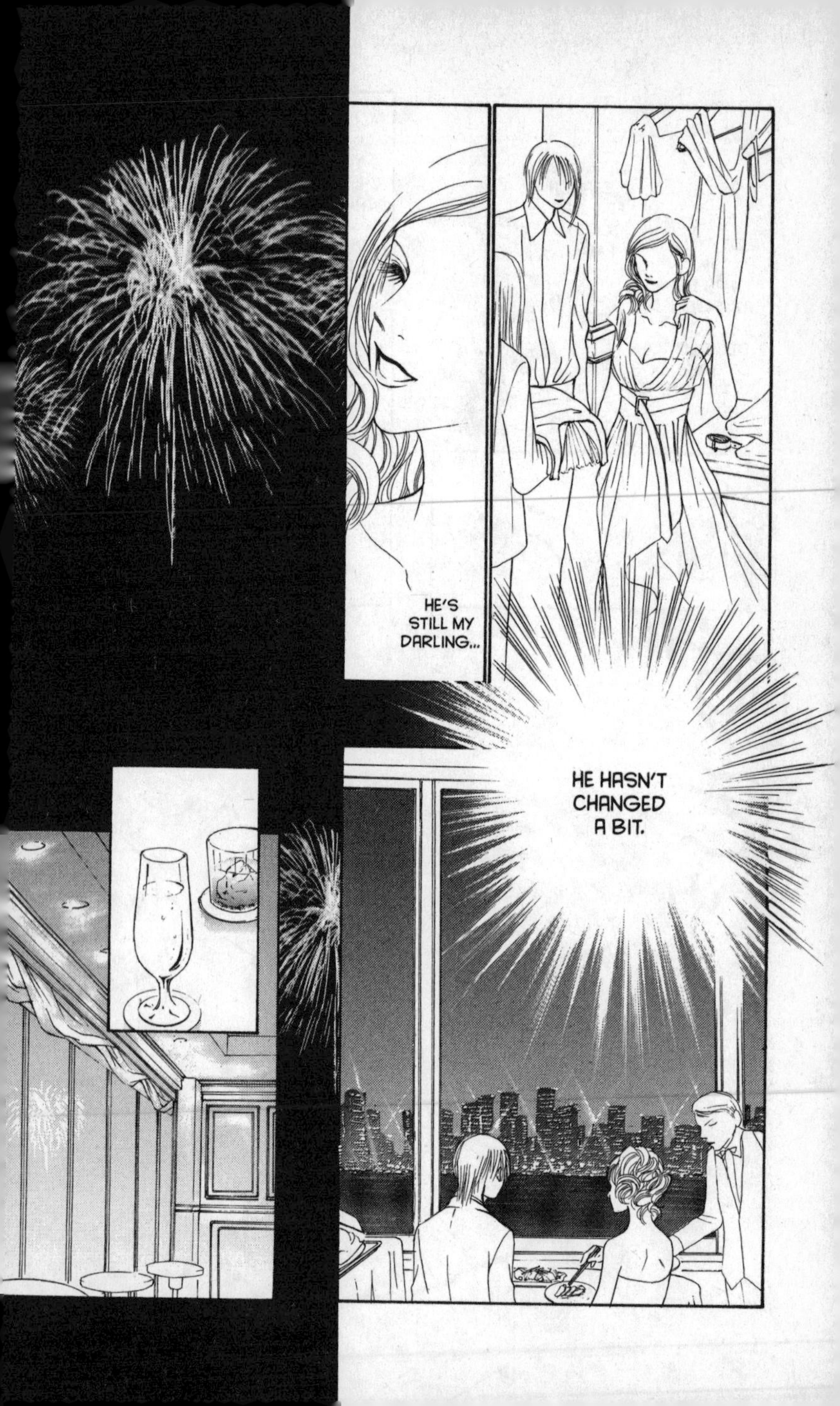
HE'S STILL MY DARLING...
HE HASN'T CHANGED A BIT.

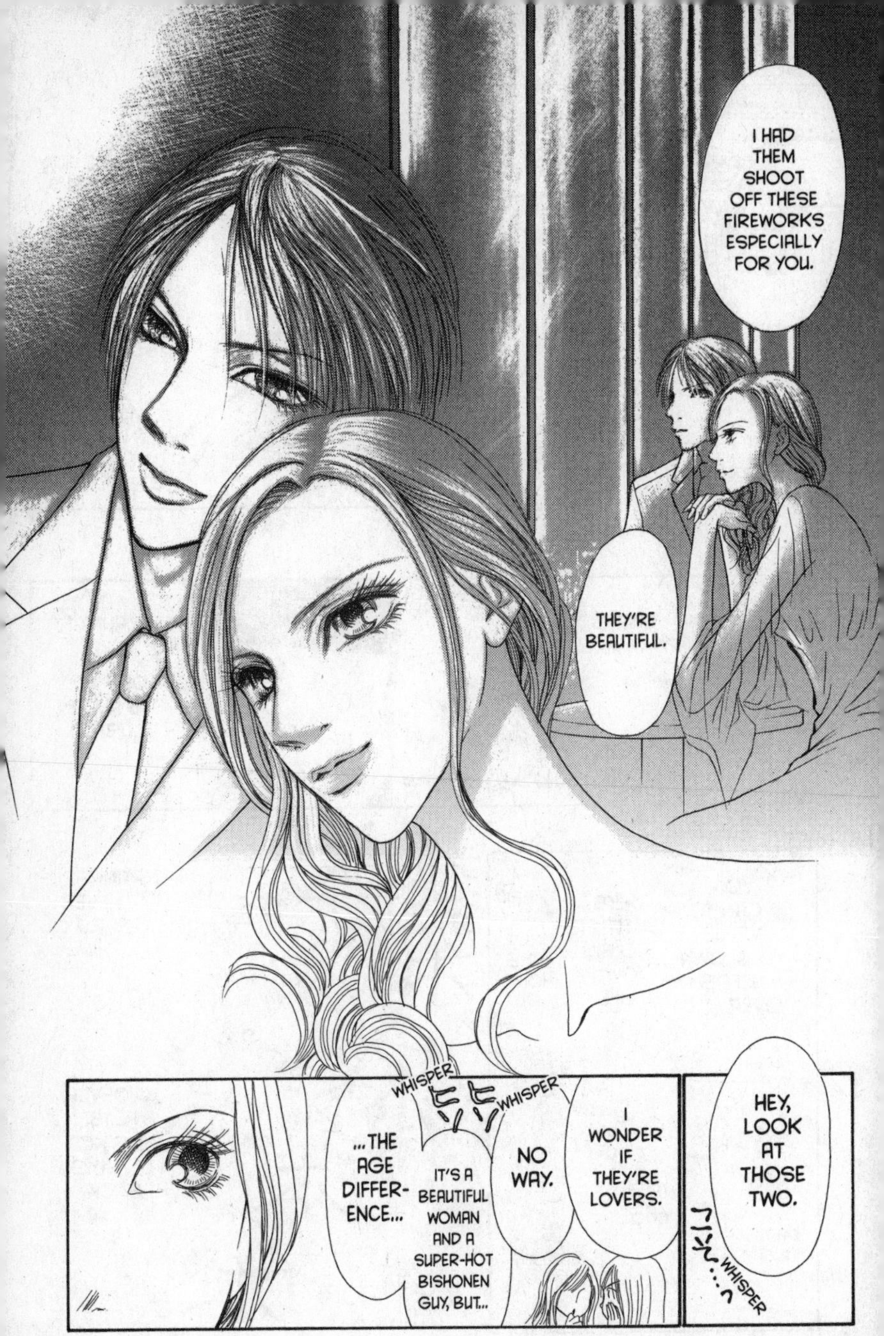
I HAD THEM SHOOT OFF THESE FIREWORKS ESPECIALLY FOR YOU.
THEY'RE BEAUTIFUL.
HEY, LOOK AT THOSE TWO.
WHISPER
I WONDER IF THEY'RE LOVERS.
NO WAY.
WHISPER
WHISPER
IT'S A BEAUTIFUL WOMAN AND A SUPER-HOT BISHONEN GUY, BUT...
...THE AGE DIFFERENCE...

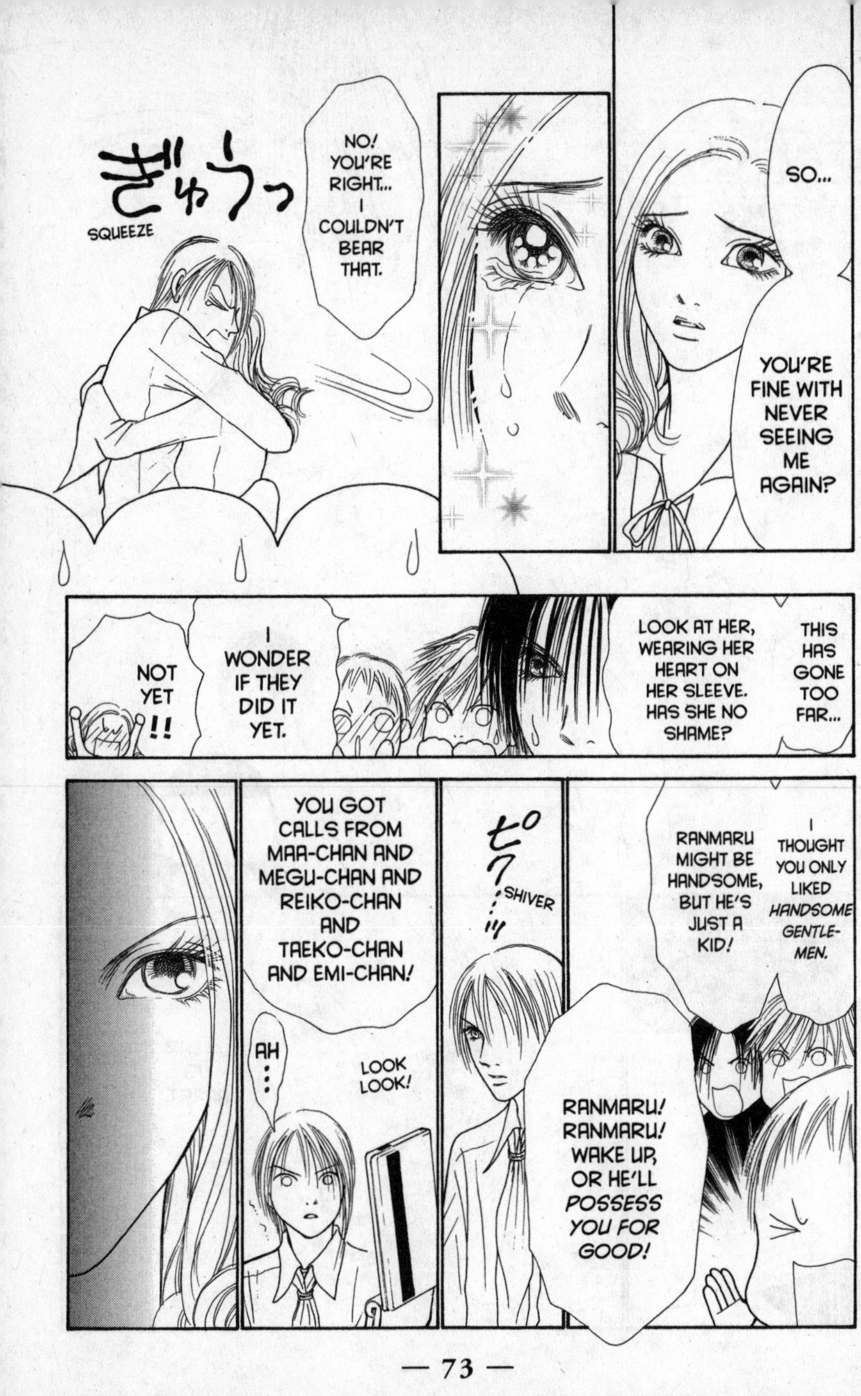
SO...
YOU'RE FINE WITH NEVER SEEING ME AGAIN?
NO! YOU'RE RIGHT... I COULDN'T BEAR THAT.
ぎゅうっ
SQUEEZE
THIS HAS GONE TOO FAR...
LOOK AT HER, WEARING HER HEART ON HER SLEEVE. HAS SHE NO SHAME?
I WONDER IF THEY DID IT YET.
NOT YET!!
I THOUGHT YOU ONLY LIKED HANDSOME GENTLEMEN.
RANMARU MIGHT BE HANDSOME, BUT HE'S JUST A KID!
RANMARU! RANMARU! WAKE UP, OR HE'LL POSSESS YOU FOR GOOD!
ピクッ
SHIVER
YOU GOT CALLS FROM MAA-CHAN AND MEGU-CHAN AND REIKO-CHAN AND TAEKO-CHAN AND EMI-CHAN!
LOOK LOOK!
AH...

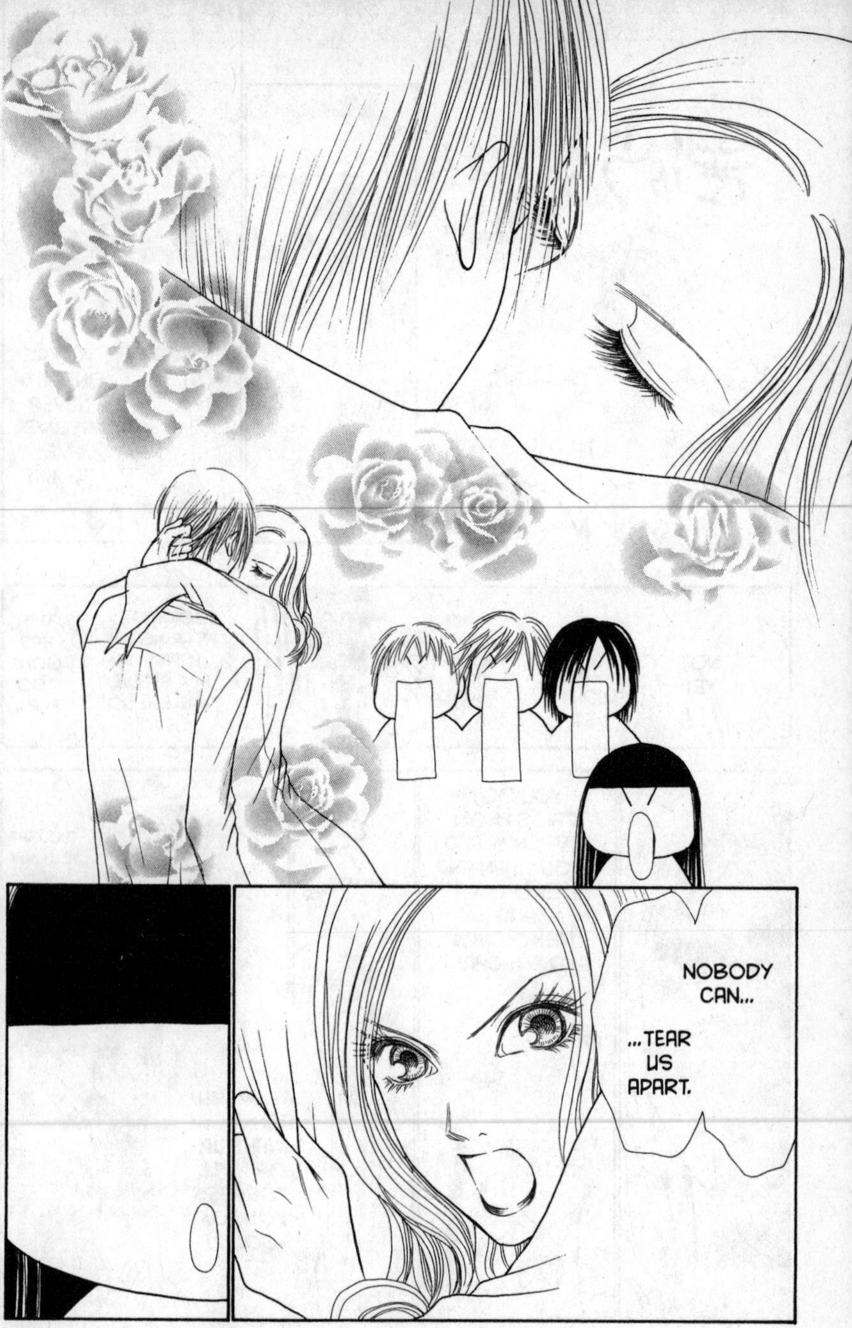
NOBODY CAN...
...TEAR US APART.

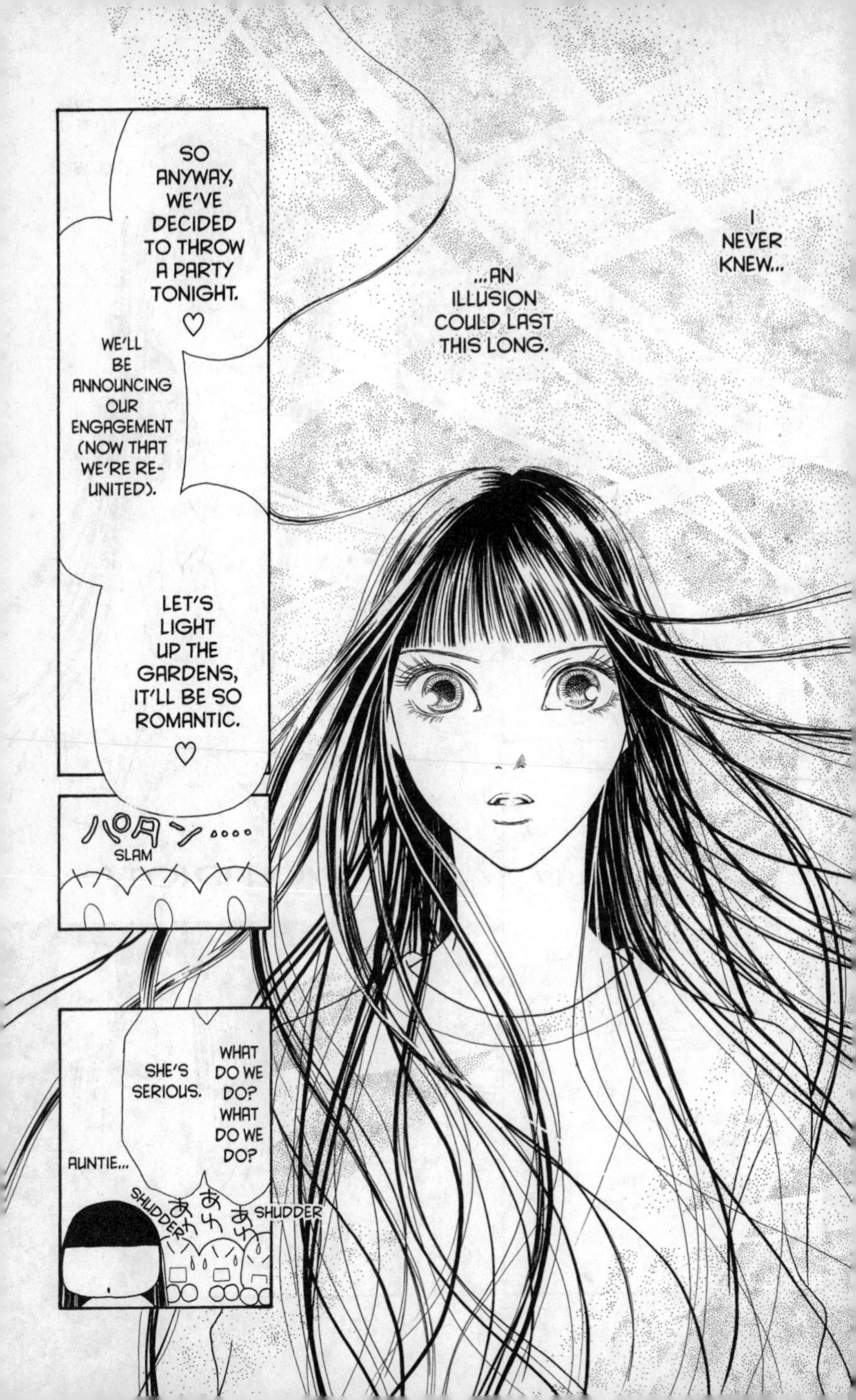
I NEVER KNEW...
...AN ILLUSION COULD LAST THIS LONG.
SO ANYWAY, WE'VE DECIDED TO THROW A PARTY TONIGHT. ♡
WE'LL BE ANNOUNCING OUR ENGAGEMENT (NOW THAT WE'RE RE-UNITED).
LET'S LIGHT UP THE GARDENS, IT'LL BE SO ROMANTIC. ♡
パタン····
SLAM
WHAT DO WE DO? WHAT DO WE DO?
SHE'S SERIOUS.
AUNTIE...
あわ あわ あわ
SHUDDER
SHUDDER

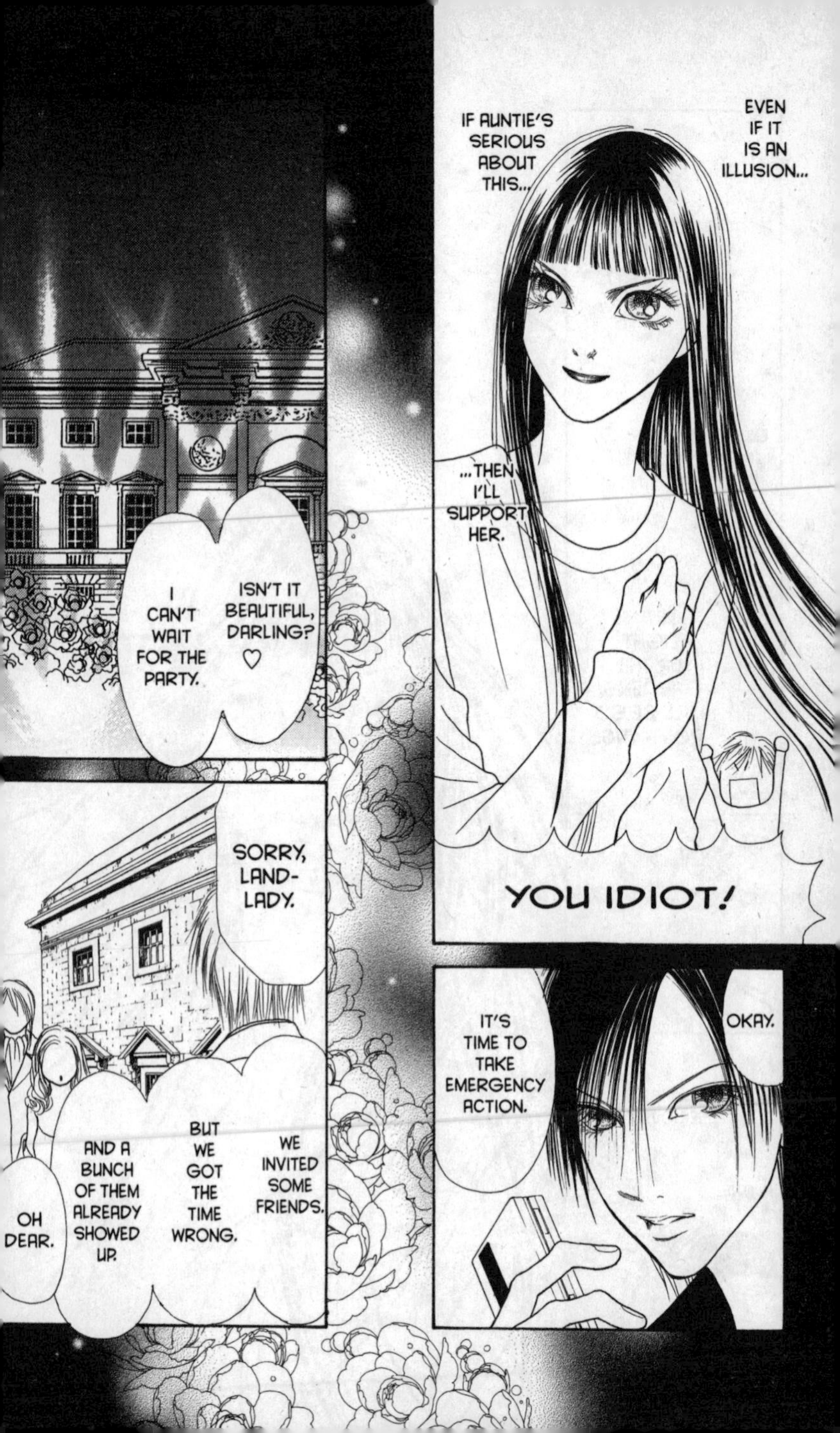
EVEN IF IT IS AN ILLUSION...
IF AUNTIE'S SERIOUS ABOUT THIS...
...THEN I'LL SUPPORT HER.
YOU IDIOT!
OKAY.
IT'S TIME TO TAKE EMERGENCY ACTION.
ISN'T IT BEAUTIFUL, DARLING? ♡
I CAN'T WAIT FOR THE PARTY.
SORRY, LAND-LADY.
WE INVITED SOME FRIENDS.
BUT WE GOT THE TIME WRONG.
AND A BUNCH OF THEM ALREADY SHOWED UP.
OH DEAR.

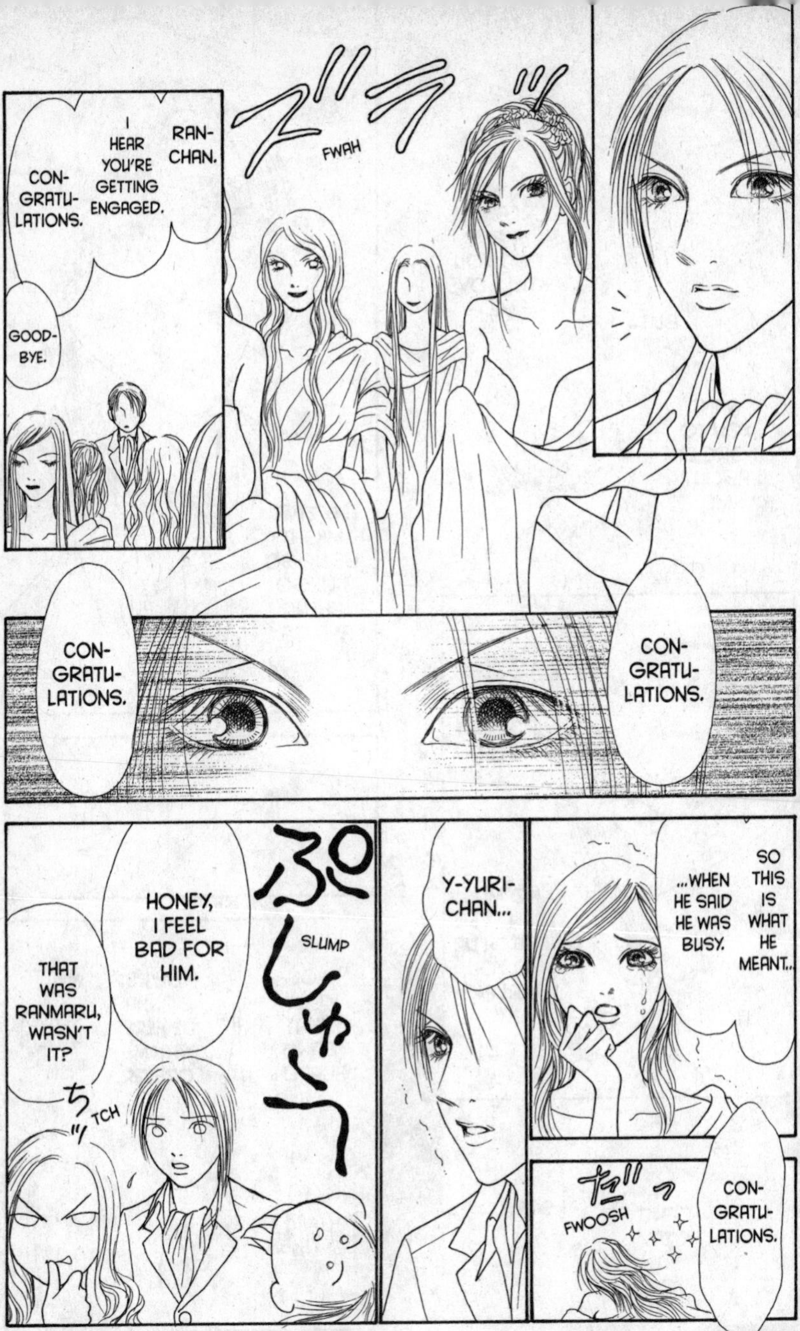
FWAH
RAN-CHAN.
I HEAR YOU'RE GETTING ENGAGED.
CON-GRATU-LATIONS.
GOOD-BYE.
CON-GRATU-LATIONS.
CON-GRATU-LATIONS.
SO THIS IS WHAT HE MEANT...
...WHEN HE SAID HE WAS BUSY.
FWOOSH
CON-GRATU-LATIONS.
Y-YURI-CHAN...
SLUMP
HONEY, I FEEL BAD FOR HIM.
THAT WAS RANMARU, WASN'T IT?
TCH

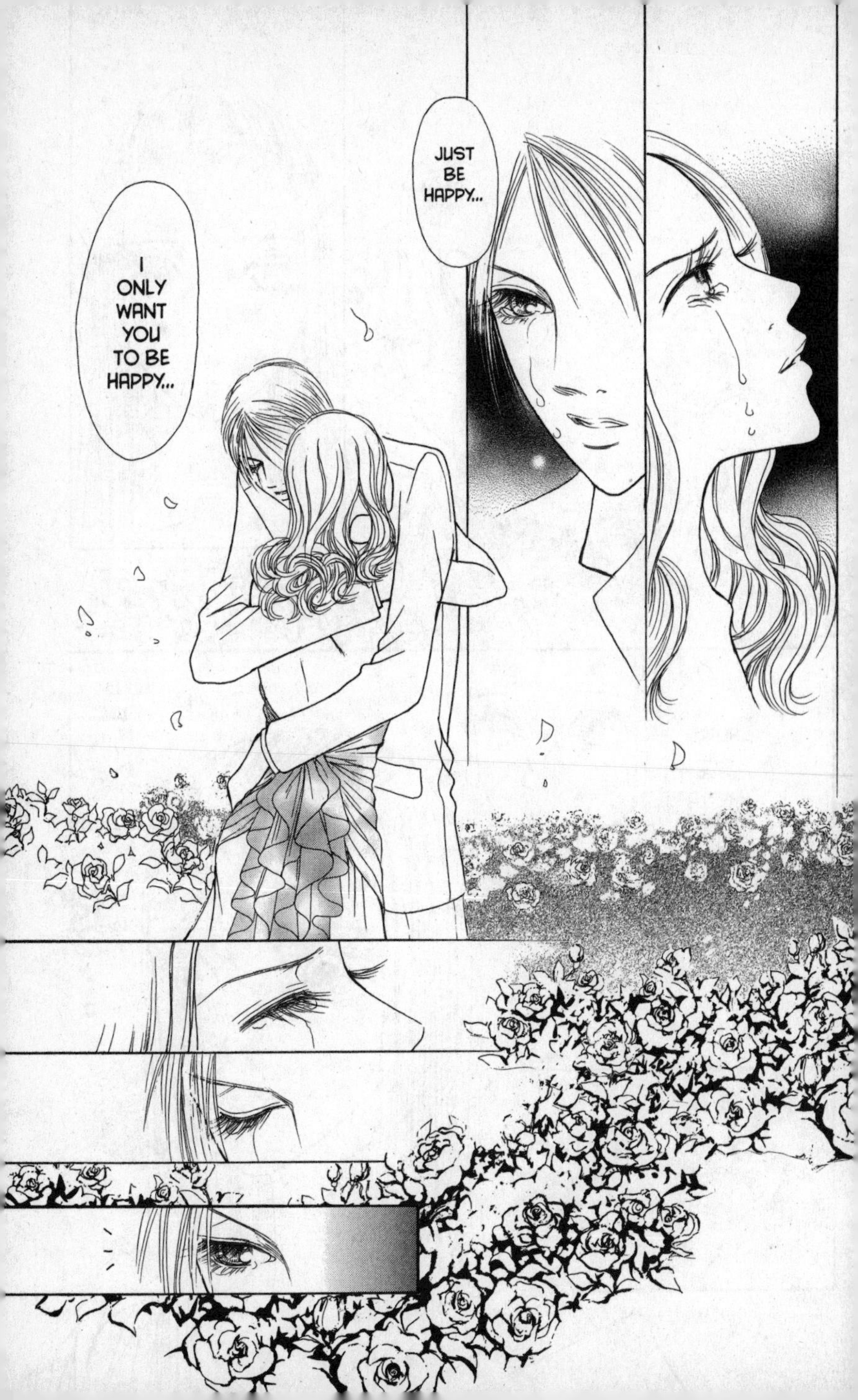
JUST BE HAPPY...
I ONLY WANT YOU TO BE HAPPY...

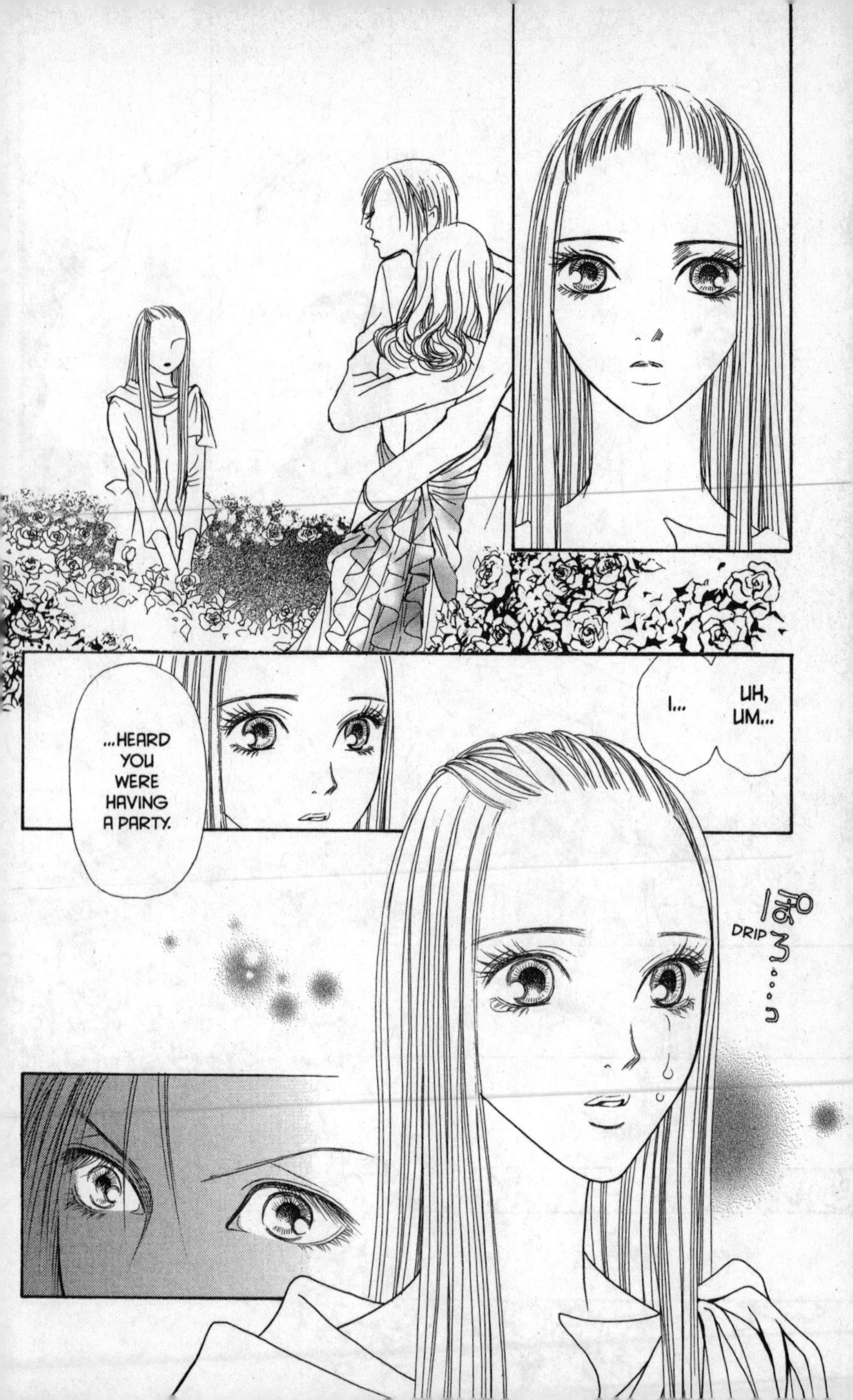
UH, UM... I...
...HEARD YOU WERE HAVING A PARTY.
DRIP

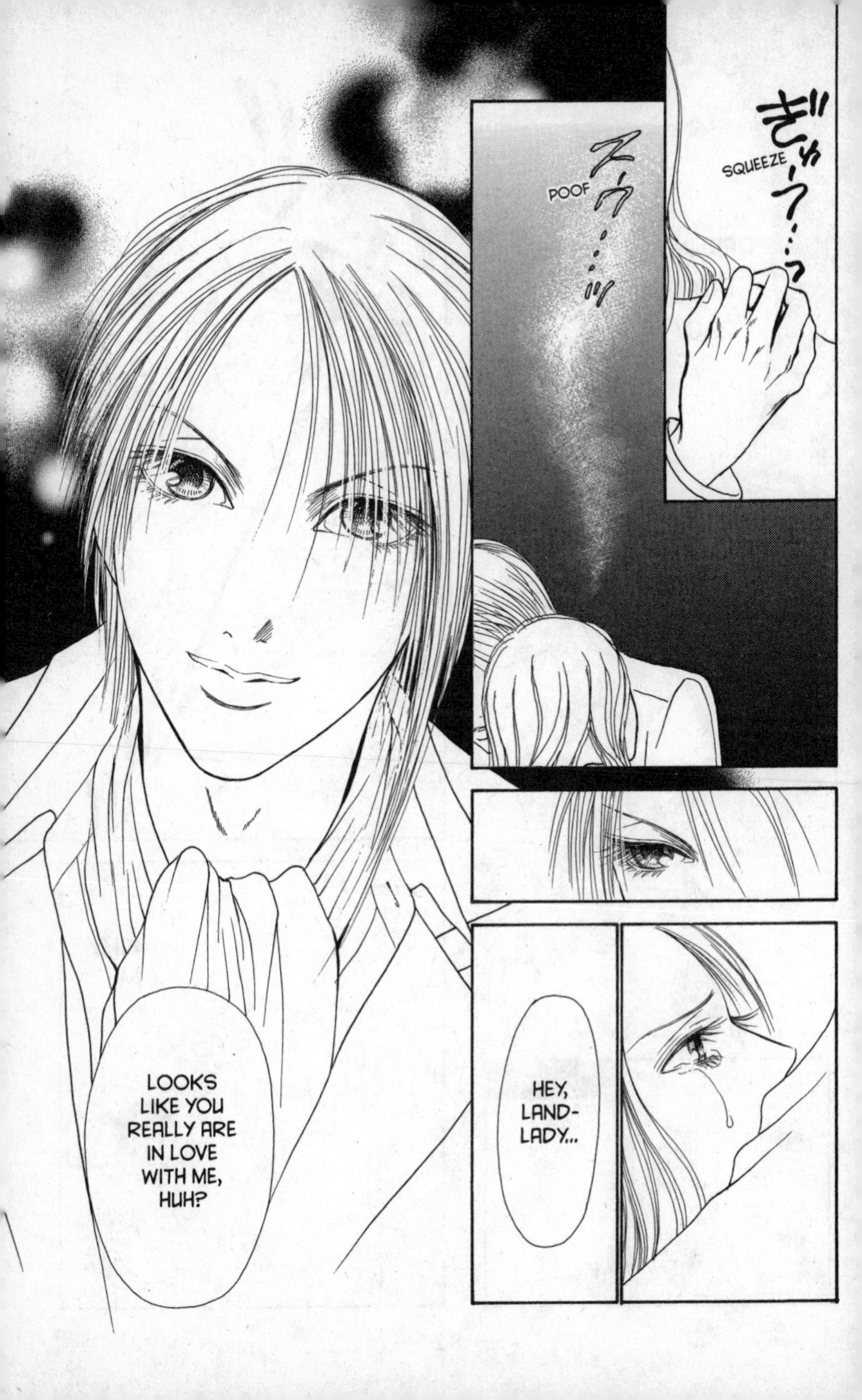
SQUEEZE
POOF
HEY, LAND-LADY...
LOOKS LIKE YOU REALLY ARE IN LOVE WITH ME, HUH?

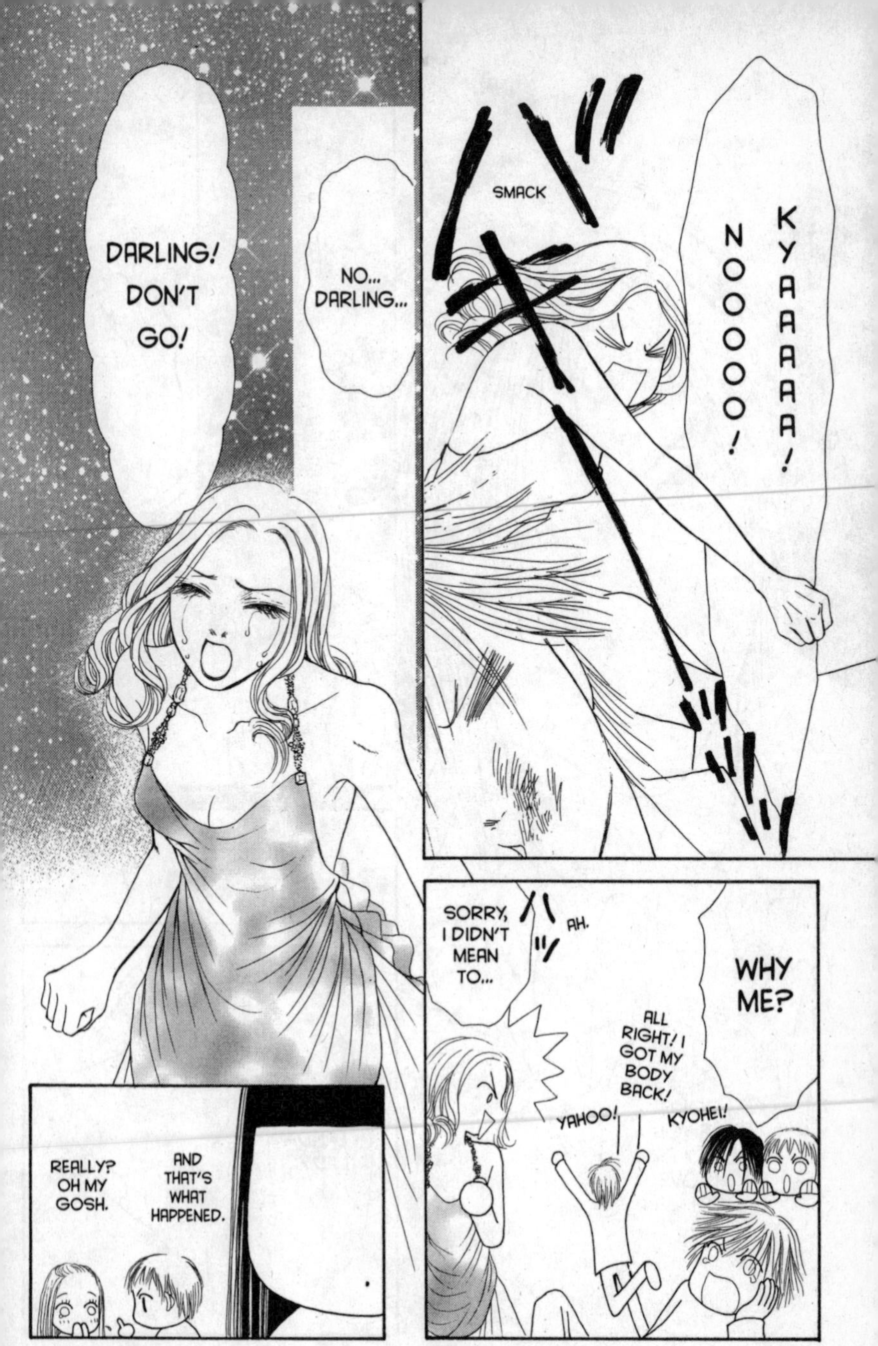
KYAAAAA! NOOOOO!
SMACK
WHY ME?
AH.
SORRY, I DIDN'T MEAN TO...
ALL RIGHT! I GOT MY BODY BACK!
KYOHEI!
YAHOO!
NO... DARLING...
DARLING! DON'T GO!
AND THAT'S WHAT HAPPENED.
REALLY? OH MY GOSH.

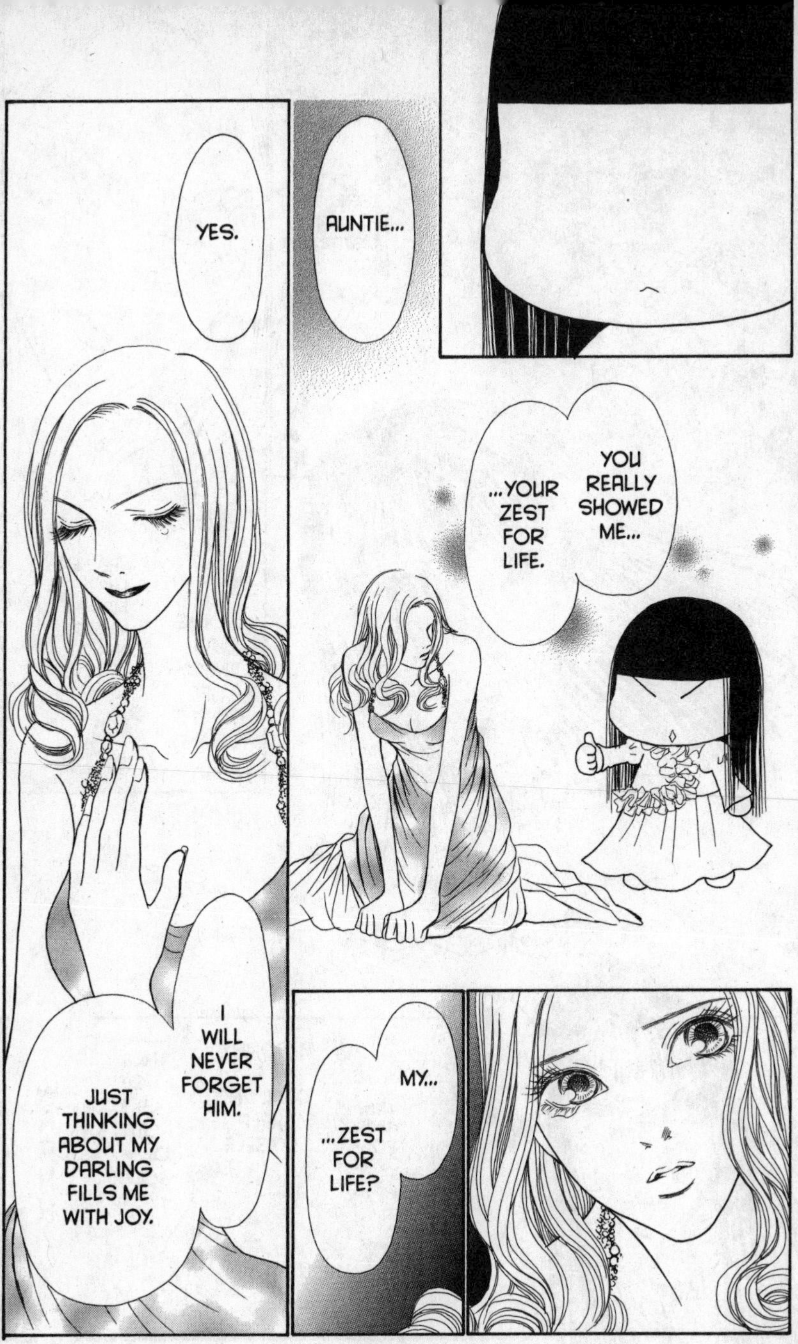
AUNTIE...
YOU REALLY SHOWED ME...
...YOUR ZEST FOR LIFE.
MY...
...ZEST FOR LIFE?
YES.
I WILL NEVER FORGET HIM.
JUST THINKING ABOUT MY DARLING FILLS ME WITH JOY.

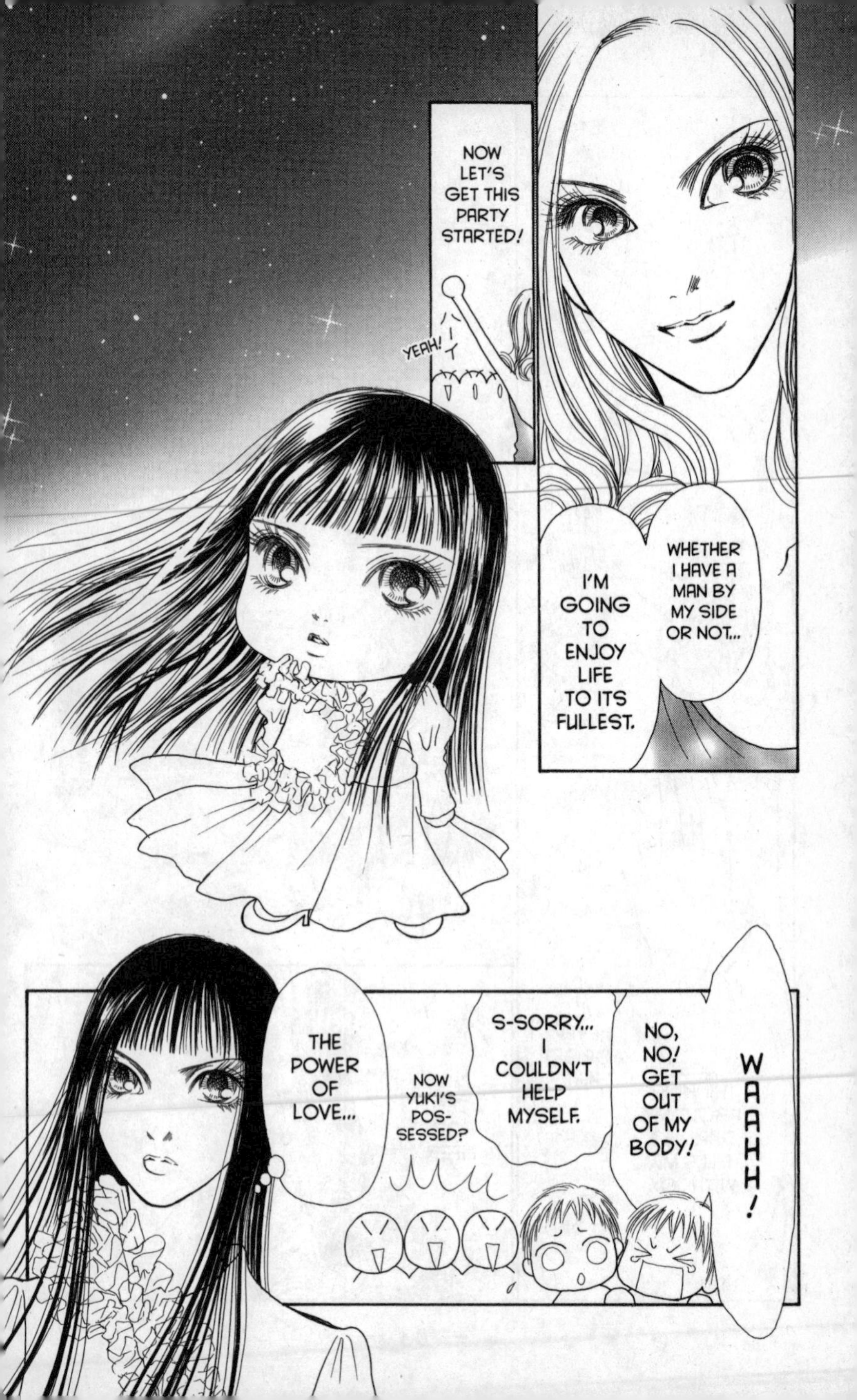
WHETHER I HAVE A MAN BY MY SIDE OR NOT...
I'M GOING TO ENJOY LIFE TO ITS FULLEST.
NOW LET'S GET THIS PARTY STARTED!
ハーイ
YEAH!
WAAHH!
NO, NO! GET OUT OF MY BODY!
S-SORRY... I COULDN'T HELP MYSELF.
NOW YUKI'S POS-SESSED?
THE POWER OF LOVE...

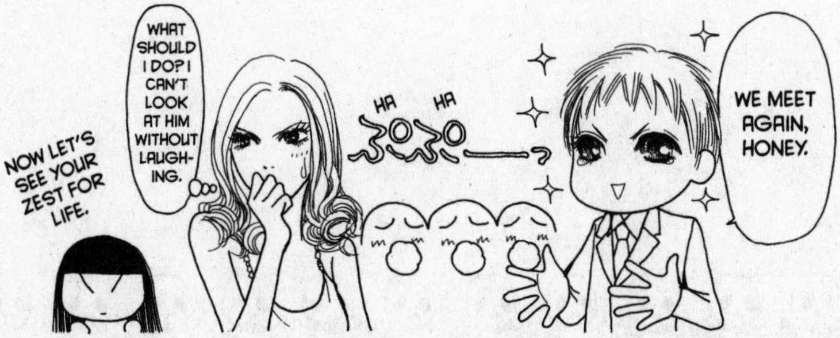
WE MEET AGAIN, HONEY.
HA HA
WHAT SHOULD I DO? I CAN'T LOOK AT HIM WITHOUT LAUGHING.
NOW LET'S SEE YOUR ZEST FOR LIFE.

apter 77 HOW TO BE A
LE DOMESTIC

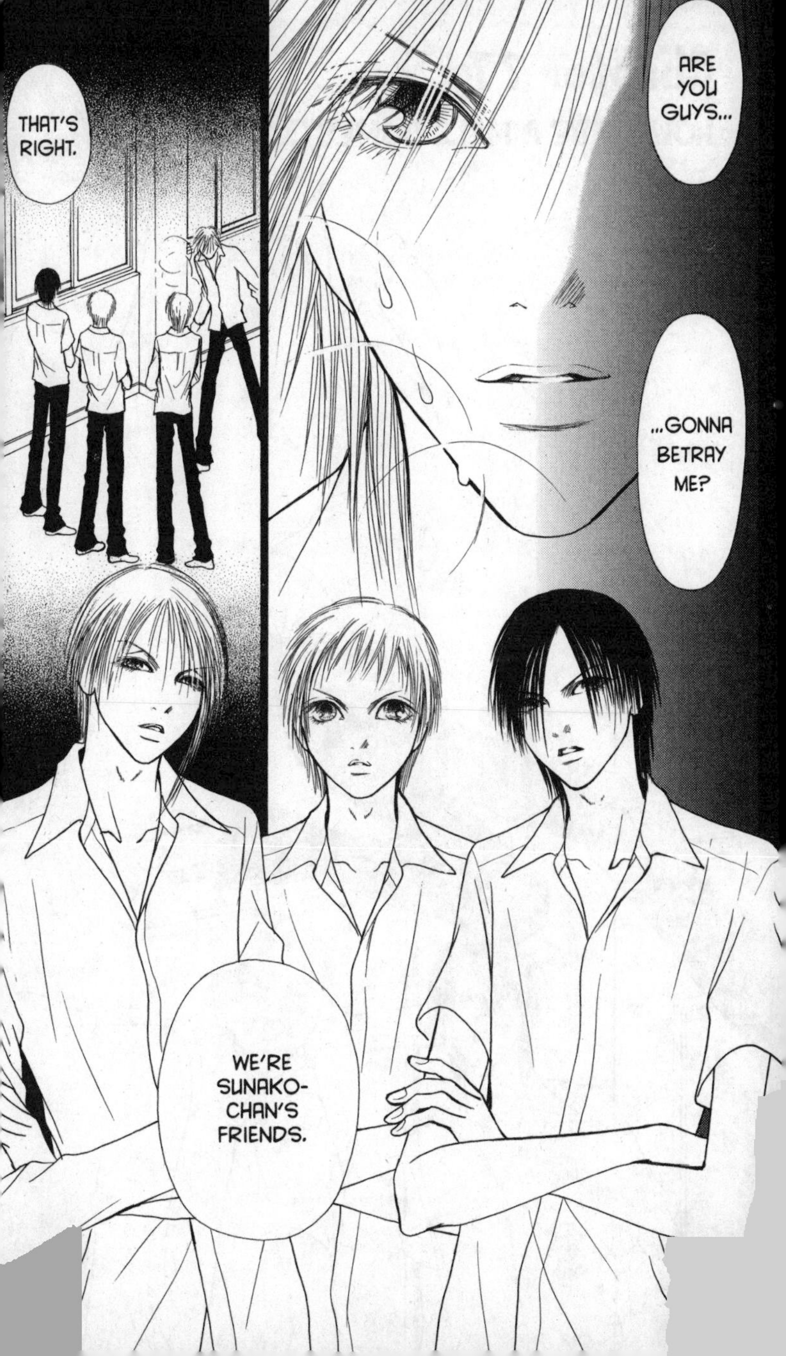
ARE YOU GUYS...
...GONNA BETRAY ME?
THAT'S RIGHT.
WE'RE SUNAKO-CHAN'S FRIENDS.

Chapter 77
HOW TO BE A MALE DOMESTIC

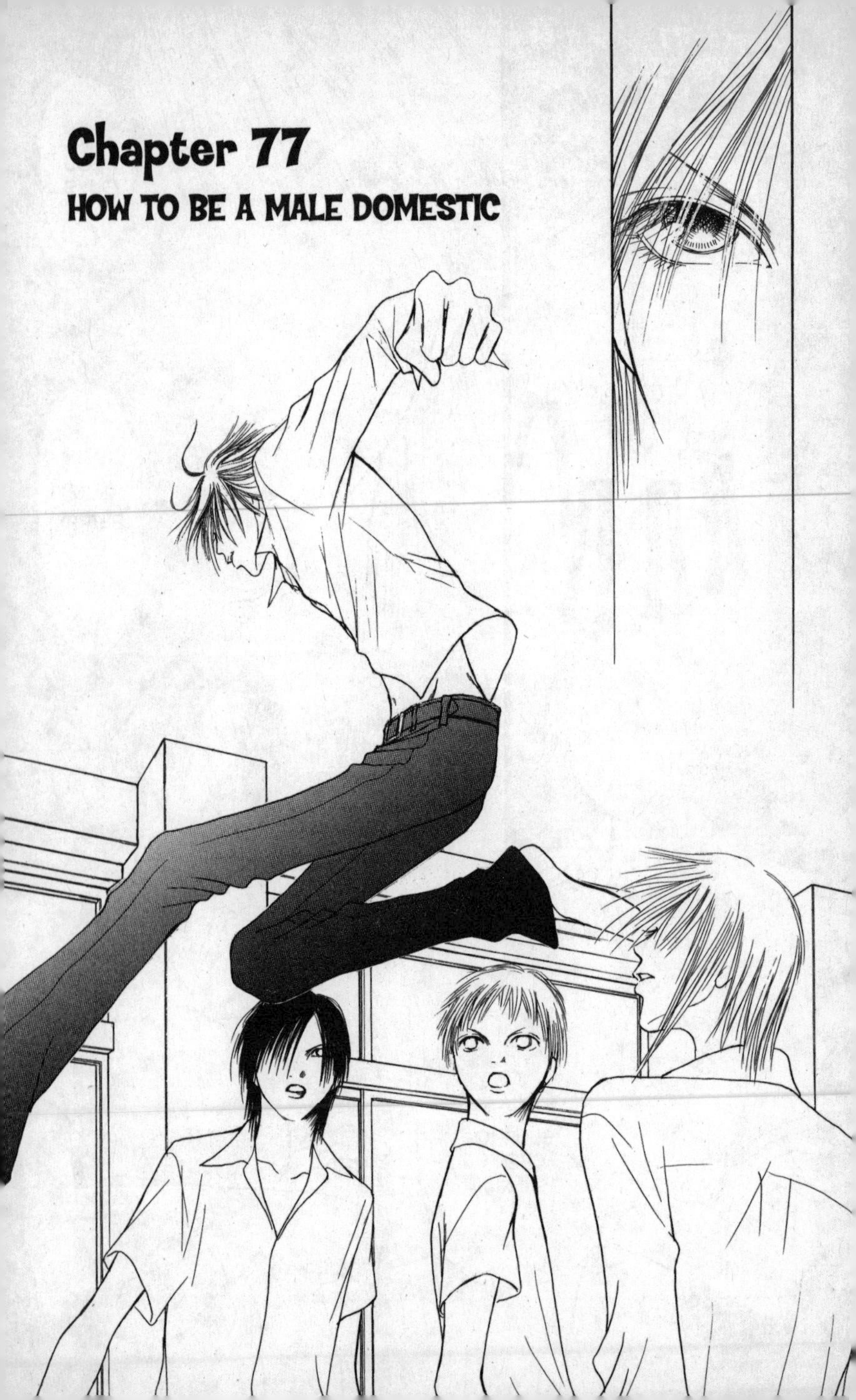

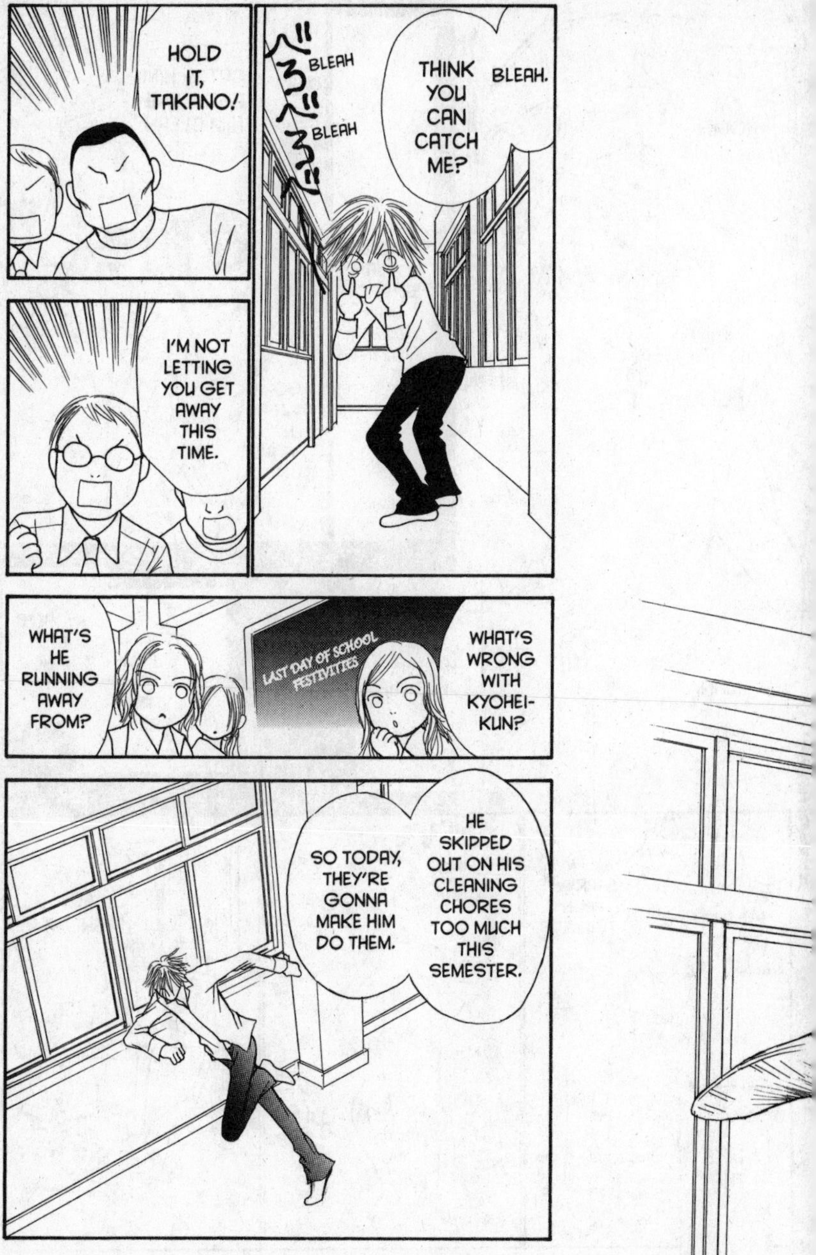
BLEAH
BLEAH
THINK YOU CAN CATCH ME?
BLEAH.
HOLD IT, TAKANO!
I'M NOT LETTING YOU GET AWAY THIS TIME.
WHAT'S WRONG WITH KYOHEI-KUN?
LAST DAY OF SCHOOL FESTIVITIES
WHAT'S HE RUNNING AWAY FROM?
HE SKIPPED OUT ON HIS CLEANING CHORES TOO MUCH THIS SEMESTER.
SO TODAY, THEY'RE GONNA MAKE HIM DO THEM.

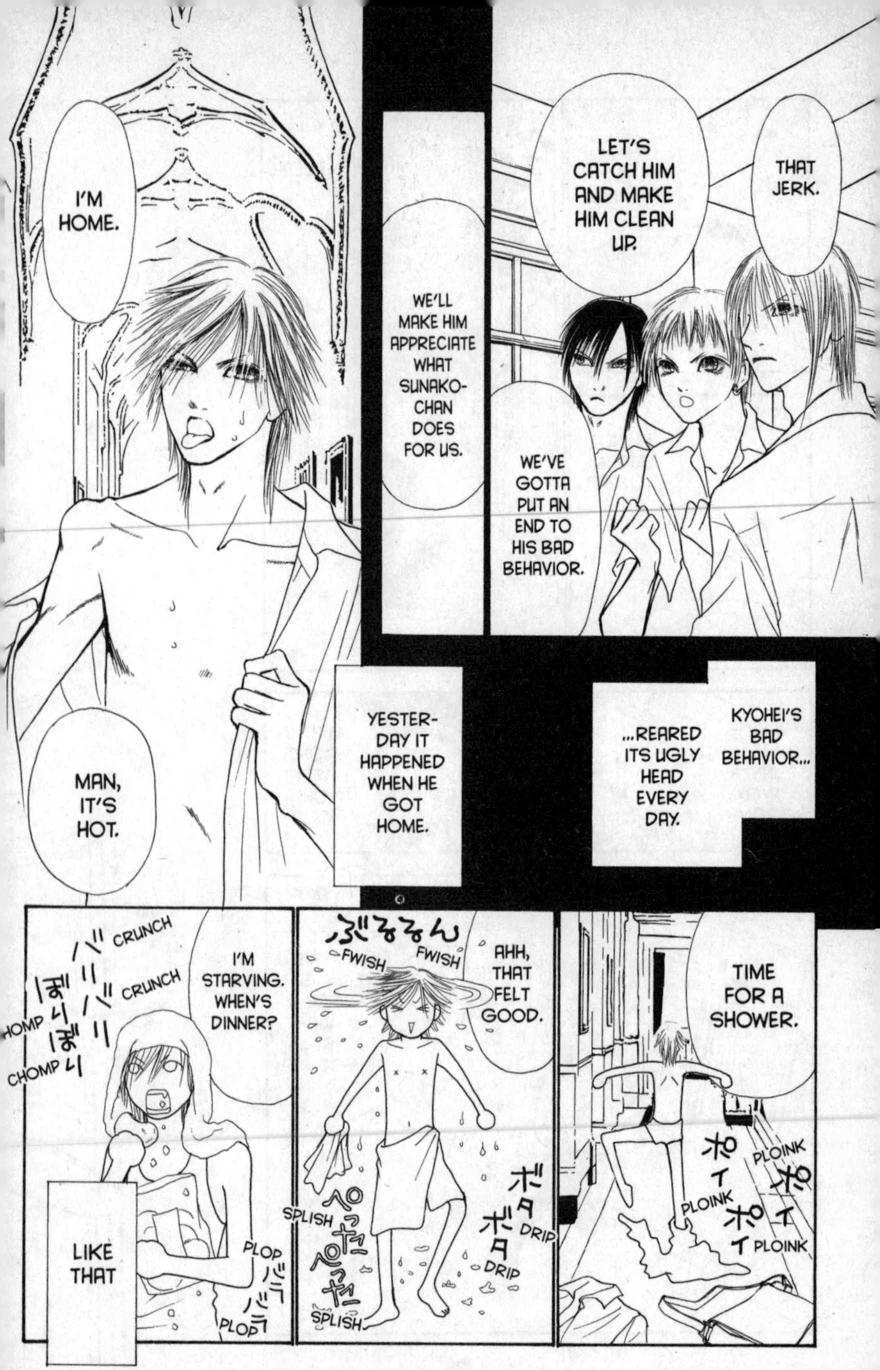
THAT JERK.
LET'S CATCH HIM AND MAKE HIM CLEAN UP.
WE'VE GOTTA PUT AN END TO HIS BAD BEHAVIOR.
WE'LL MAKE HIM APPRECIATE WHAT SUNAKO-CHAN DOES FOR US.
KYOHEI'S BAD BEHAVIOR...
...REARED ITS UGLY HEAD EVERY DAY.
YESTER-DAY IT HAPPENED WHEN HE GOT HOME.
I'M HOME.
MAN, IT'S HOT.
TIME FOR A SHOWER.
PLOINK
PLOINK
PLOINK
AHH, THAT FELT GOOD.
FWISH
FWISH
DRIP
DRIP
SPLISH
SPLISH
I'M STARVING. WHEN'S DINNER?
CRUNCH
CRUNCH
CHOMP
CHOMP
PLOP
PLOP
LIKE THAT

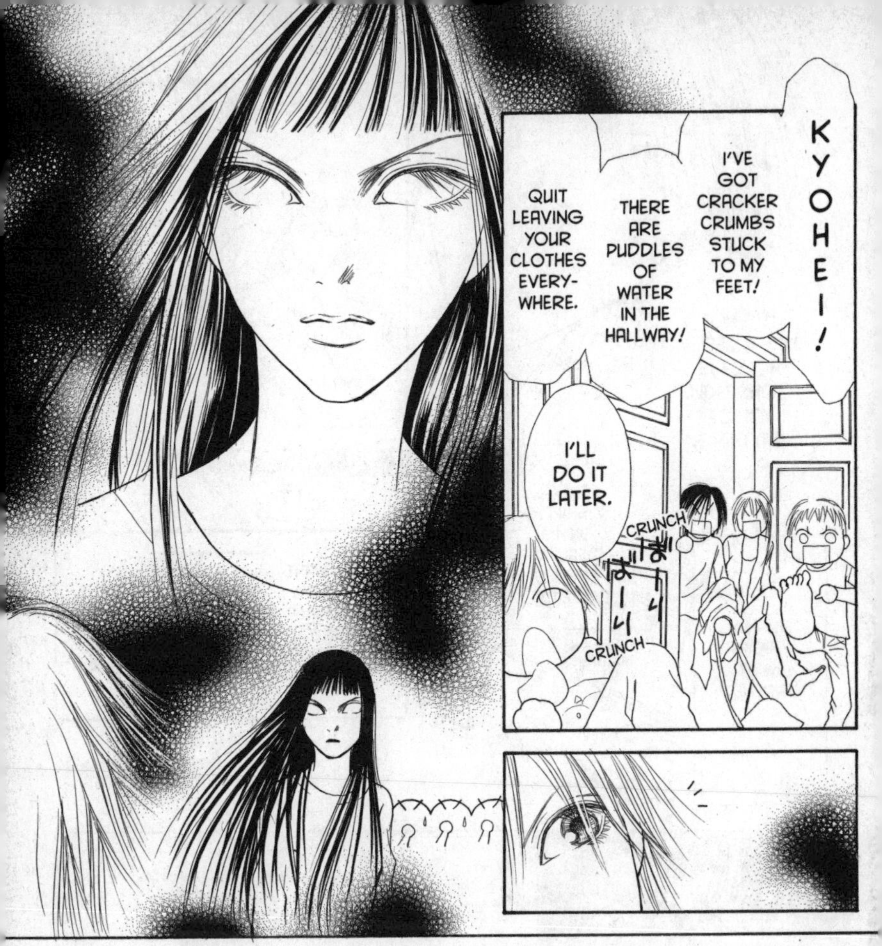
KYOHEI!
I'VE GOT CRACKER CRUMBS STUCK TO MY FEET!
THERE ARE PUDDLES OF WATER IN THE HALLWAY!
QUIT LEAVING YOUR CLOTHES EVERY-WHERE.
I'LL DO IT LATER.
CRUNCH
CRUNCH

BEHIND THE SCENES

CONTINUED FROM PAGE 48.

OF COURSE EVERYBODY ON THE STAFF WAS REALLY NICE TOO. ♡ NABESHIN-SAMA, THE DIRECTOR, AND HARUKA-SAN, THE WRITER, AND EVERYBODY ELSE WAS REALLY COOL. ♡ THERE WAS ONE PERSON THERE WHO WAS JUST MY TYPE. ♡ I'M FEELING REALLY LONELY BECAUSE I HAVEN'T SEEN THAT PERSON SINCE. ♡

I WONDER HOW I CAN LEARN TO SOCIALIZE IN PUBLIC BETTER. AS SOON AS I'M STANDING IN FRONT OF PEOPLE, MY MIND GOES BLANK. I'D LIKE TO GET OVER MY NERVES. I'M REALLY TERRIBLE. I EMBARRASS EVERYBODY. AT MY AGE, I SHOULD BE OVER THIS.

ANYWAY, IT WAS A FUN PARTY. I WAS SAD TO SEE THE SHOW END. I'D LIKE TO THANK EVERYONE INVOLVED FROM THE BOTTOM OF MY HEART!

IT'S NOT LIKE A MESSY HOUSE IS GONNA KILL YOU OR ANYTHING.

THAT'S HOW HE BEHAVED AT HOME.

AT SCHOOL, HE SKIPPED ON HIS CLEANING CHORES EVERY TIME.

FINALLY, THIS IS WHAT HAPPENED.

IF YOU WANT TO MAKE A MESS, WHY DON'T YOU DO IT IN YOUR OWN ROOM?

WHY DON'T YOU HELP HER?

APOLO-GIZE TO HER!

FWEESH

FWEESH

LA LA LA

THEME FROM HISATSU SHIGOTONIN.

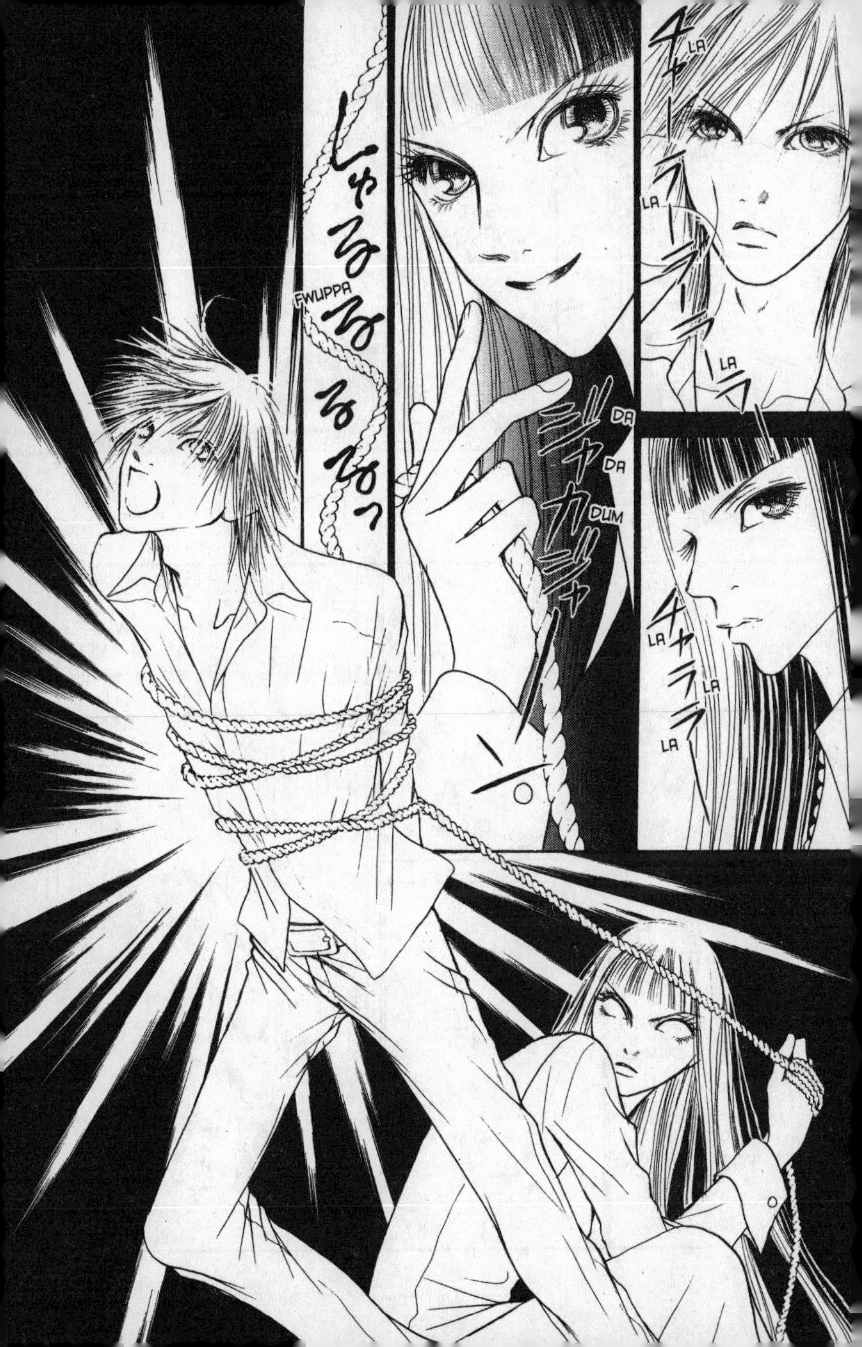
LA
LA
LA
LA
LA
LA
DA
DA
DUM
FWUPPA

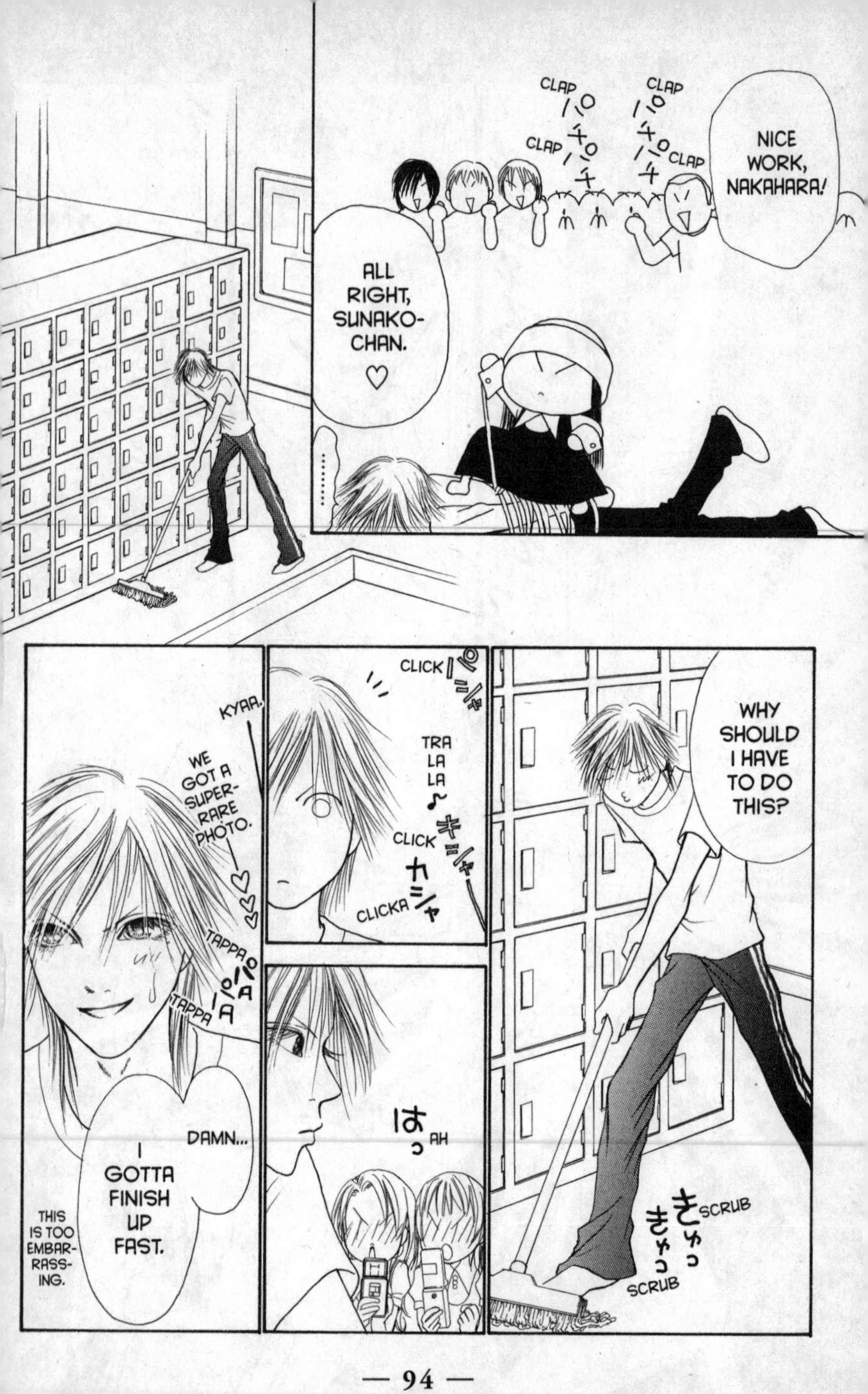
NICE WORK, NAKAHARA!
CLAP
CLAP
CLAP
CLAP
ALL RIGHT, SUNAKO-CHAN. ♡
......
WHY SHOULD I HAVE TO DO THIS?
SCRUB
SCRUB
CLICK
TRA LA LA ♪
CLICK
CLICKA
AH
KYAA.
WE GOT A SUPER-RARE PHOTO. ♡ ♡ ♡
TAPPA
TAPPA
DAMN...
I GOTTA FINISH UP FAST.
THIS IS TOO EMBARRASSING.

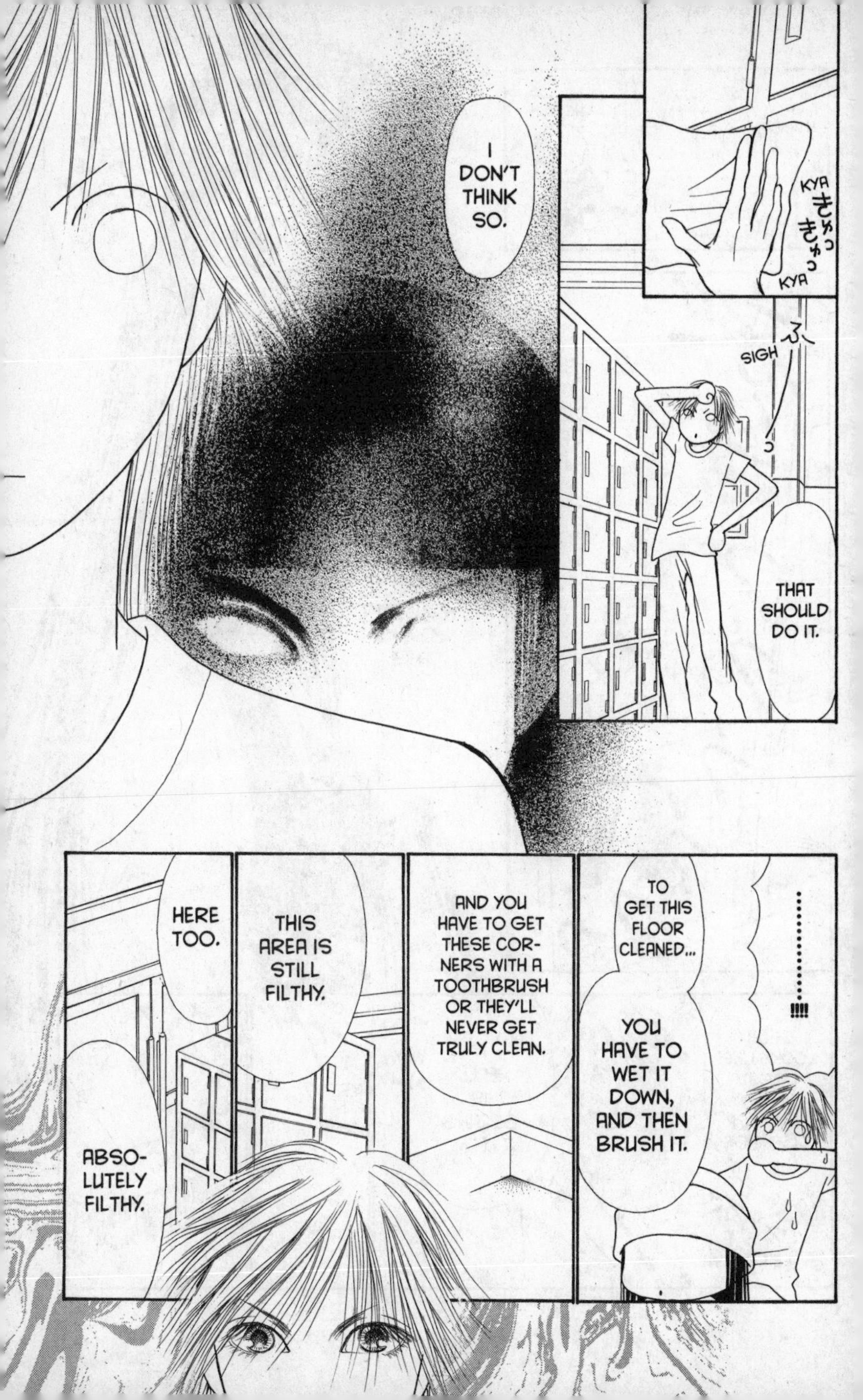
KYA
KYA
SIGH
THAT SHOULD DO IT.
I DON'T THINK SO.
......!!!!
TO GET THIS FLOOR CLEANED...
YOU HAVE TO WET IT DOWN, AND THEN BRUSH IT.
AND YOU HAVE TO GET THESE COR-NERS WITH A TOOTHBRUSH OR THEY'LL NEVER GET TRULY CLEAN.
THIS AREA IS STILL FILTHY.
HERE TOO.
ABSO-LUTELY FILTHY.

— 96 —

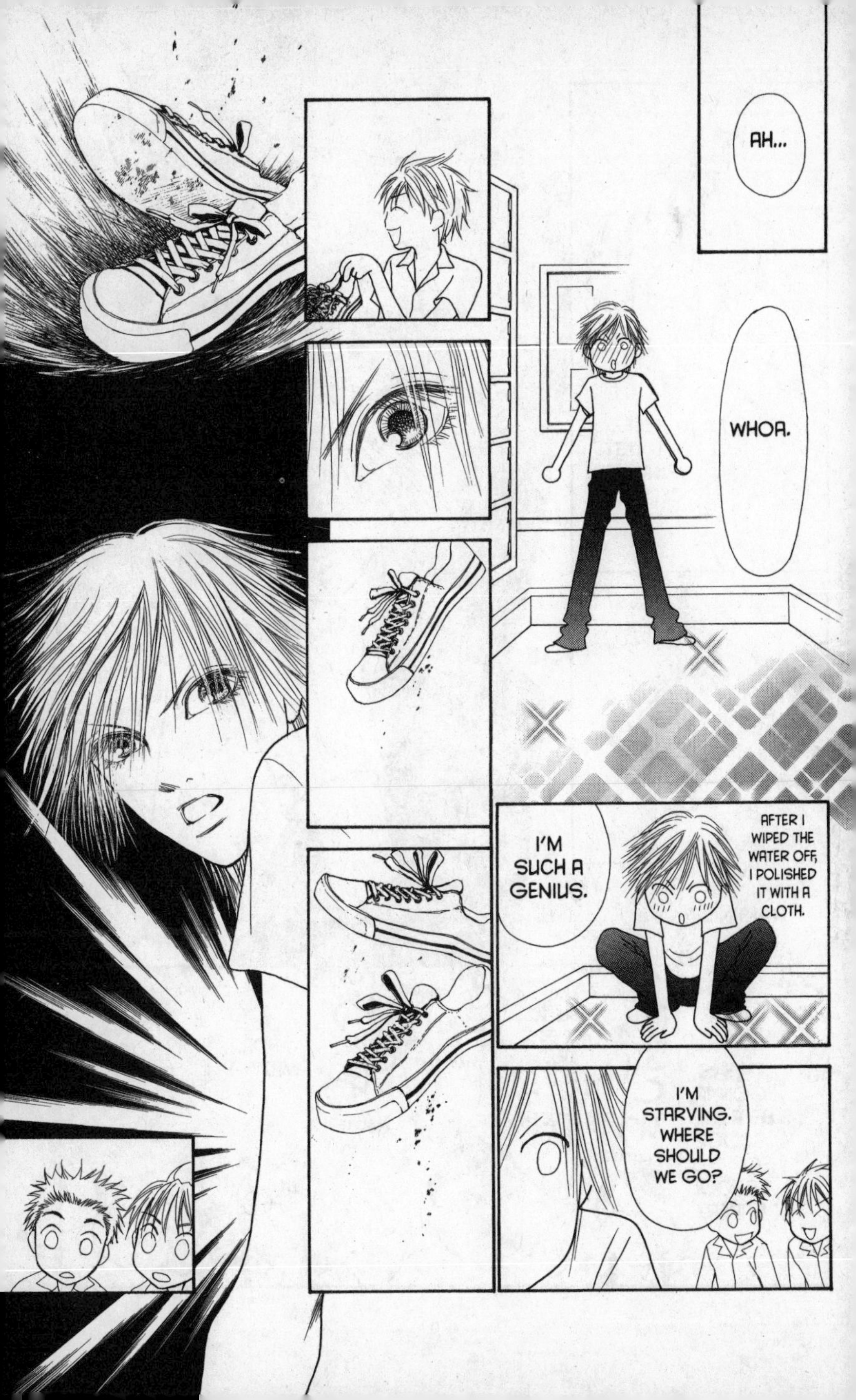
AH...
WHOA.
AFTER I WIPED THE WATER OFF, I POLISHED IT WITH A CLOTH.
I'M SUCH A GENIUS.
I'M STARVING. WHERE SHOULD WE GO?

AHHHH

WE'RE SORRY!

GEEZ, I JUST FINISHED CLEANING.

HMMPH.

SCRUB

SCRUB

HUH? IS THAT TAKANO?

CHATTER

CHATTER

THIS IS GONNA BE A BIG SCOOP FOR THE SCHOOL PAPER!

I'M HERE TO WITNESS THIS MIRACLE ON BEHALF OF THE STUDENT BODY.

WOW!

WHOA, AMAZING.

TAKANO IS ACTUALLY CLEANING.

CHATTER

CHATTER

CHATTER

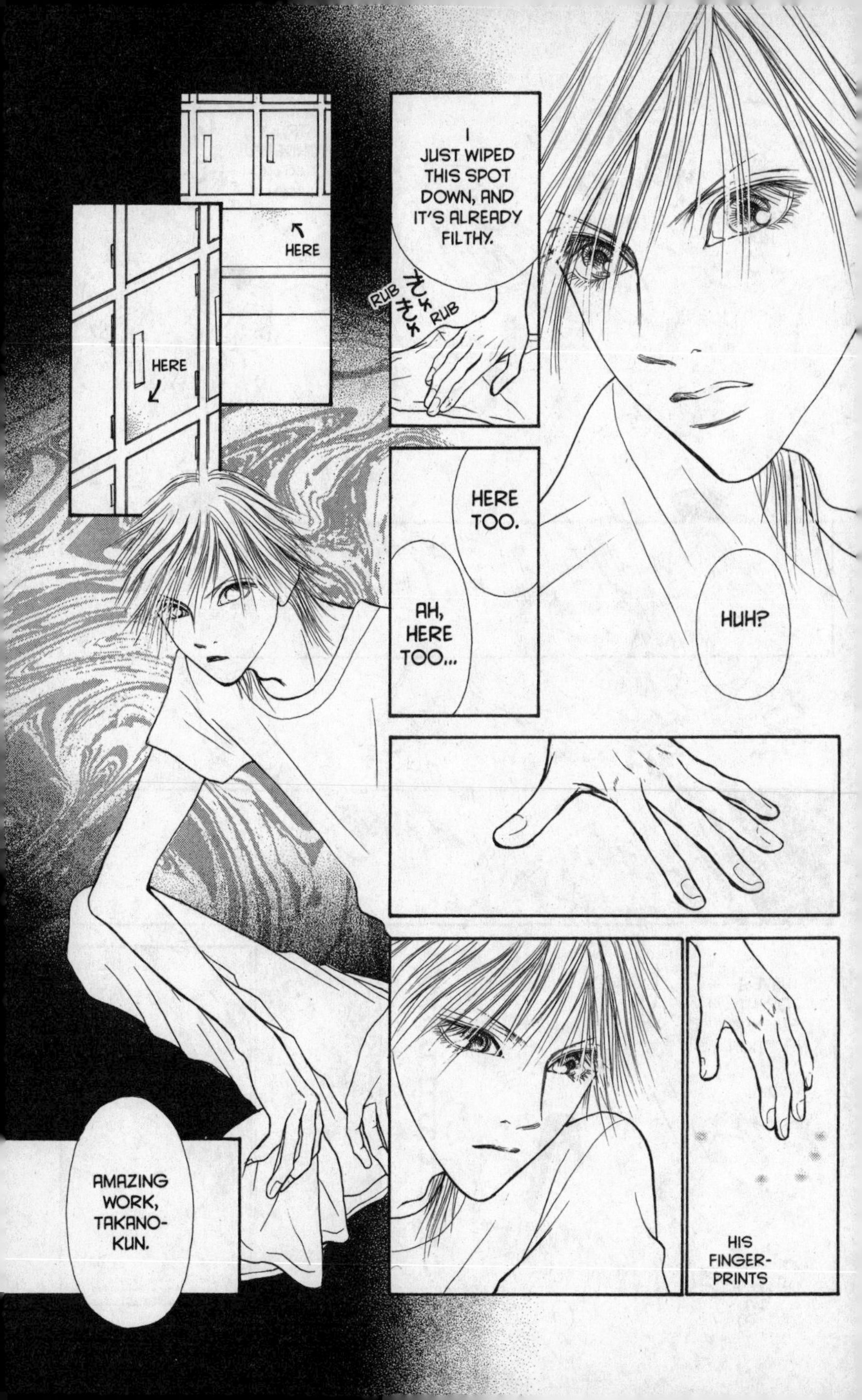
I JUST WIPED THIS SPOT DOWN, AND IT'S ALREADY FILTHY.
RUB
RUB
HUH?
HERE TOO.
AH, HERE TOO...
HIS FINGER-PRINTS
HERE
HERE
AMAZING WORK, TAKANO-KUN.

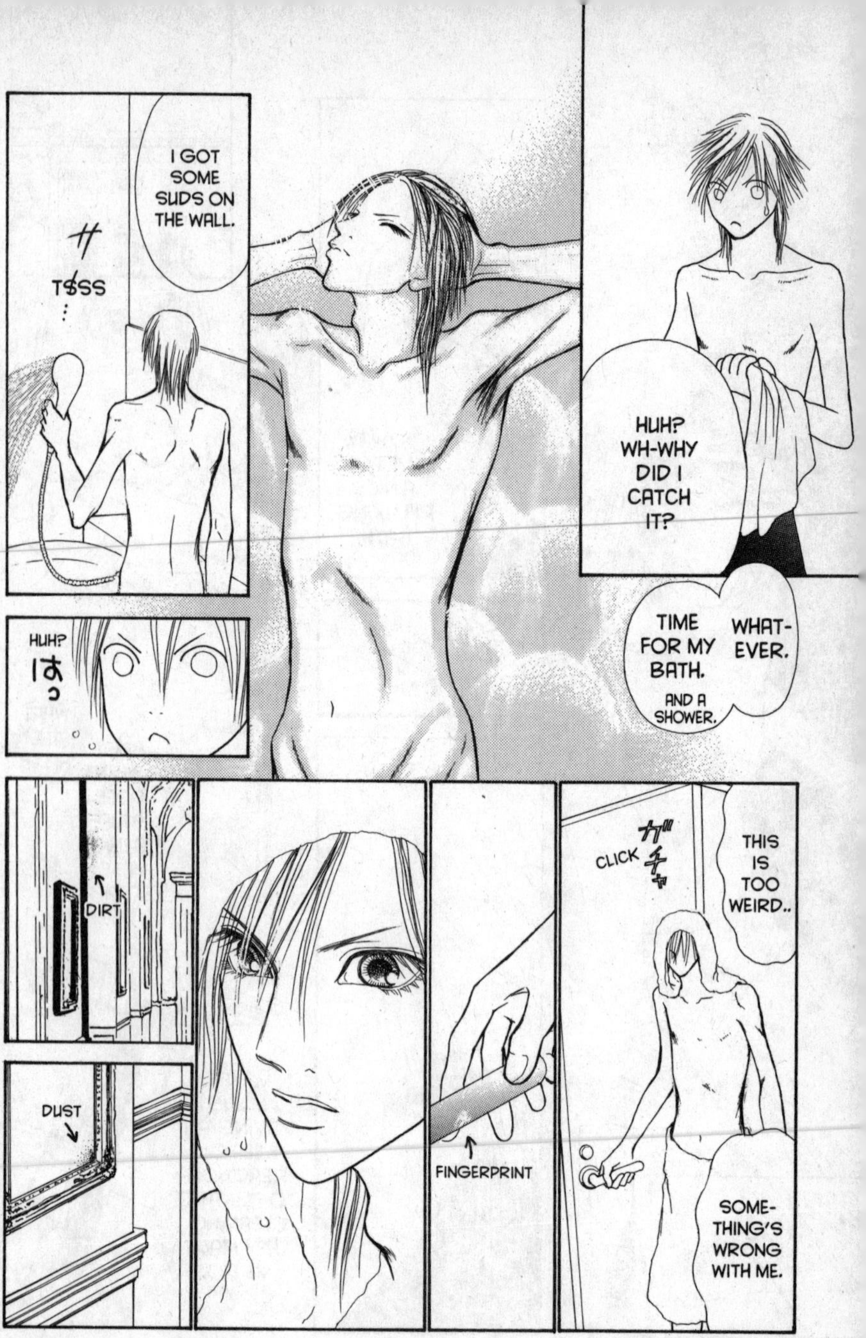
HUH? WH-WHY DID I CATCH IT?
WHAT-EVER.
TIME FOR MY BATH.
AND A SHOWER.
I GOT SOME SUDS ON THE WALL.
ザ
TSSS...
HUH?
はっ
CLICK
ガチャ
THIS IS TOO WEIRD..
SOME-THING'S WRONG WITH ME.
FINGERPRINT
DIRT
DUST

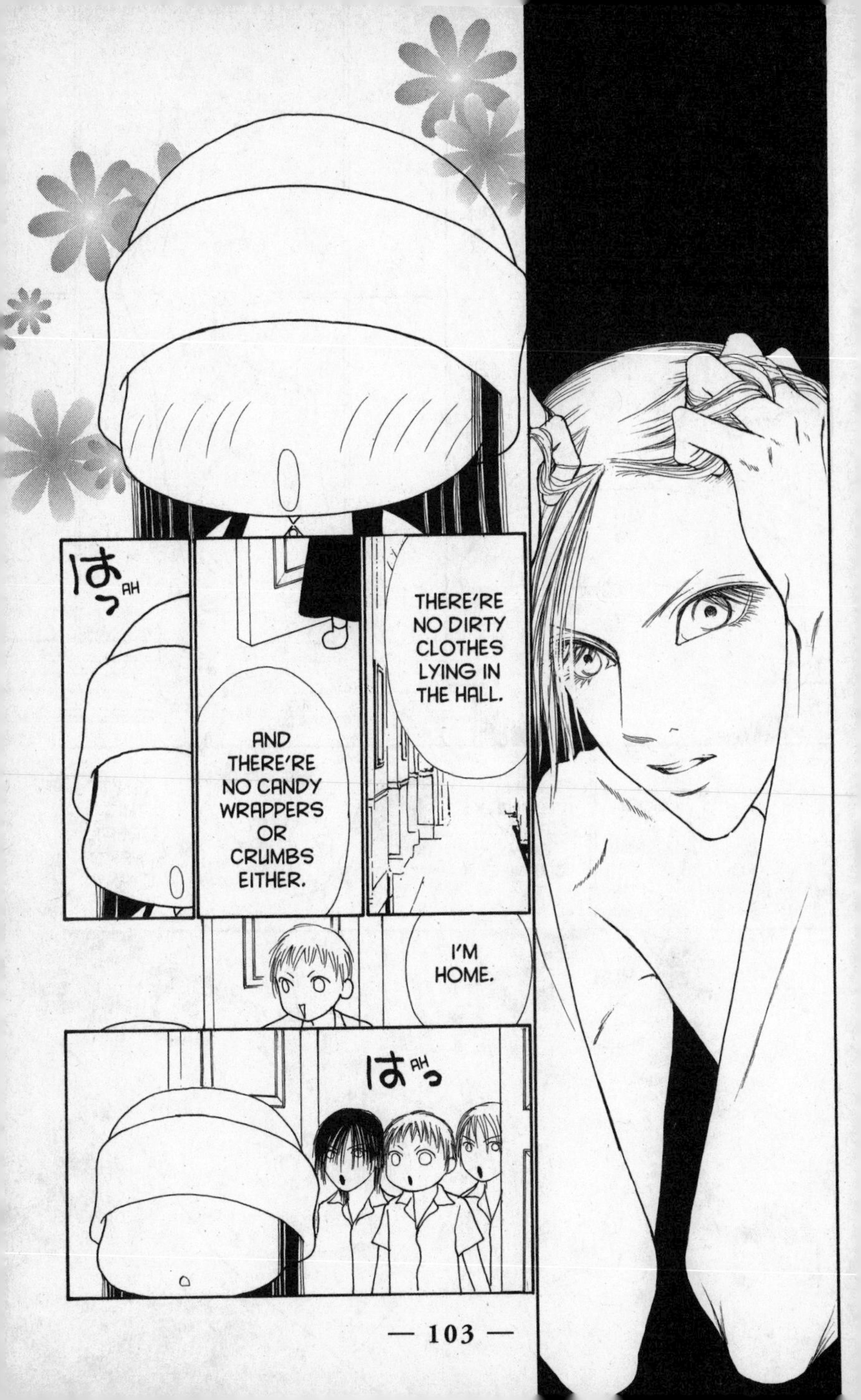
THERE'RE NO DIRTY CLOTHES LYING IN THE HALL.
AND THERE'RE NO CANDY WRAPPERS OR CRUMBS EITHER.
はっ AH
I'M HOME.
はっ AH

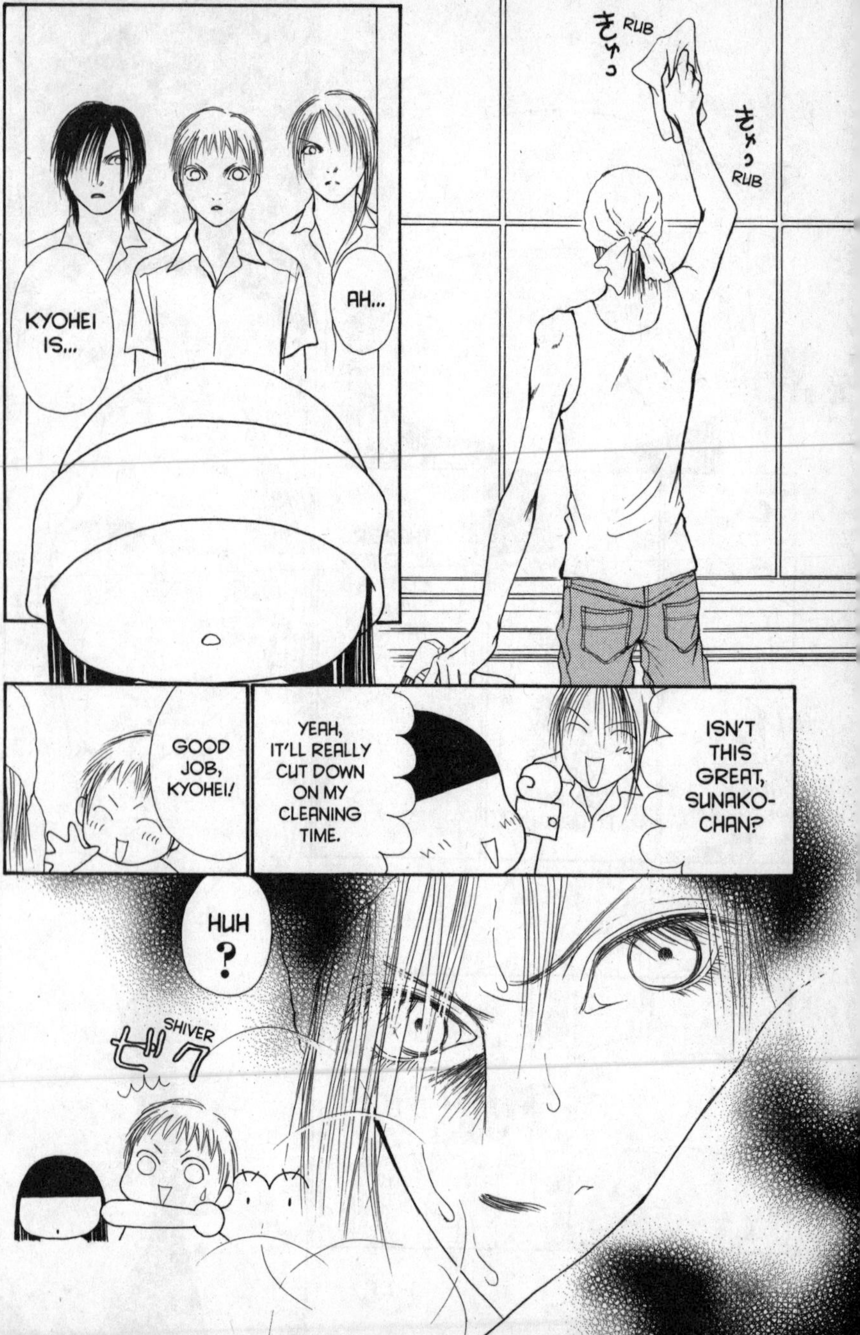

きゅっ RUB
きゅっ RUB
AH...
KYOHEI IS...
ISN'T THIS GREAT, SUNAKO-CHAN?
YEAH, IT'LL REALLY CUT DOWN ON MY CLEANING TIME.
GOOD JOB, KYOHEI!
HUH?
SHIVER

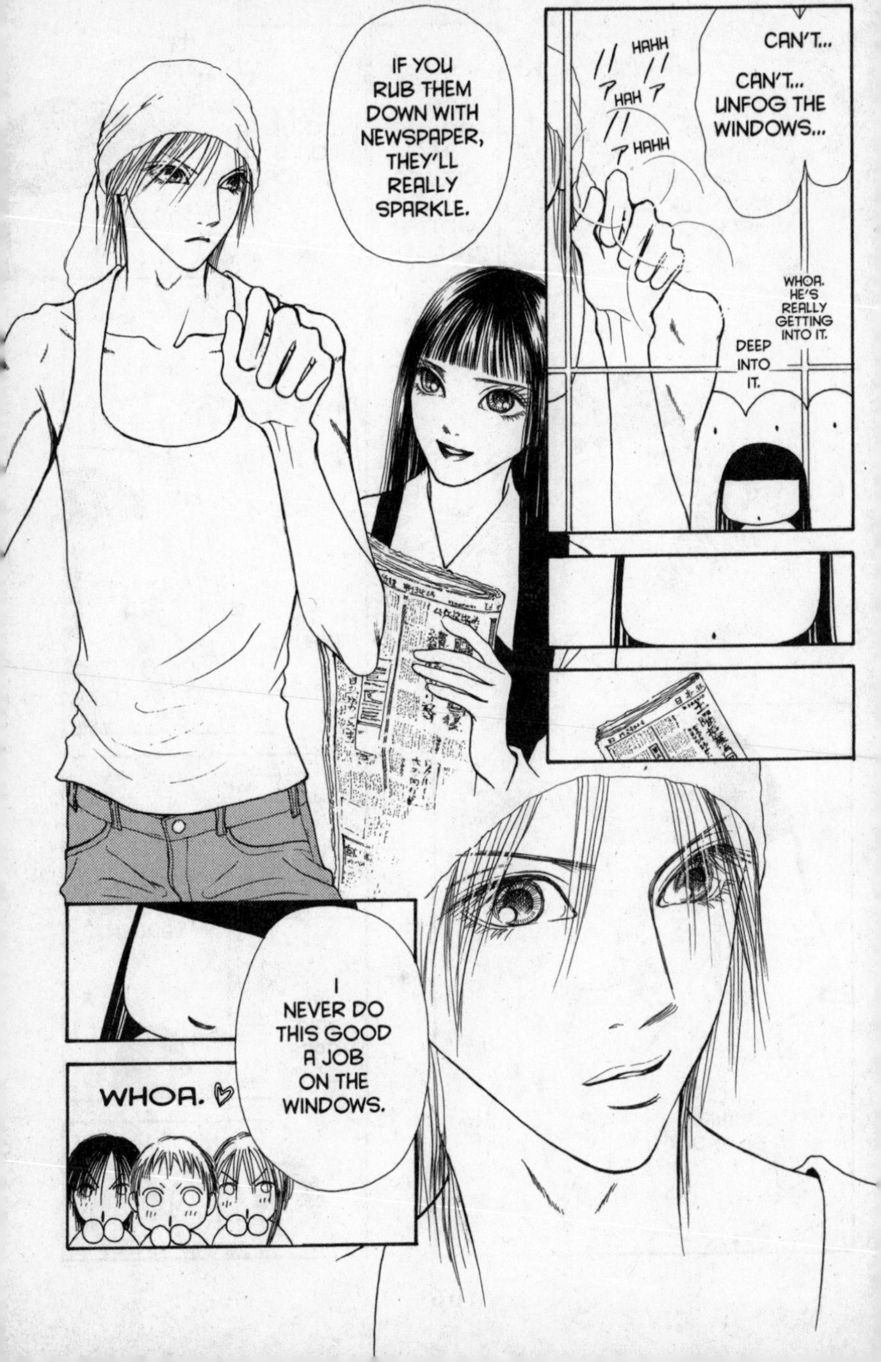
CAN'T...
CAN'T... UNFOG THE WINDOWS...
HAHH
HAH
HAHH
WHOA. HE'S REALLY GETTING INTO IT.
DEEP INTO IT.
IF YOU RUB THEM DOWN WITH NEWSPAPER, THEY'LL REALLY SPARKLE.
I NEVER DO THIS GOOD A JOB ON THE WINDOWS.
WHOA. ♡

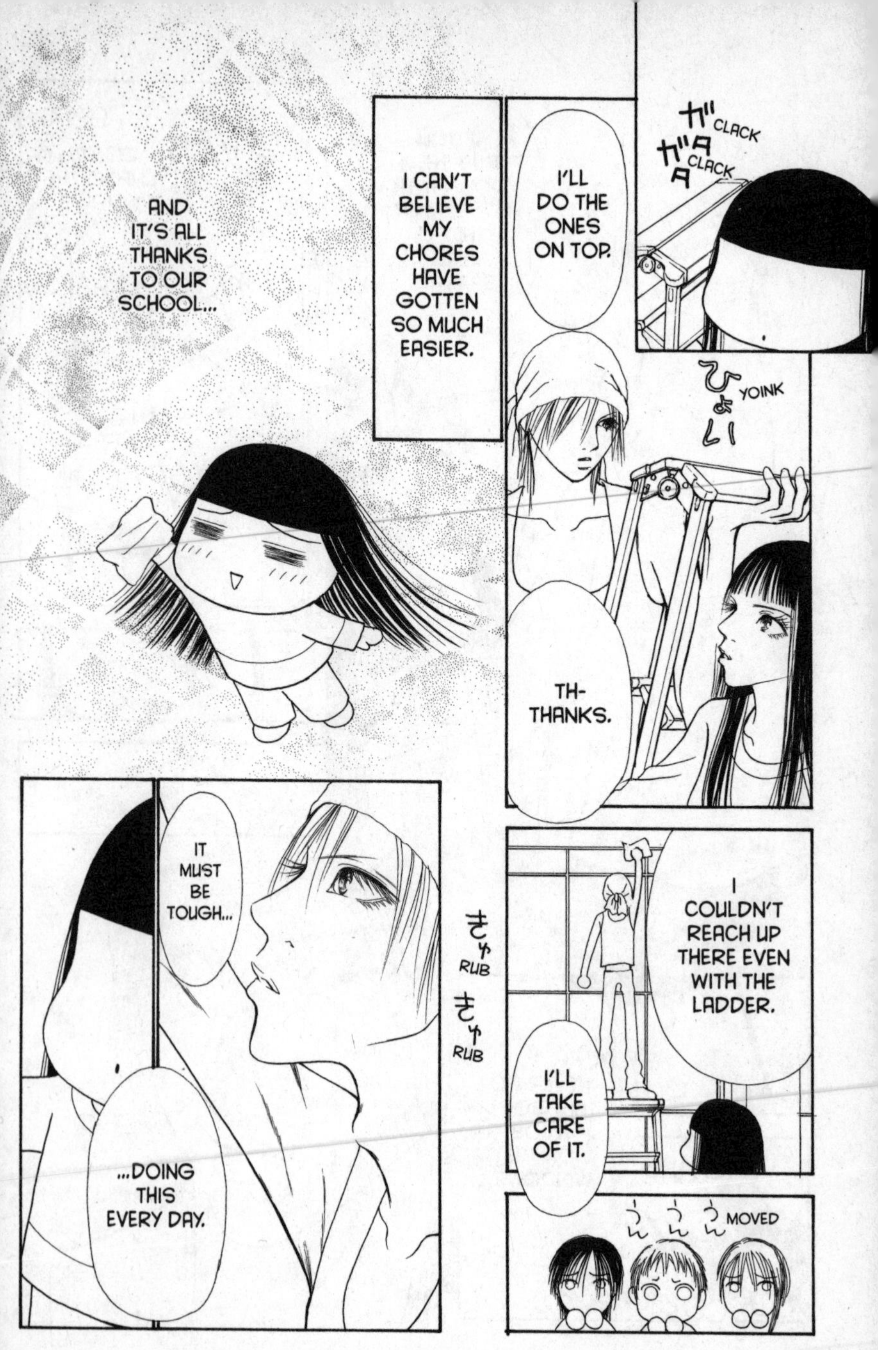
ガ CLACK
ガタ CLACK
ひょい YOINK
I'LL DO THE ONES ON TOP.
TH-THANKS.
I CAN'T BELIEVE MY CHORES HAVE GOTTEN SO MUCH EASIER.
AND IT'S ALL THANKS TO OUR SCHOOL...
I COULDN'T REACH UP THERE EVEN WITH THE LADDER.
I'LL TAKE CARE OF IT.
うんうんうん MOVED
きゅ RUB
きゅ RUB
IT MUST BE TOUGH...
...DOING THIS EVERY DAY.

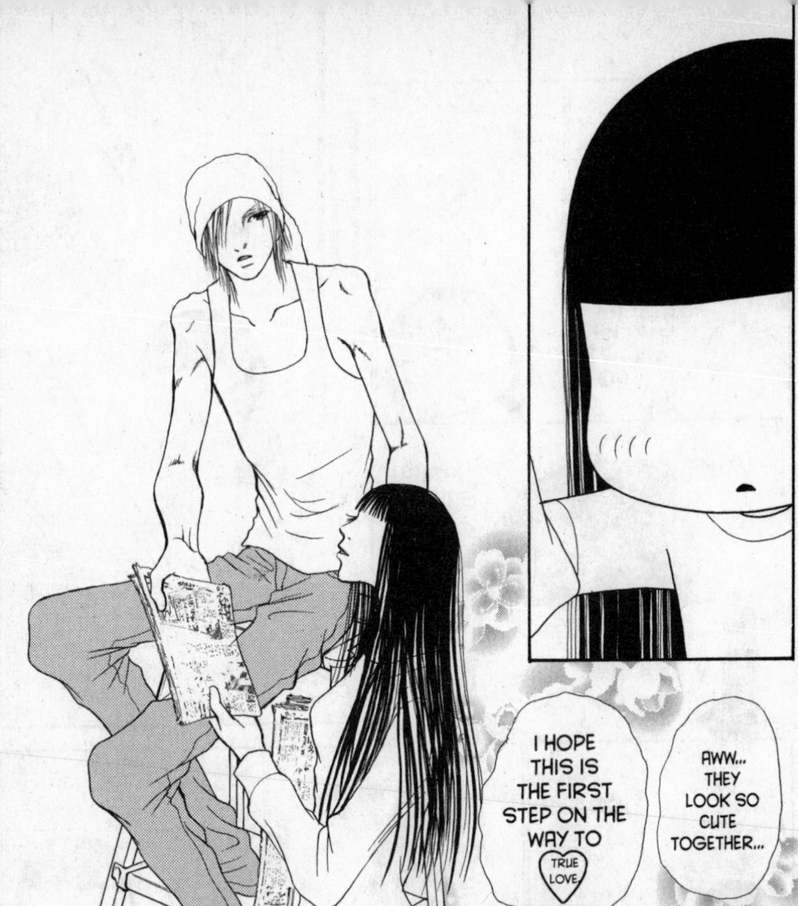
AWW... THEY LOOK SO CUTE TOGETHER...
I HOPE THIS IS THE FIRST STEP ON THE WAY TO TRUE LOVE
OH NO! OH NO!
I WAS SO BUSY WITH CLEANING THAT DINNER IS GONNA BE LATE!
ころん
PLOINK

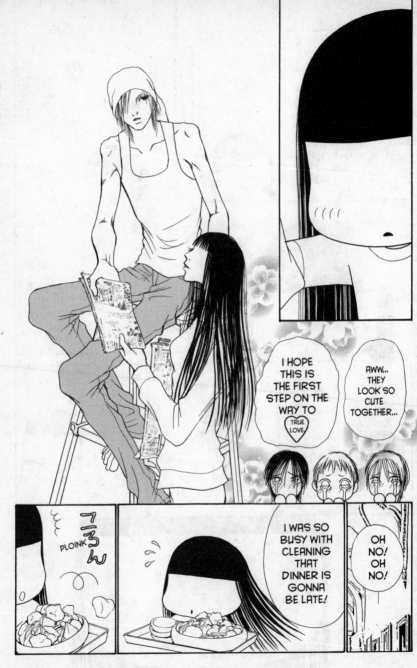

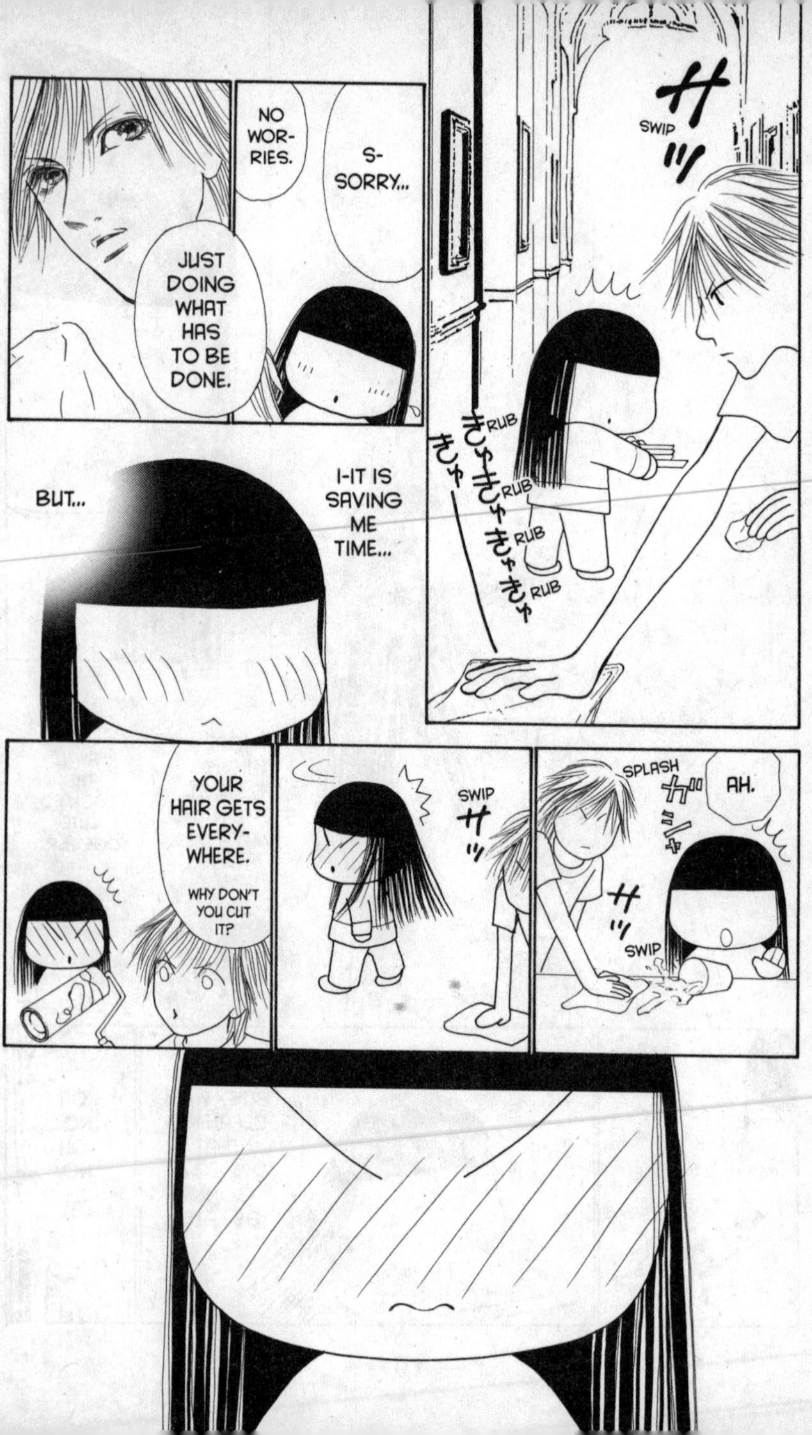
SWIP
RUB
RUB
RUB
RUB
S-SORRY...
NO WORRIES.
JUST DOING WHAT HAS TO BE DONE.
I-IT IS SAVING ME TIME...
BUT...
AH.
SPLASH
SWIP
SWIP
YOUR HAIR GETS EVERYWHERE.
WHY DON'T YOU CUT IT?

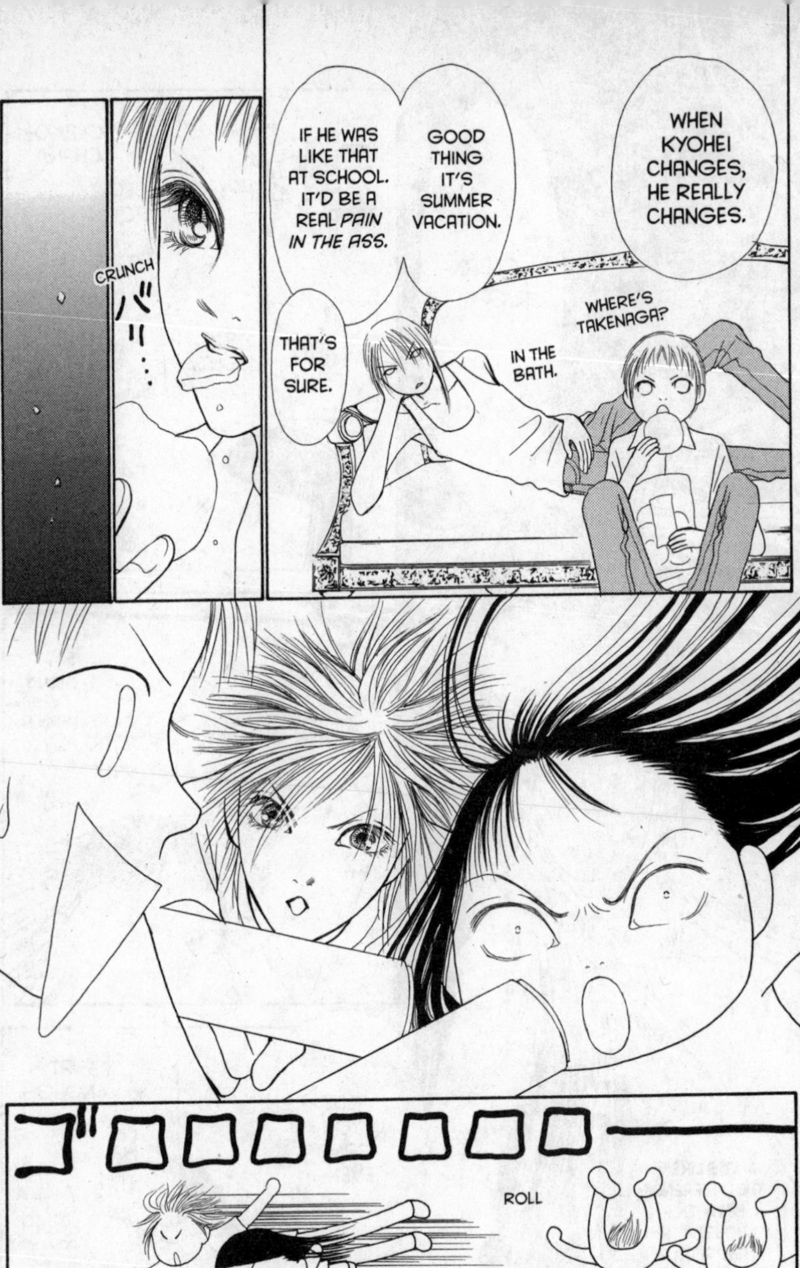
WHEN KYOHEI CHANGES, HE REALLY CHANGES.
GOOD THING IT'S SUMMER VACATION.
IF HE WAS LIKE THAT AT SCHOOL. IT'D BE A REAL *PAIN IN THE ASS.*
WHERE'S TAKENAGA?
IN THE BATH.
THAT'S FOR SURE.
CRUNCH
バリ…
ゴロロロロロロロ——
ROLL

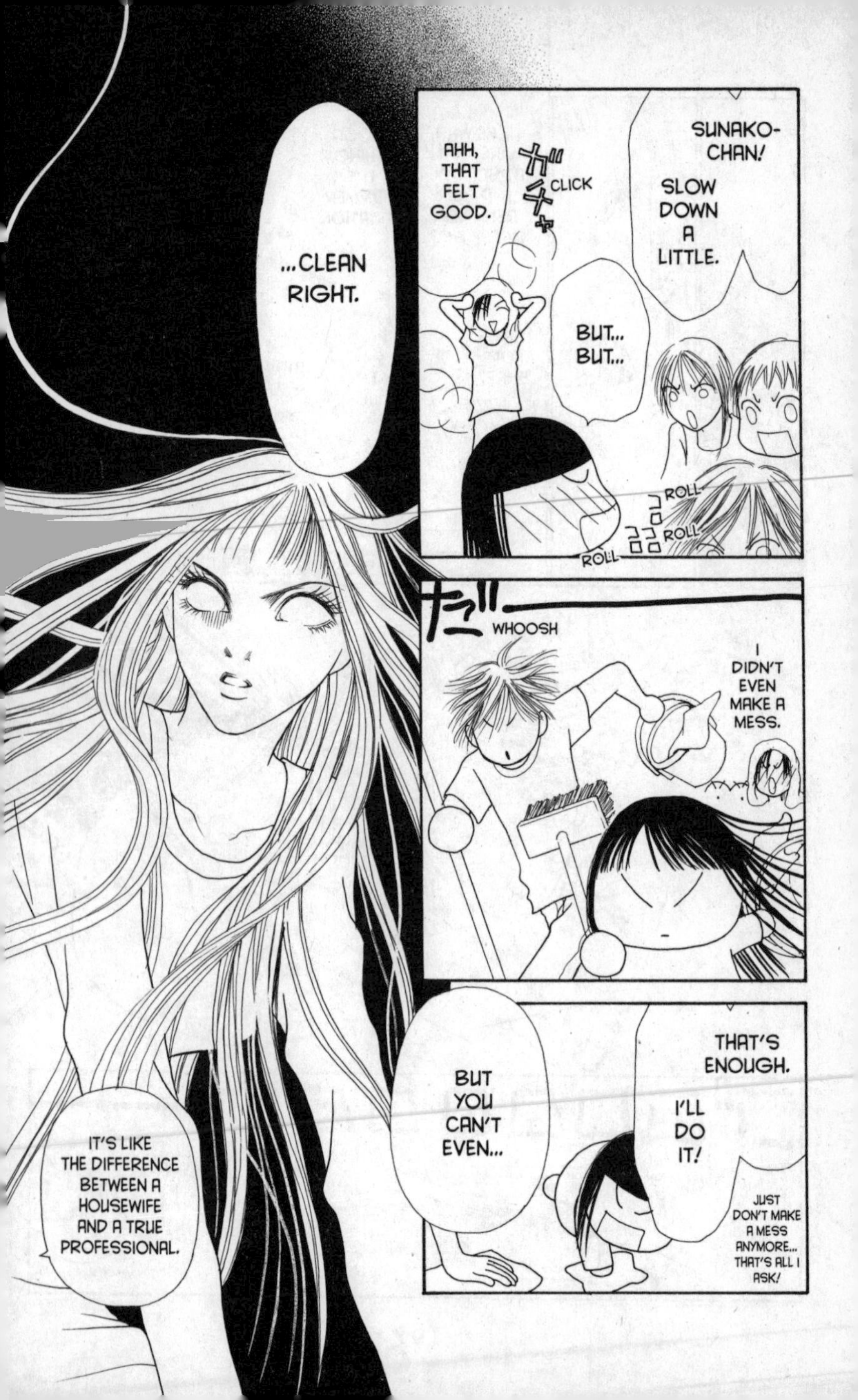
SUNAKO-CHAN!
SLOW DOWN A LITTLE.
AHH, THAT FELT GOOD.
CLICK
BUT... BUT...
ROLL
ROLL
ROLL
WHOOSH
I DIDN'T EVEN MAKE A MESS.
THAT'S ENOUGH.
I'LL DO IT!
JUST DON'T MAKE A MESS ANYMORE... THAT'S ALL I ASK!
BUT YOU CAN'T EVEN...
...CLEAN RIGHT.
IT'S LIKE THE DIFFERENCE BETWEEN A HOUSEWIFE AND A TRUE PROFESSIONAL.

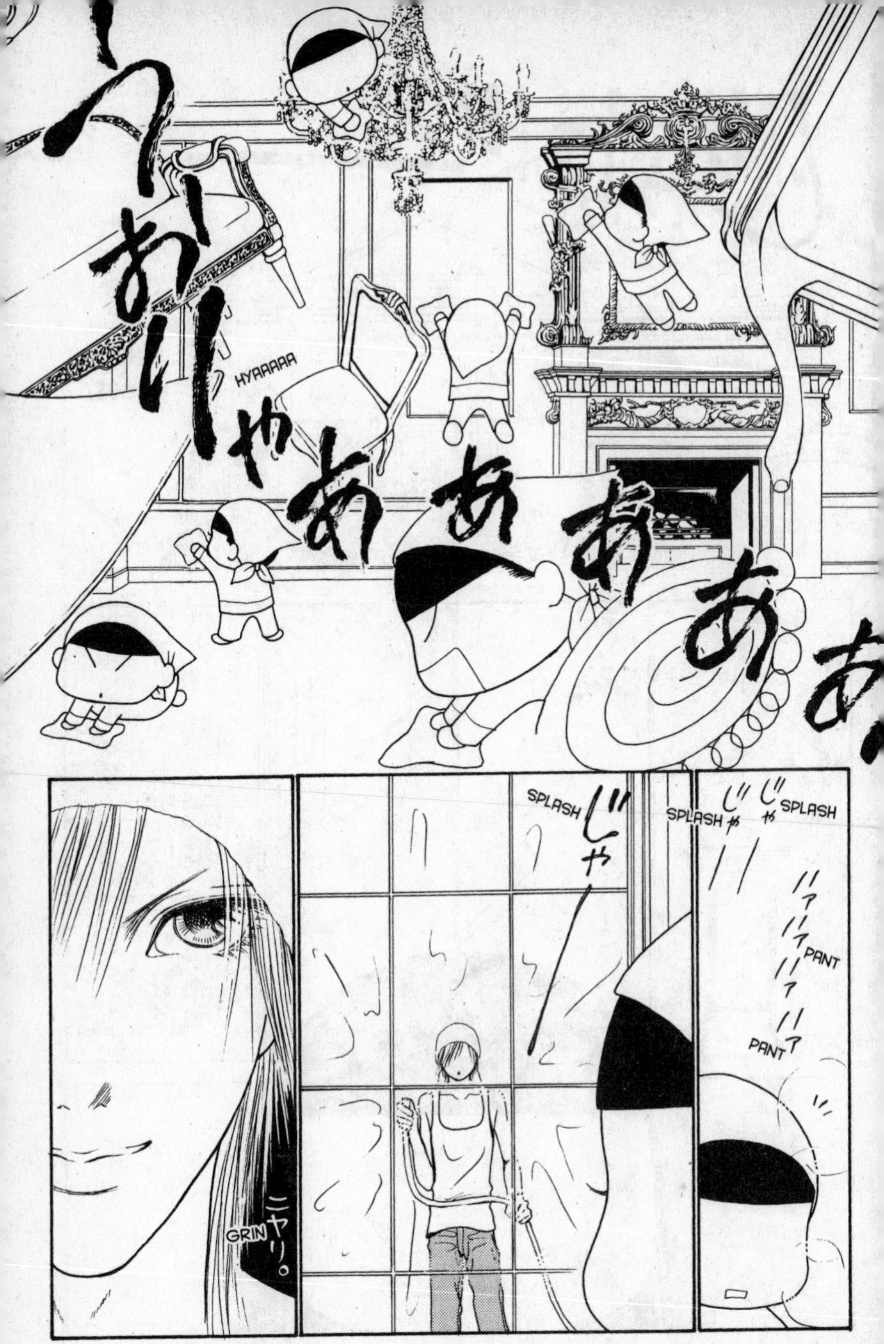
HYAAAAA
じゃ
SPLASH
SPLASH
じゃ
ハァハァ
PANT
ハァハァ
PANT
じゃー
SPLASH
ニヤリ。
GRIN

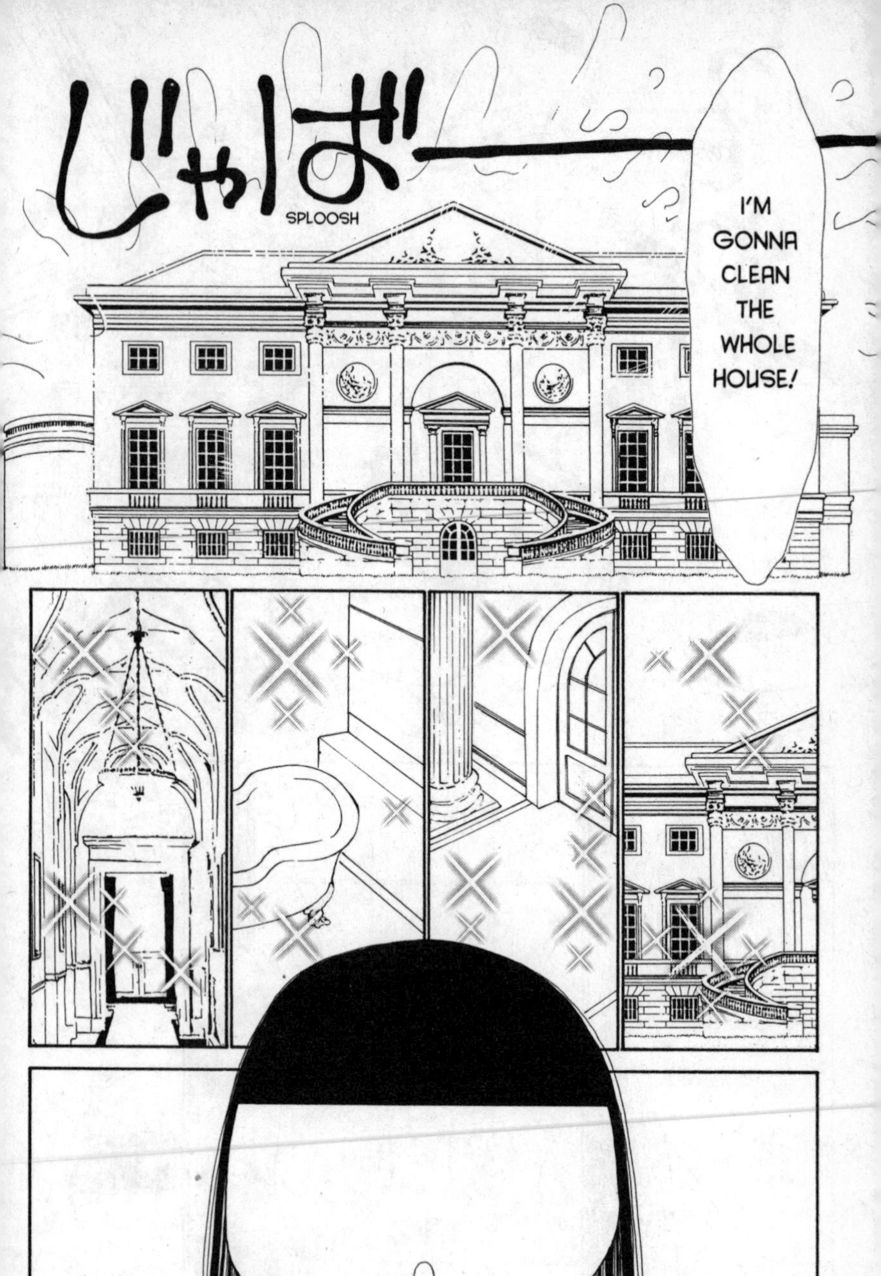
I'M GONNA CLEAN THE WHOLE HOUSE!
じゃばー
SPLOOSH

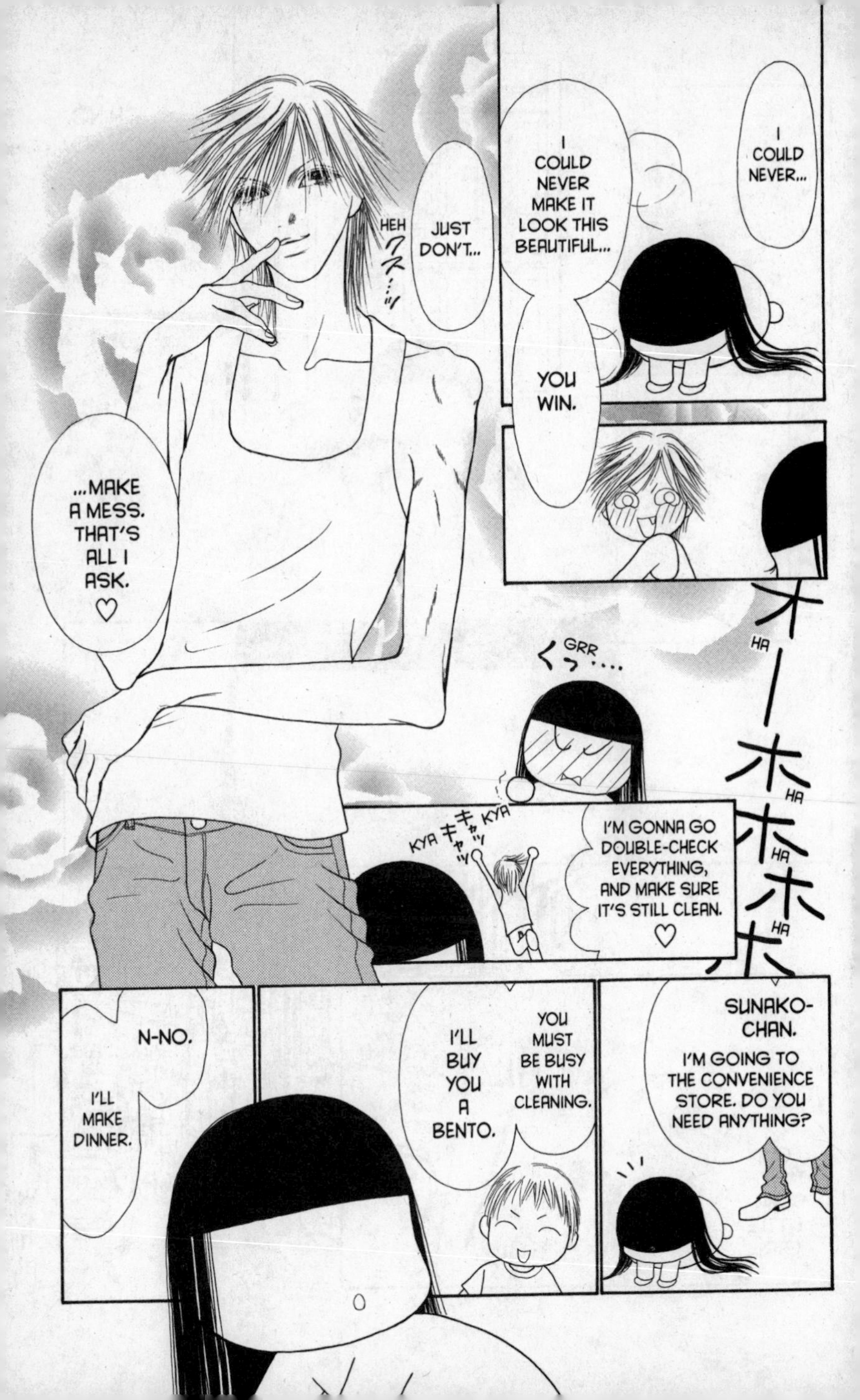

I COULD NEVER...
I COULD NEVER MAKE IT LOOK THIS BEAUTIFUL...
YOU WIN.
GRR
HA HA HA HA
I'M GONNA GO DOUBLE-CHECK EVERYTHING, AND MAKE SURE IT'S STILL CLEAN. ♡
KYA KYA
JUST DON'T...
HEH
...MAKE A MESS. THAT'S ALL I ASK. ♡
SUNAKO-CHAN.
I'M GOING TO THE CONVENIENCE STORE. DO YOU NEED ANYTHING?
YOU MUST BE BUSY WITH CLEANING.
I'LL BUY YOU A BENTO.
N-NO.
I'LL MAKE DINNER.

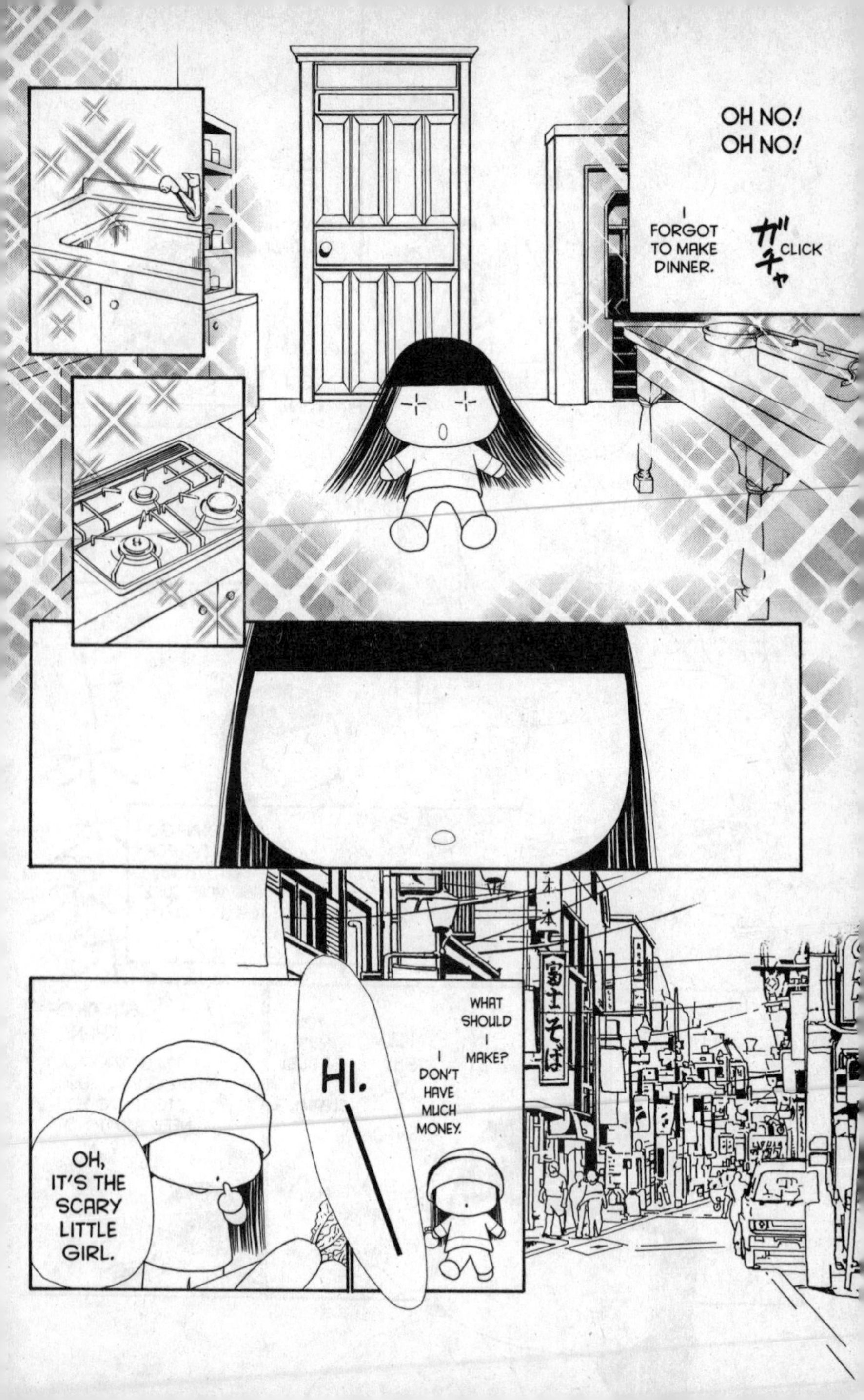
OH NO!
OH NO!
I FORGOT TO MAKE DINNER.
ガチャ CLICK
富士そば
WHAT SHOULD I MAKE?
I DON'T HAVE MUCH MONEY.
HI.
OH, IT'S THE SCARY LITTLE GIRL.

SIZZLE

SIZZLE

HEY, KYOHEI!

LOOK AT ALL THESE SHRIMP.

AND THERE'S MORE WHERE THAT CAME FROM.

YOU CAN FRY STUFF UP AT YOUR OWN TABLE. ♡

IT'S CALLED HOT OIL FONDUE.

WH-WHAT'S THIS?

NOW WE DON'T HAVE TO WORRY ABOUT THE OIL OR THE SMOKE.

SO HE JUST WANTS TO KEEP IT THAT WAY.

I UNDERSTAND.

WELL, HE WORKED REALLY HARD TO CLEAN THE PLACE UP.

CANDLES?

A PLASTIC TARP?

IT'S A LITTLE CLAUSTRO-PHOBIC.

くら WOBBLE ‥‥‥つ

BUT YOU DIDN'T EVEN EAT.

THANKS FOR DINNER.

WHO'D WANNA EAT IN A PLACE LIKE THIS?

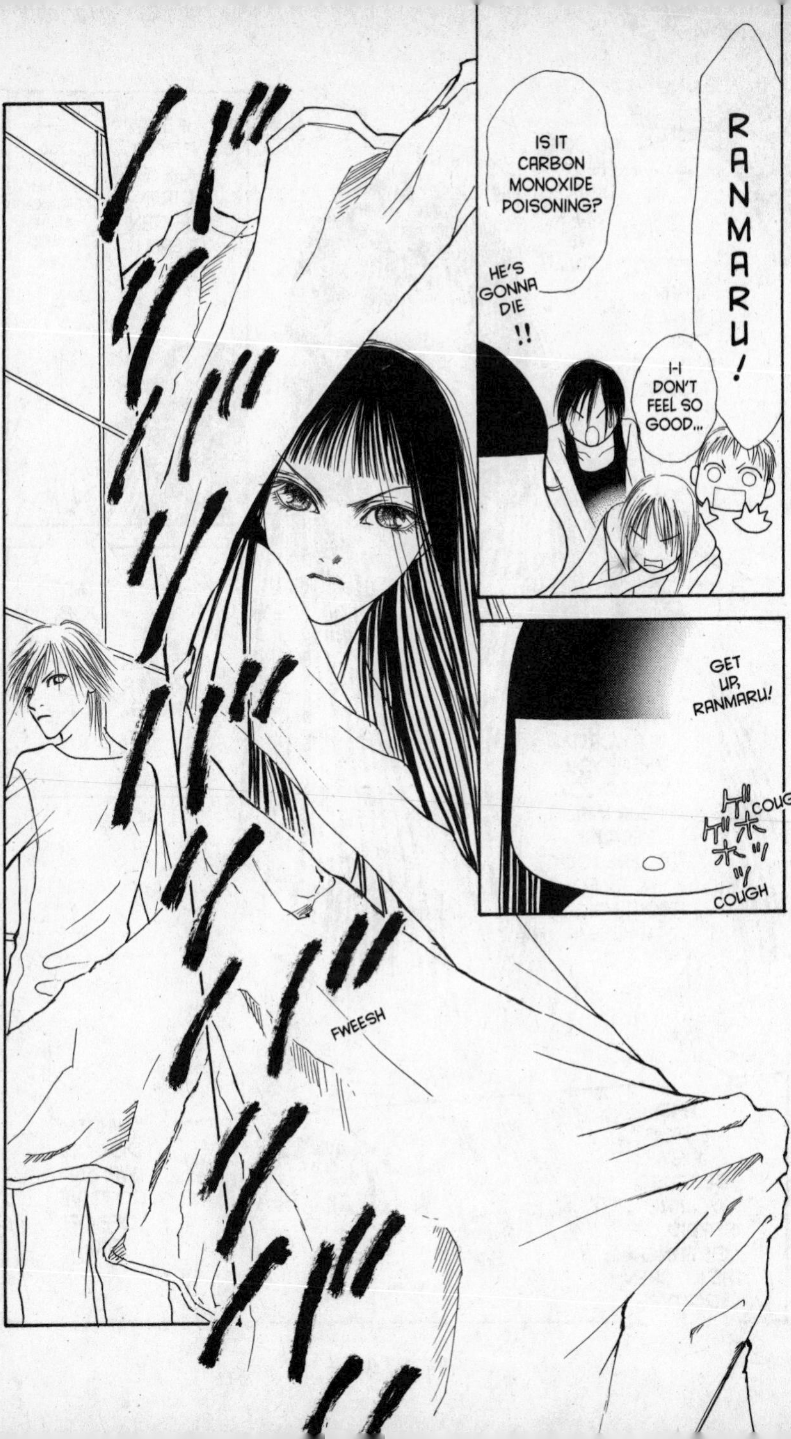
RANMARU!
IS IT CARBON MONOXIDE POISONING?
I-I DON'T FEEL SO GOOD...
HE'S GONNA DIE!!
GET UP, RANMARU!
ゲホッ COUGH
ゲホッ COUGH
FWEESH

- 120 -

WHEN IT TURNS GOLDEN BROWN, TAKE IT OUT.

IT SMELLS GOOD.

THE CRUST...

...SHOULD BE NICE AND CRUNCHY...

...WHILE THE INSIDE IS FIRM AND JUICY. AND THERE YOU HAVE IT.

THE TAIL IS CRUNCHY AND DELICIOUS.

ALL RIGHT. LET'S GIVE IT A TRY. ♡

FOR ME?

WE HAVE DIFFERENT SAUCES TOO, BUT...

...THE SHRIMP IS ALREADY SEASONED, TRY IT WITHOUT SAUCE FIRST.

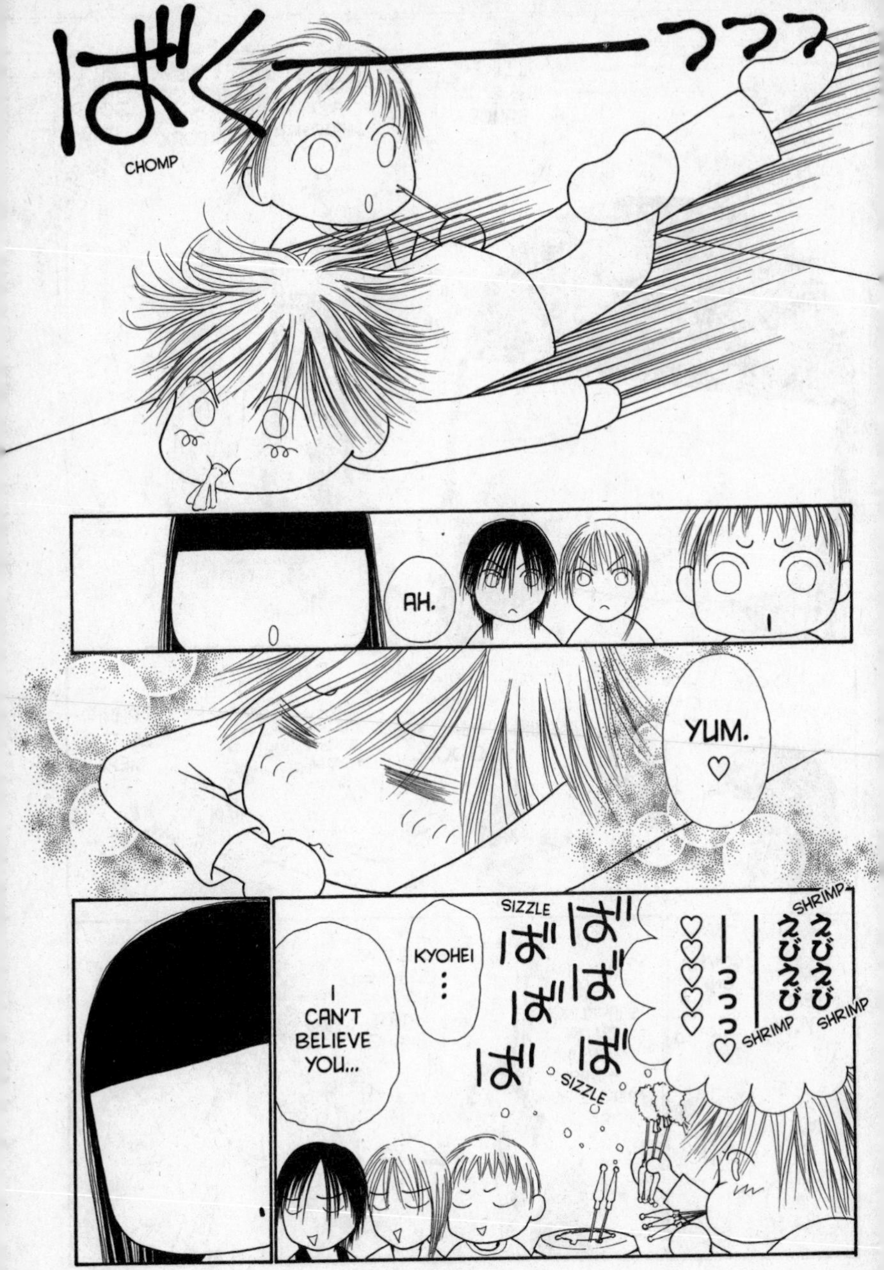
ばくーーっっっ
CHOMP
AH.
YUM. ♡
えびえびえびえびーーっっっ♡
♡♡♡♡♡
SHRIMP SHRIMP
SHRIMP SHRIMP
ばばばばばば
SIZZLE
SIZZLE
KYOHEI...
I CAN'T BELIEVE YOU...

I LIKE THE PLUM SAUCE. ♡

THE ASPARAGUS AND TOMATO ARE YUMMY TOO. ♡

THE MUSHROOM WRAPPED IN PORK. ♡

THIS ONE'S GOOD TOO.

OKAY.

I'LL HELP CLEAN UP.

LET'S DO IT AGAIN.

THIS WAS REALLY GOOD.

NO MORE SHRIMP FOR ME. ♡

I'M STUFFED.

AHH, WHAT A MEAL.

TIME TO CLEAN UP, KYOHEI.

COME ON.

WE'VE GOTTA GET IT SPARKLING CLEAN AGAIN LIKE IT WAS BEFORE WE ATE.

SHOULD WE ALL WIPE IT DOWN WITH A DISHRAG?

THERE'RE BREAD CRUMBS ALL OVER THE FLOOR.

A LITTLE MESS NEVER KILLED ANYBODY.

THIS PUDDING'S REALLY YUMMY.

NOW HE'LL GO RIGHT BACK TO THE WAY HE WAS.

NOOO......

YUP, THAT'S KYOHEI ALL RIGHT.

THAT'S KYOHEI FOR YA.

YUP, RIGHT
BACK TO THE
WAY HE WAS.

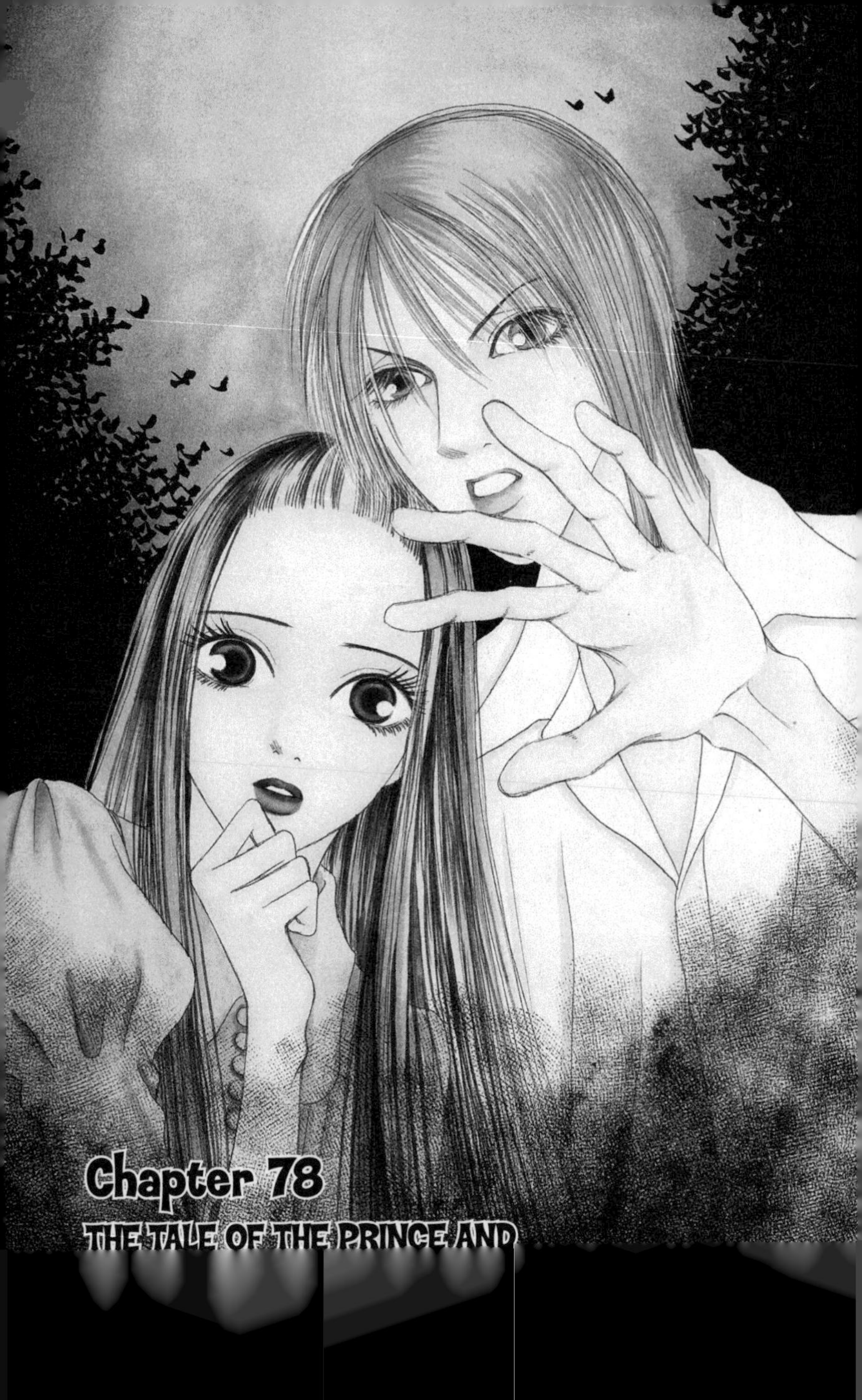
Chapter 78
THE TALE OF THE PRINCE AND

SIGH...

...MY WAY WITH WORDS, MY ABILITY TO REALLY LISTEN...

MY GOOD LOOKS, MY GENTLE PERSONALITY...

...MY RICH FATHER AND HIS NUMEROUS VACATION HOMES.

WELL, HE'S NOT THAT RICH, BUT...

I'M SO PERFECT THAT IT'S ALMOST SCARY.

AHH, SOMETIMES I ALMOST FEEL GUILTY.

THIS IS PRETTY FUNNY. LET'S WATCH. ♡

WHAT'S WITH RANMARU?

I MEAN, HE'S ALWAYS LIKE THIS, BUT...

NO, YOU DIDN'T!!

I JUST SAID THAT!!

WHAT!?

HE'S EVEN PROVIDING THE TRANSPORTATION.

...INVITED US TO STAY AT HIS SUMMER HOME.

AND SO...

RANMARU'S DAD...

I DON'T THINK I'M INCLUDED.

IT'S NICE AND COOL.

IT SURE IS RELAXING UP HERE.

IT'S HUGE.

HE'S SO SPOILED.

THE GANG HEADED FOR RANMARU'S SUMMER HOME, HIGH UP IN THE MOUNTAINS.

THE MOUNTAIN WIND IS SO NICE AND COOL.

HYUU

AT FIRST I DIDN'T WANNA COME, BUT...

I HATE AIR-CONDITIONING, SO...

WE DRAGGED HER ALONG.

I THOUGHT YOU HATED GOING OUTSIDE, SUNAKO-CHAN.

I'M SLEEPY.

BEHIND THE SCENES

THERE ARE NO BONUS PAGES IN THIS VOLUME, SO I'M GONNA HAVE TO THANK EVERYBODY HERE. SPECIAL THANKS TO...

CHOBI-SAN-SAMA, TOMMY-SAMA, NABEKO-SAMA, TENKO-SAMA, MORI-SAN-SAMA, SAKURA-SAMA

MINE-SAMA, INO-SAMA, INNAN-SAMA, EVERYBODY FROM THE EDITING DEPARTMENT

AND ALL MY FRIENDS WHO CAME TO VISIT ME, AND STUCK AROUND TO HELP. AND ALL OF YOU READING THIS RIGHT NOW. AND EVERYBODY WHO WROTE TO ME. ♡

THANK YOU ALL. ♡

THERE'S NO POOL HERE, BUT...

AND...

HEY, LET'S GO FISHING.

OUR PLACE IN CHIBA HAS A GOLF COURSE AND A MINERAL SPRINGS.

THAT FOREST LOOKS HAUNTED. I CAN'T WAIT FOR IT TO GET DARK. ...... ♡

LOOK, THE DRIVER GAVE ME THIS.

...OUR PLACE IN KARUIZAWA HAS ONE.

777 HEH HEH HEH

QUIT TRYING TO SCARE US. !!

WHY DO I HAVE TO COME ALONG?

WHERE IS EVERY-ONE?

PLEASE GO OFF ON YOUR OWN, AND LEAVE RANMARU AT HOME AROUND 1 O'CLOCK.

NOW, まま NOW. まま

OUR PLACE IN NIIGATA IS GREAT IN THE WINTERTIME. IT'S RIGHT ON THE SLOPES.

RANMARU'S DAD AND MOM ♡

HUH?

YES, MADAM.

WELL, I'LL SEE YOU TOMORROW NIGHT.

GIVE US A RIDE TO THE LAKE.

AK, ODA-SAMA.

HEY!

THUMP

I GET IT.

CATCH AND RELEASE!!

AHH!

THE YOUNG MADAM AND RANMARU-SAMA'S RELATIONSHIP HASN'T BEEN PROGRESSING QUITE FAST ENOUGH.

THE STRATEGY IS TO GET THE TWO OF THEM ALONE IN THE SUMMER-HOUSE.

YES... YOU'RE RIGHT, ODA-SAMA.

I DON'T KNOW HOW TO SAY THIS, BUT...

TICK カ"チ
コッチ TOCK
カッチ TICK

IT'S LIKE HE CAN'T FIGURE OUT WHAT TO DO OR SAY.

HE'S TOTALLY HOPELESS WHEN HE'S AROUND HER.

DON'T WORRY.

YEAH, YEAH.

UH... WELL...

ARE YOU WORRIED THAT RANMARU MIGHT MOVE A LITTLE TOO FAST?

UM...

TOCK コッチ ..... カッチ TICK

G-GO AHEAD.

WHAT'RE YOU DOING? HURRY UP, AND COME BACK HERE.

HELLO, TAK-ENAGA?

CLICK CLICK
カカカ
チチチ
CLICK

I'M GONNA GO TO THE BATH-ROOM.

I-I WONDER WHAT'S TAKING EVERYBODY SO LONG...

SPOKEN AT THE SAME TIME.

YOUR MOM, YOUR DAD, YOUR BUTLER... THEY ALL GAVE YOU GUYS THEIR BLESSING. ♡

HUH?

HER PARENTS TOO.

NICE JOB, ODA-SAMA!

I GOT ONE !!!

CLAP 4/10 4/10 7 CLAP

HOW'RE YOU FEELING? ♡

HEY, RANMARU. IT'S YUKI. ♡

WE'LL LET YOU TWO BE ALONE A LITTLE LONGER. ♡

TH—

BEEP
BEEP

THEY TRICKED ME.

GOOD ♡ LUCK ♡

CLICK

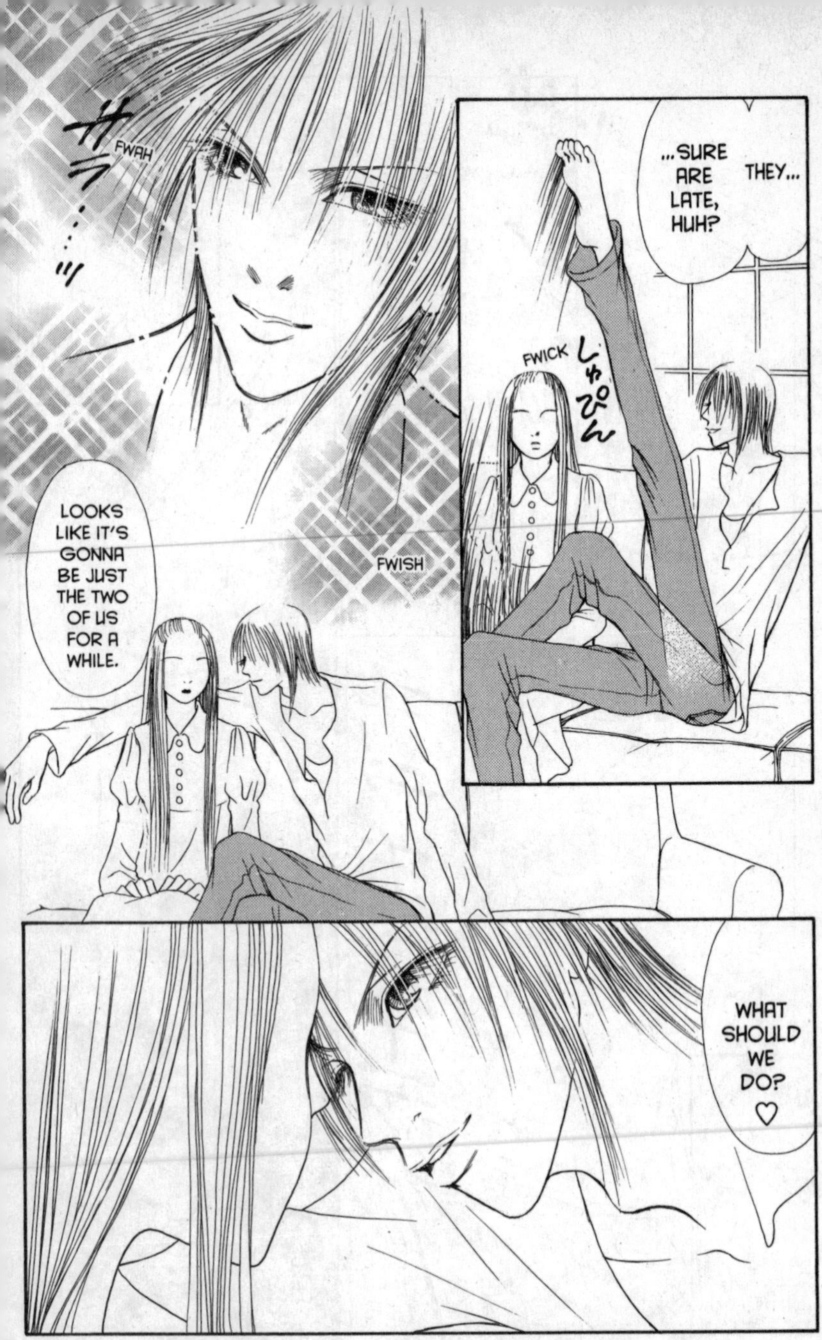
THEY...
...SURE ARE LATE, HUH?
FWICK
しゅぴん
FWAH
サラ…ッ
LOOKS LIKE IT'S GONNA BE JUST THE TWO OF US FOR A WHILE.
FWISH
WHAT SHOULD WE DO? ♡

I HAD A FEELING SHE'D REACT THAT WAY, BUT STILL...

MY ATTACK WAS A TOTAL FAILURE...

I'LL GO MAKE SOME TEA.

TIME TO SPLIT

PLAP PLAP

THUD

AH.

IF ALL WENT AS PLANNED, THEY'VE PROBABLY ALREADY DONE IT TWICE.

SHOULD WE GO BACK TO THE VACATION HOUSE?

THERE'S NOTHING TO DO IN THE MOUNTAINS.

I'M BORED.

T-TWICE?

SOFT-SERVE ICE CREAM

PLOP

YES, I'LL SEND THEM OFF TO TOKYO.

THESE VEGETABLES ARE SO FRESH.

AND LOOK AT THIS HOMEMADE JAM.

THAT MOUNTAIN...

WELL, YOU'D BETTER HURRY HOME.

THOSE BOYS LOOK LIKE REAL-LIFE PRINCES.

DID YOU COME FROM THE VACATION HOME ON TOP OF THE MOUNTAIN, YOUNG LADY?

...IS HAUNTED.

YES.

AND A PORK BUN AND A CORN DOG, AND A SWEET MOCHI RICE BALL.

FWUPPA FWUPPA

AND THESE CRACKERS, AND THESE LITTLE PIES.

I-I-I'LL TAKE THESE CHOCOLATE-COVERED COOKIES AND THESE TOO.

L-LET'S GO BACK RIGHT NOW!

FWUPPA

HAUNTED?

WHAT'RE YOU GONNA DO WITH ALL THAT STUFF?

FWUPPA

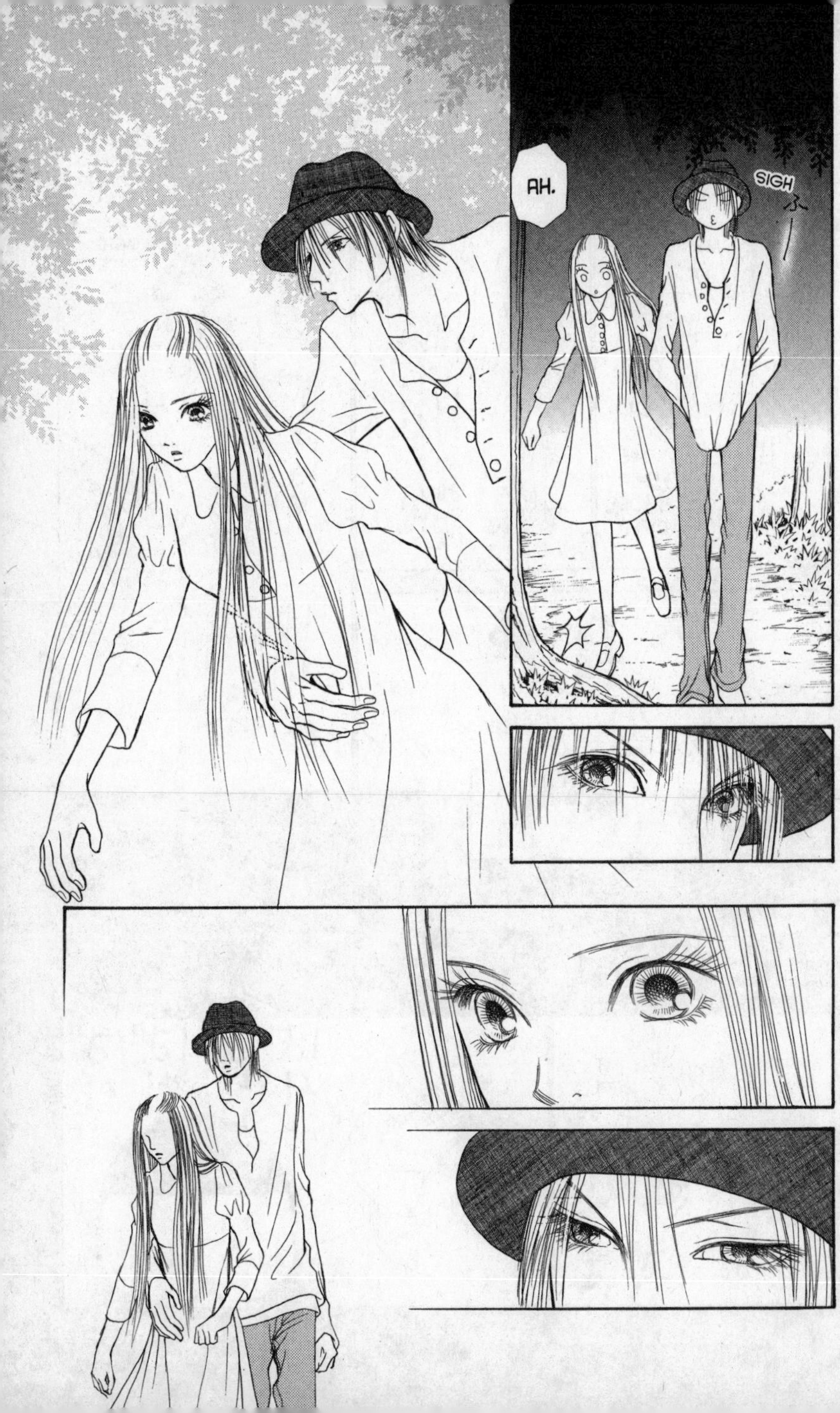
SIGH
ふー
AH.

SHOCK

D-DID YOU TAKE YOUR SHOES OFF?

HUH?

CLOP CLOP

AH... YOU'RE RIGHT.

OH, I'M WEARING DRESS SHOES TOO...

THAT'S WHAT HAPPENS WHEN YOU WEAR SHOES LIKE THAT.

NO...

HANG ON, I'LL GO GET THEM.

DOESN'T IT HURT?

SIGH

WHY DO THOSE TWO ONLY GET ALONG AT TIMES LIKE THIS?

YEAH. ♡

IT REALLY DOES LOOK HAUNTED. ♡

SQUEEZE

CRUNCH CRUNCH CRUNCH

FLAPPA

KYAA!

FLAPPA

SCARY, MAYBE WE SHOULD GO BACK.

IT REALLY DOES LOOK HAUNTED OUT HERE.

BUT I CAN'T EVEN TELL IF WE'RE NEAR THE TOP OF THE MOUNTAIN OR THE BOTTOM.

A-ARE YOU OKAY?

PANT

PANT

O-OH, IT WAS JUST A CROW.

THUMP-THUMP

I'M FINE... TOTALLY FINE.

FWIP

EV—

EVEN AT TIMES LIKE THIS, SHE'S TOTALLY EXPRESSIONLESS.

BLUSH

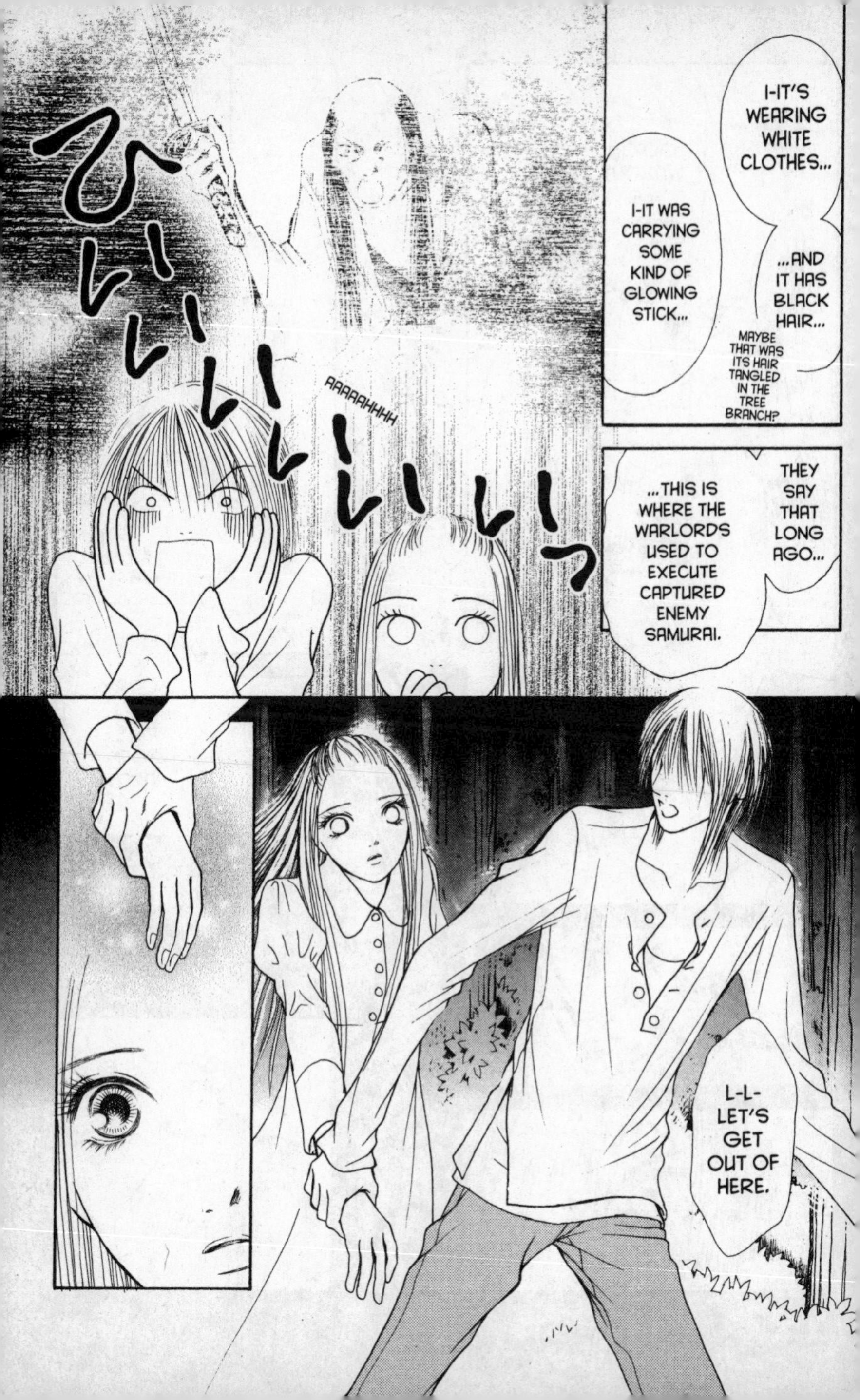
I-IT'S WEARING WHITE CLOTHES...
I-IT WAS CARRYING SOME KIND OF GLOWING STICK...
...AND IT HAS BLACK HAIR...
MAYBE THAT WAS ITS HAIR TANGLED IN THE TREE BRANCH?
THEY SAY THAT LONG AGO...
...THIS IS WHERE THE WARLORDS USED TO EXECUTE CAPTURED ENEMY SAMURAI.
ひぃぃぃぃぃっ
AAAAAHHHH
L-L-LET'S GET OUT OF HERE.

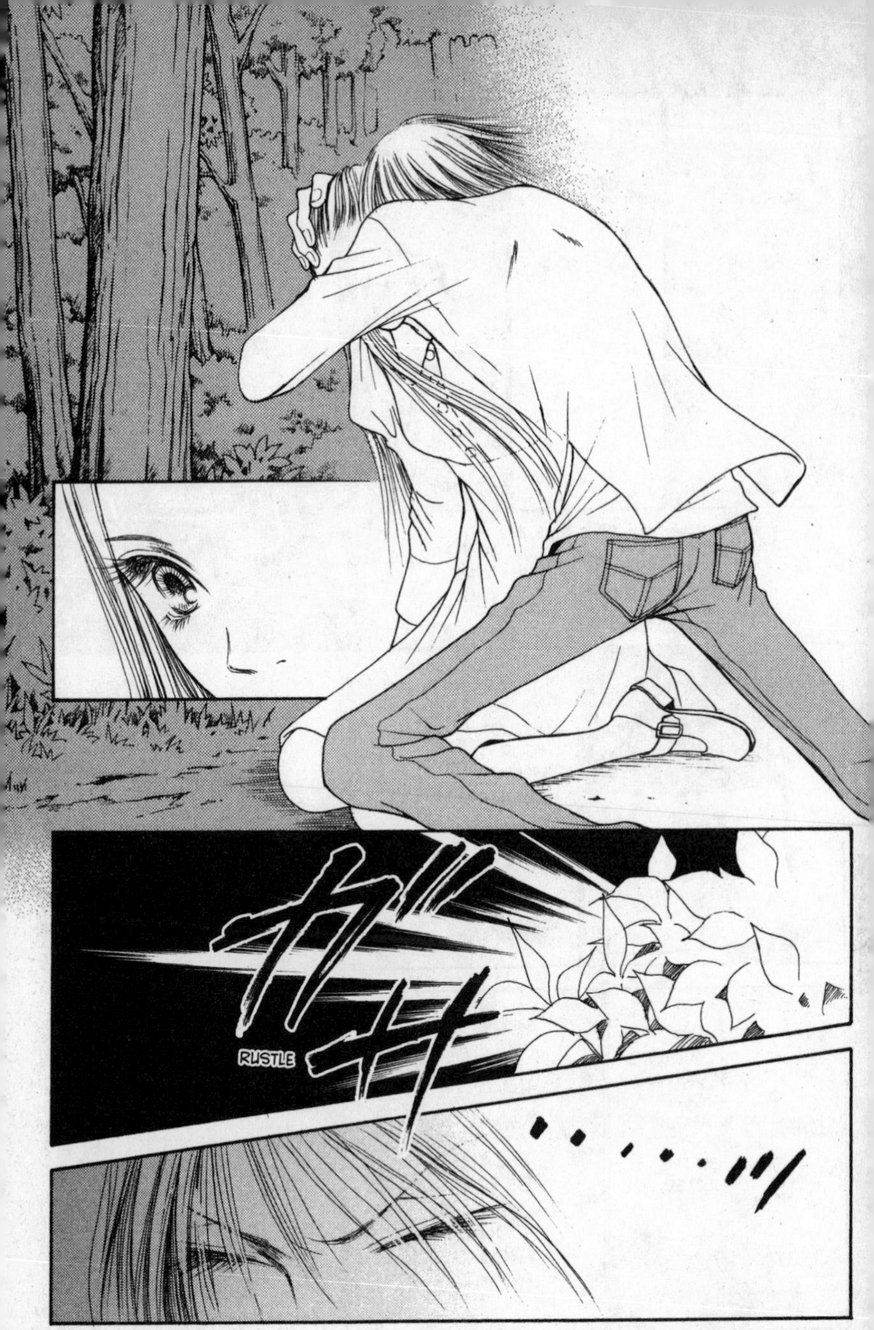
ガサ
RUSTLE
......!!

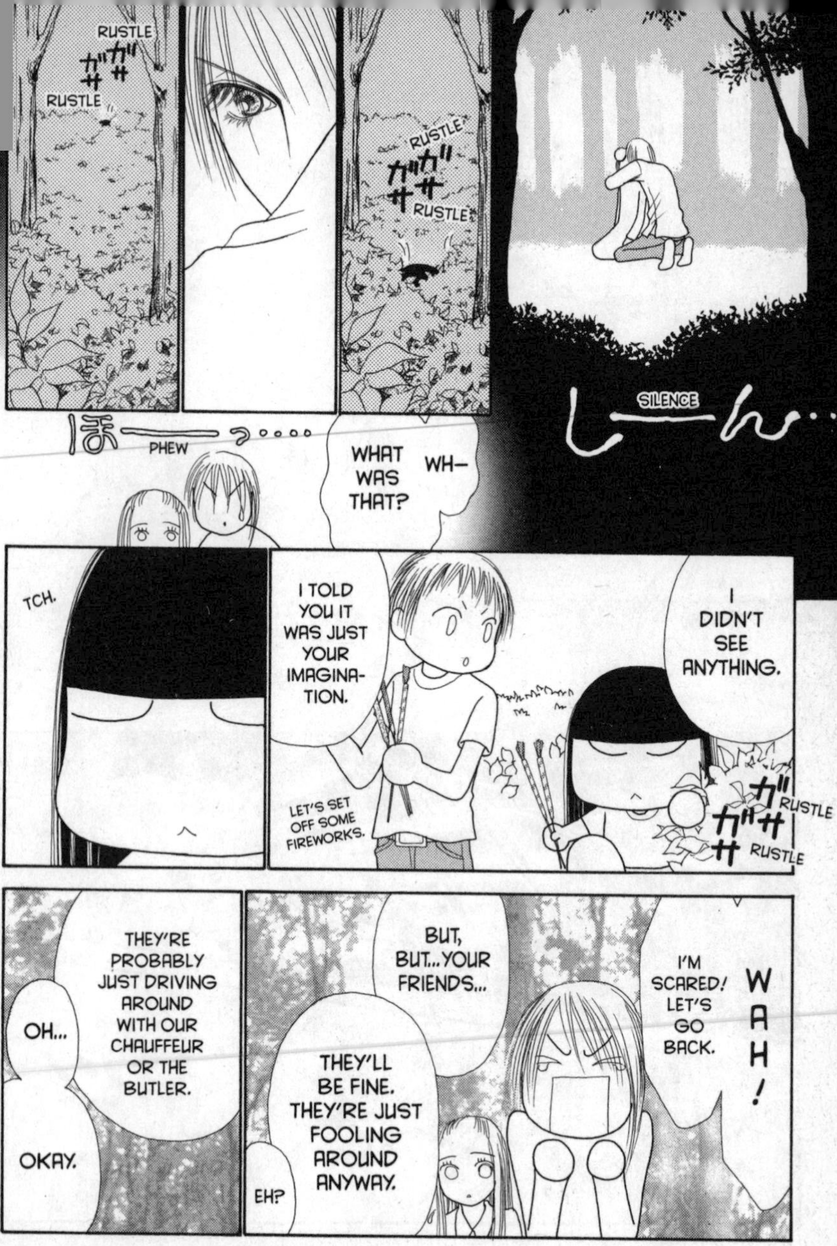
SILENCE
し—ん…
RUSTLE
ガサ
ガサ
RUSTLE
RUSTLE
ガサ
ガサ
RUSTLE
WH–
WHAT WAS THAT?
ほ——っ……
PHEW
I DIDN'T SEE ANYTHING.
ガサ
ガサ
RUSTLE
RUSTLE
I TOLD YOU IT WAS JUST YOUR IMAGINATION.
LET'S SET OFF SOME FIREWORKS.
TCH.
WAH!
I'M SCARED! LET'S GO BACK.
BUT, BUT...YOUR FRIENDS...
THEY'LL BE FINE. THEY'RE JUST FOOLING AROUND ANYWAY.
EH?
THEY'RE PROBABLY JUST DRIVING AROUND WITH OUR CHAUFFEUR OR THE BUTLER.
OH...
OKAY.

OF COURSE...

I COULD NEVER LEAVE A GIRL ALL ALONE IN THE WOODS LIKE THIS.

GLARE

I....

I'M SORRY...

I WAS ONLY TEASING.

AH...

WELL, THEN LET'S GO BACK.

I—

?

RUB RUB

I WASN'T BEING STUBBORN.

I....

AND MY LEG REALLY ISN'T BAD AT ALL...

I WANNA GO BACK.

I THINK IT'S SCARY OUT HERE TOO.

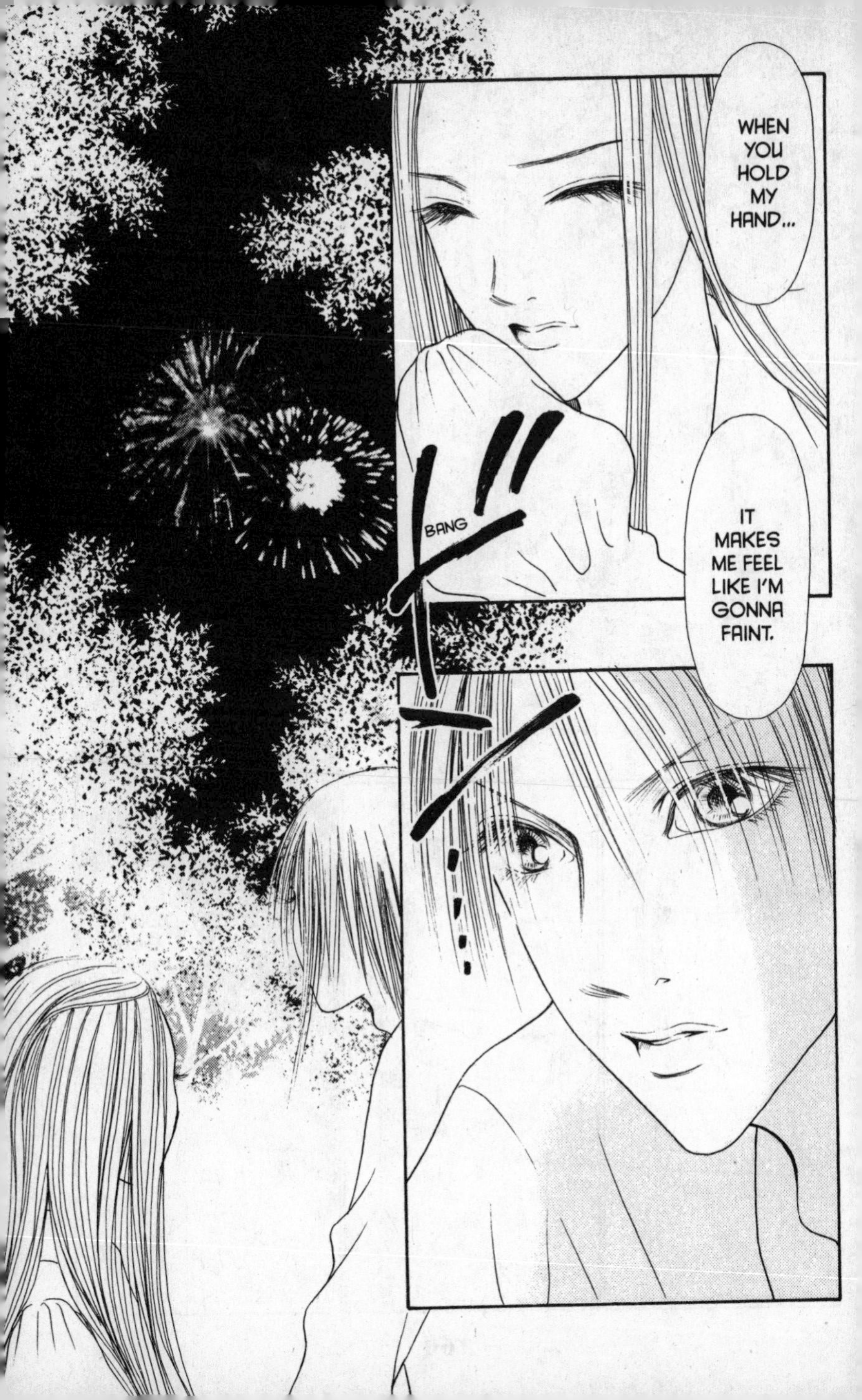
WHEN YOU HOLD MY HAND...
BANG
IT MAKES ME FEEL LIKE I'M GONNA FAINT.

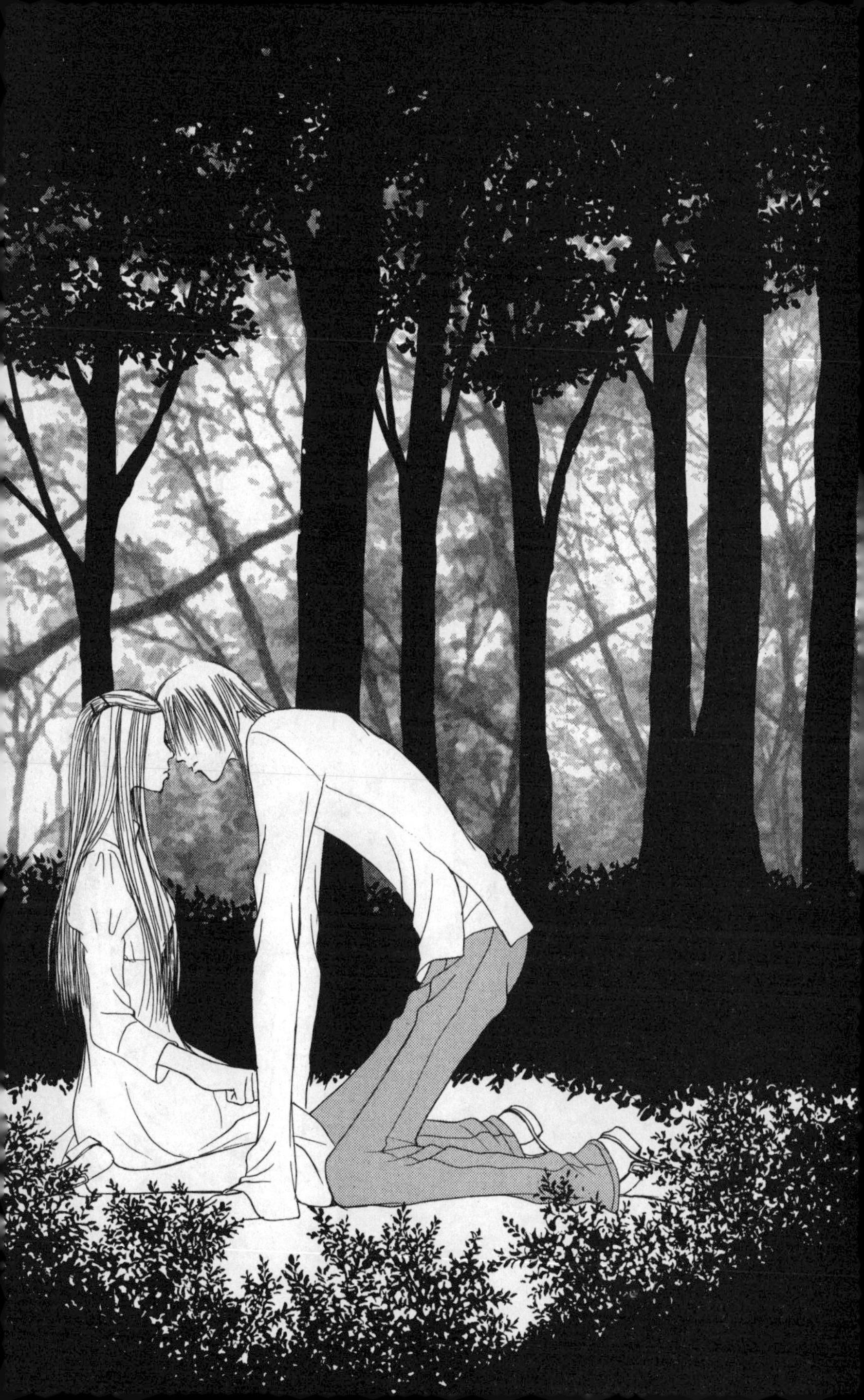

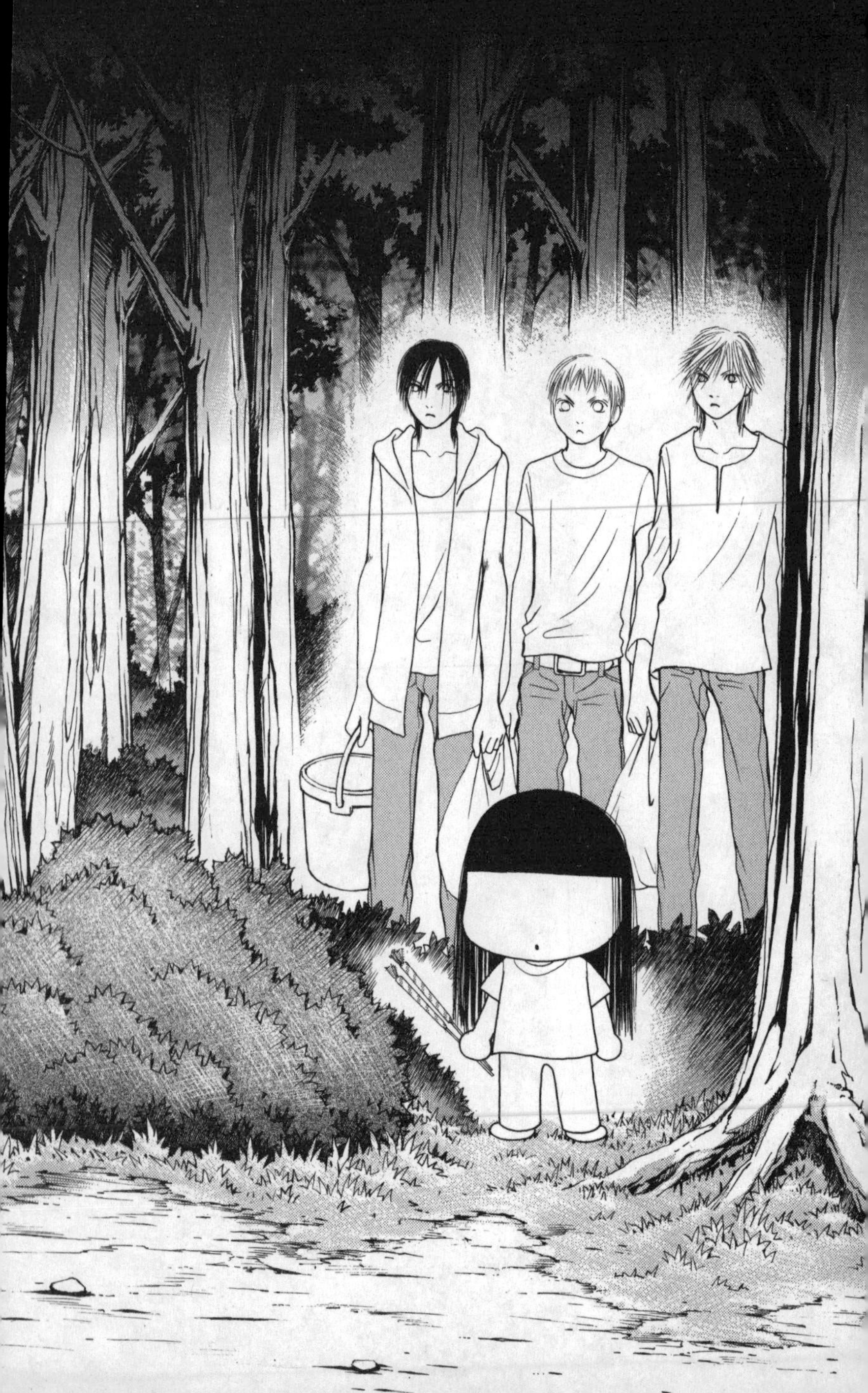

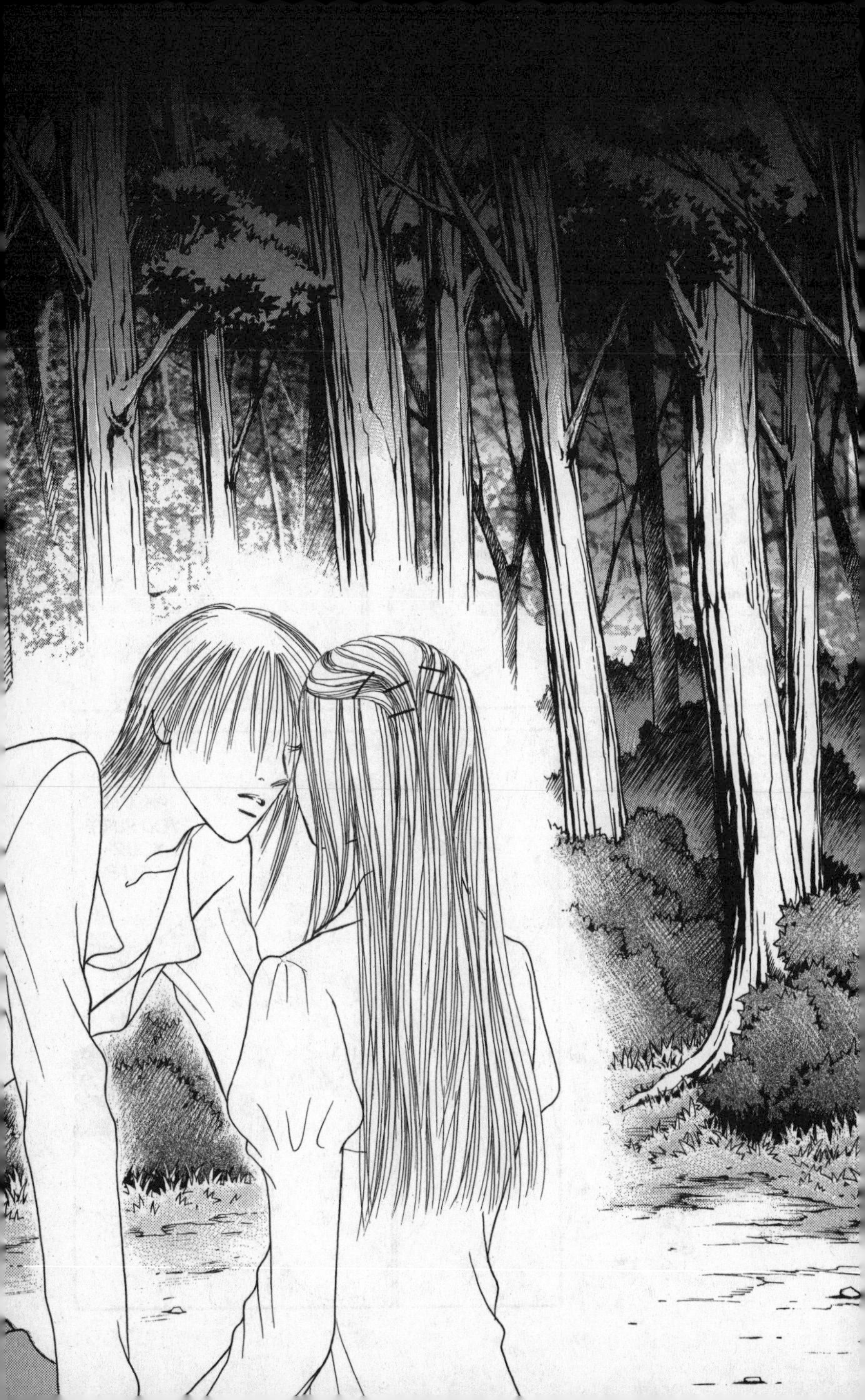

IN THE MIDDLE OF IT !?

YEAH, BUT I WOULDN'T WANNA WALK IN ON THEM WHILE THEY'RE IN THE MIDDLE OF IT.

GUESS WE SHOULD'VE COME BACK A LITTLE LATER.

SORRY, RAN-MARU...

BLUSH
カ

....

!!!!!!

DON'T BLAME US.

HA HA HA HA HA HA

DID HE JUST CALL ME STUPID HEAD?

バカっ

I'M GOING HOME.

WHAT-EVER.

STUPID HEAD.

I'LL GO FIND SOME MEDICINAL HERBS TO KILL THE PAIN.

AH, DID YOU HURT YOUR-SELF?

OH NO !!

AH, I'M FINE.

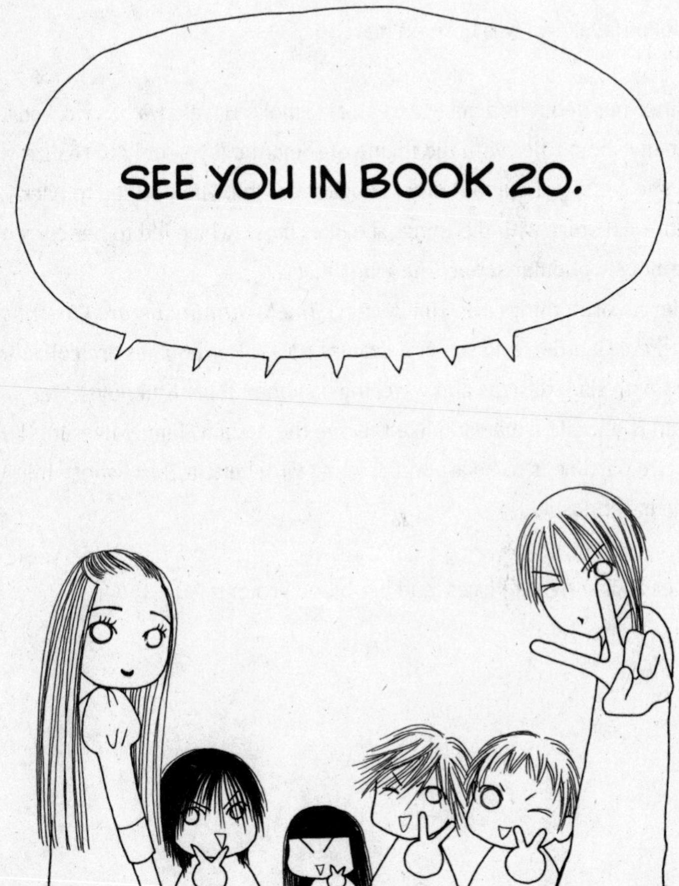
SEE YOU IN BOOK 20.

About the Creator

Tomoko Hayakawa was born on March 4.

Since her debut as a manga creator, Tomoko Hayakawa has worked on many shojo titles with the theme of romantic love—only to realize that she could write about other subjects as well. She decided to pack her newest story with the things she likes most, which led to her current, enormously popular series, *The Wallflower*.

Her favorite things are: Tim Burton's *The Nightmare Before Christmas*, Jean-Paul Gaultier, and samurai dramas on TV. Her hobbies are collecting items with skull designs and watching bishonen (beautiful boys). Her dream is to build a mansion like the one the Addams family lives in. Her favorite pastime is to lie around at home with her cat, Ten (whose full name is Tennosuke).

Her zodiac sign is Pisces, and her blood group is AB.

Translation Notes

Japanese is a tricky language for most Westerners, and translation is often more art than science. For your edification and reading pleasure, here are notes on some of the places where we could have gone in a different direction in our translation of the work, or where a Japanese cultural reference is used.

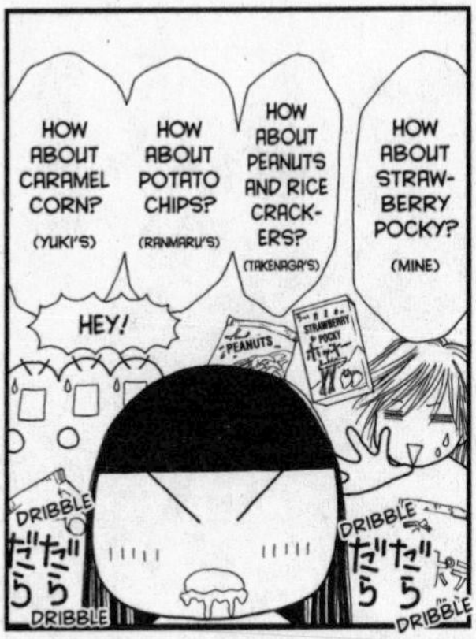
HOW ABOUT STRAW-BERRY POCKY?
(MINE)
HOW ABOUT PEANUTS AND RICE CRACK-ERS?
(TAKENAGA'S)
HOW ABOUT POTATO CHIPS?
(RANMARU'S)
HOW ABOUT CARAMEL CORN?
(YUKI'S)
HEY!
STRAWBERRY POCKY
PEANUTS
DRIBBLE
DRIBBLE
DRIBBLE
DRIBBLE

Strawberry Pocky, page 15

Pocky are a brand of thin, stick-shaped cookies covered with chocolate, strawberry, or other flavors.

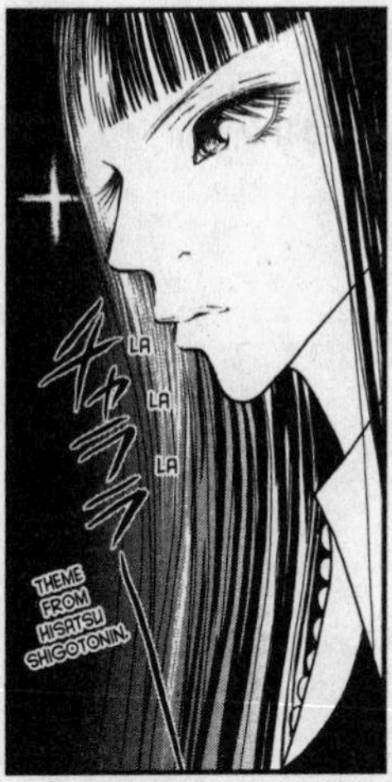
LA
LA
LA
THEME FROM HISATSU SHIGOTONIN

***Hisatsu Shigotonin,* page 92**

Hisastsu Shigotonin is a popular Japanese TV crime drama.

Karuizawa, page 131

Karuizawa is a famous hot springs resort area located in the mountains of Nagano Prefecture, a few hours outside of Tokyo.

THERE'S NO POOL HERE, BUT...

HEY, LET'S GO FISHING.

OUR PLACE IN CHIBA HAS A GOLF COURSE AND A MINERAL SPRINGS.

LOOK, THE DRIVER GAVE ME THIS.

...OUR PLACE IN KARUIZAWA HAS ONE.

PLEASE GO OFF ON YOUR OWN, AND LEAVE RANMARU AT HOME AROUND 1 O'CLOCK.

OUR PLACE IN NIIGATA IS GREAT IN THE WINTER TIME. IT'S RIGHT ON THE SLOPES.

RANMARU'S DAD AND MOM ♡

Niigata, page 131

Niigata is a coastal prefecture famous for its ski resorts and hot springs and frequent earthquakes.

Oden, page 141

Oden is a tasty dish made up of various ingredients boiled in soup stock. Common ingredients include daikon radish, hard-boiled eggs, konyaku (yam cake), and fish cakes.

Preview of volume 20

We're pleased to present you a preview from volume 20. Enjoy!.

LONG AGO, THEY USED TO BRING THE DEAD HERE.

DURING MY GRANDFATHER'S GENERATION, IT WAS USED AS A COMMUNAL CEMETERY.

PANT. PANT

S-SORRY, I WAS OVERWHELMED WITH HAPPINESS.

SU-SUNAKO!

FWUMP

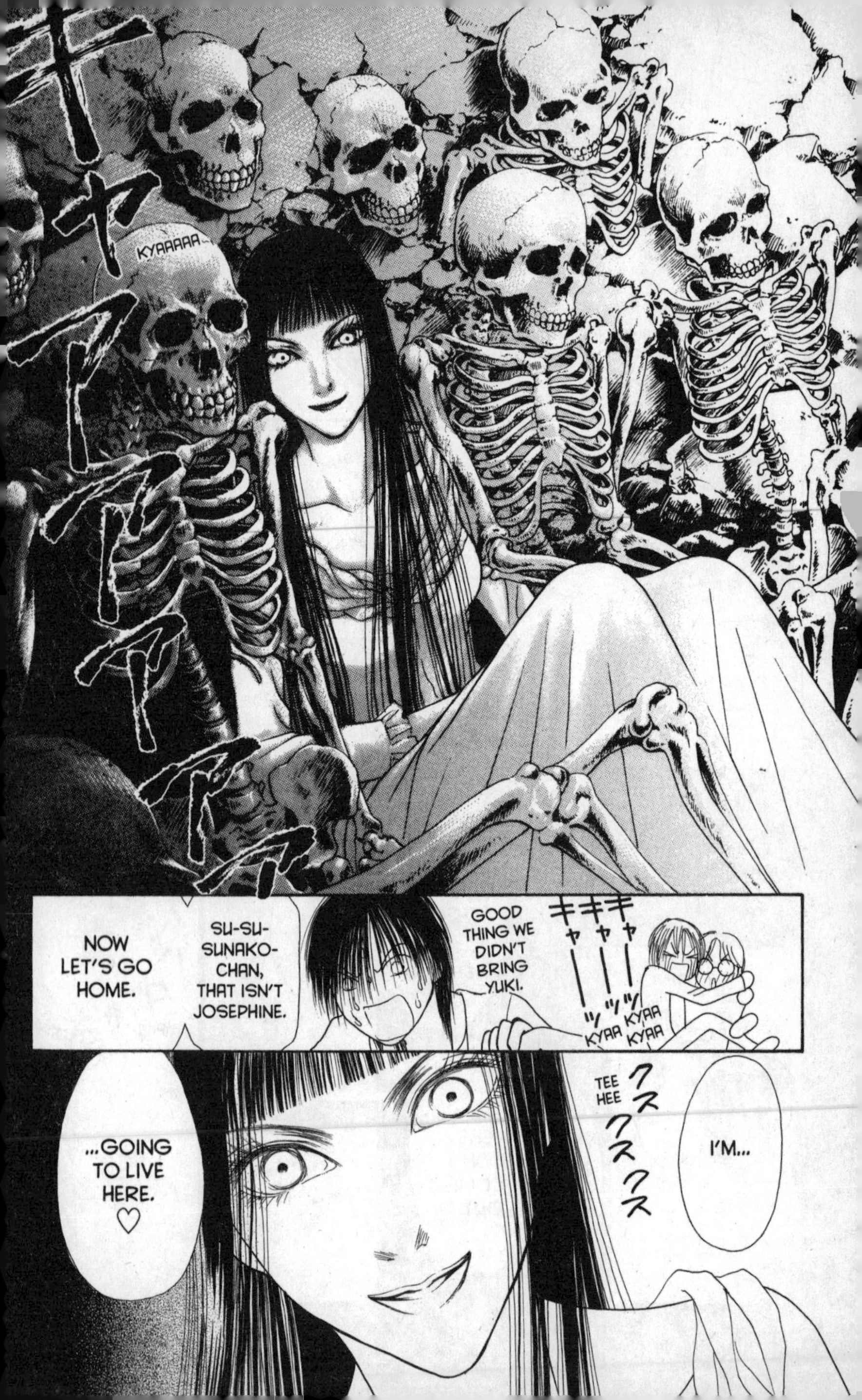

キャアアアアア
KYAAAAA
キャーッ
キャーッ
キャーッ
KYAA KYAA KYAA
GOOD THING WE DIDN'T BRING YUKI.
SU-SU-SUNAKO-CHAN, THAT ISN'T JOSEPHINE.
NOW LET'S GO HOME.
I'M...
クスクスクスクス
TEE HEE
...GOING TO LIVE HERE. ♡

TOMARE!

[STOP!]

You're going the wrong way!

Manga is a completely different type of reading experience.

To start at the *beginning*, go to the *end*!

That's right! Authentic manga is read the traditional Japanese way—from right to left. Exactly the *opposite* of how American books are read. It's easy to follow: Just go to the other end of the book, and read each page—and each panel—from right side to left side, starting at the top right. Now you're experiencing manga as it was meant to be!